Central and Eastern European Perspectives on International Relations

Series Editors

Michal Onderco
Erasmus University Rotterdam
Rotterdam, The Netherlands

Monika Sus
Center for International Security
Hertie School
Wroclaw, Poland

CEEPIR, the foundational book series of the Central and East European International Studies Association (CEEISA), is an interdisciplinary forum for scholarship that straddles traditional and novel approaches, advancing cutting-edge scholarship in global international relations.

The series invites proposals in the spirit of epistemological and methodological pluralism and in a range of traditional and innovative formats: research monographs, edited collections, textbooks and Pivots which aim at succinct and timely scholarly interventions.

The editorial focus is twofold

(1) The CEEISA book series retains its long-standing objective to sustain and showcase excellent research in and on Central and Eastern Europe. We are interested in innovative scholarly perspectives on contemporary social and political transformations in the region, in how knowledge is produced about such transformations, and in how Central and Eastern Europe interacts with the wider European and global contexts. We are interested in advancing the scholarly discussion between Central and Eastern Europe and the discipline more broadly. In cooperation with CEEISA, we maintain a subseries of works which received distinction of excellence by the Association (e.g. the best doctoral dissertation, the best paper at the CEEISA convention, the best thematic panel).

(2) We seek in particular outstanding empirical work which advances conceptual and methodological innovation in International Relations theory, European Studies and International Political Sociology, particularly when related to Central and Eastern Europe. We welcome novel research techniques and approaches that explore diverse sites and engage diverse challenges of contemporary world politics.

As a devoted team dedicated to excellence and timeliness in the editorial and peer review process, we rely on the support of Palgrave Macmillan, and liaise with the *Journal of International Relations and Development* to develop a platform for scholars who can reinvigorate existing research in global international relations.

For a correct copy of the proposal form, please contact Isobel Cowper-Coles, Editor for International Studies, at isobel.cowpercoles@palgrave.com

Faris Kočan

Identity, Ontological Security and Europeanisation in Republika Srpska

palgrave
macmillan

Faris Kočan
Faculty of Social Sciences
University of Ljubljana
Ljubljana, Slovenia

ISSN 2947-7980   ISSN 2947-7999 (electronic)
Central and Eastern European Perspectives on International Relations
ISBN 978-3-031-46168-2   ISBN 978-3-031-46169-9 (eBook)
https://doi.org/10.1007/978-3-031-46169-9

This Palgrave Macmillan imprint is published by the registered company Springer Nature Switzerland AG.
The registered company address is: Gewerbestrasse 11, 6330 Cham, Switzerland

Paper in this product is recyclable.

FUNDING

This book has been funded by the Slovenian Research Agency's research and infrastructure programme called Slovenia and its actors in international relations and European integrations (P5-0177). The work was also supported by the project Anxieties in Cities of Southeast European Post-conflict Societies: Introducing an Integrative Approach to Peacebuilding (Grant N5-0178).

CONTENTS

LIST OF FIGURES

LIST OF TABLES

CHAPTER 1

Introduction

Achieving (transformative) peace in post-conflict societies has proven to be exceptionally hard to achieve for the international community, including the European Union (EU). The ideas underpinning European integration that arose after the Second World War were to bring the states together on the Continent politically, economically and socially, and to create a common (European) space without antagonism. This description resonates with the 'Old Europe' narrative (Manners & Murray, 2016) that refers to the narrative of peace and the post-war reconstruction of Western Europe. The symbolic power held by this narrative stems from the ability to redefine the concept of sovereignty of the member states (MS) via the transformation of the 'Self–Other' dialectic in reproducing national autobiographies. Subotić (2013, p. 611) defines the latter as "stories that countries talk about themselves with aim of maintaining a sense of identity security of their citizens". This redefinition was accomplished by "blurring" national borders, which traditionally represented a clear dividing line between the collective perception of 'Self' in relation to the 'Other', thus enabling the space for the MS' coexistence. Such process was possible due to the need to create space for the new roles of the MS in the European community (EC) (Marks & Hooghe, 2003; Kaufmann, 2009; Stanley, 2013). By so doing, the MS put the (political) opportunities of the present and the future at the forefront, enabling the gradual depoliticisation of

© The Author(s), under exclusive license to Springer Nature Switzerland AG 2023
F. Kočan, *Identity, Ontological Security and Europeanisation in Republika Srpska*, Central and Eastern European Perspectives on International Relations,
https://doi.org/10.1007/978-3-031-46169-9_1

historically determined antagonisms (Sanders et al., 2012; Lavdas, 2018). One could argue that the goal of the 'old Europe' narrative with respect to the above-mentioned identity antagonism is the transformation into *agonism*.

Having given meaning to the European integration process, this interpretation of the 'old Europe' narrative indicates that European integration should be understood not only as cooperation between European countries in supranational institutions and decision-making processes in the EU, but additionally as a successful attempt to overcome identity-based debates based on a violent past (Williams & Kelstrup, 2000; Nancheva, 2012; Biermann, 2014). As a result of interest-based cooperation, European integration offered nation-states an alternative interpretation of their roles and national/ethnic identities during various transitions, and Europeanisation as an inherent part of this has offered the potential for reconciliation and peacebuilding (Tocci, 2007; Recchia, 2007; Nancheva, 2012). Europeanisation, which is generally regarded as a process of transferring, projecting (or uploading) and converging rules, interests, practices, policies and processes to the EU level and vice versa, follows the logic of instrumental rationality[1] (Lajh & Kajnč, 2009, pp. 26–27; Bojinović Fenko & Stahl, 2019, p. 46). On top of the relevant legal, political and institutional logic of projecting EU norms, Europeanisation has another important dimension; namely, the normative rationality or the logic of appropriateness, based on transformation of the collective identity of the actor and thereby their interests (March & Olsen, 1989; Finnemore, 1996; Johnston & Acharya, 2007; Björkdahl et al., 2015).

In this respect, the idea that Europeanisation holds the potential to reconstruct antagonistic ethnic identities primarily rests on the argument put forward by Spohn and Eder (2005) that the European integrational identity facilitated the reconstruction of collective identities in Eastern Europe as they engaged in the enlargement process. This logic is embedded in what Risse (2001, p. 203) portrays as "European collective nation-state identity", resonating in the modern Western concept of Europe as a liberal community whereby the European collective nation-state identity is

---

[1] Instrumental rationality emphasised that it is rational to do what will help us to achieve our desires and goals (Hanžek, 2012, p. 413). The antipode of instrumental rationality is epistemological rationality, which stresses that it is rational to believe only in solid evidence. The difference between epistemological and instrumental rationality therefore lies in the rationality of trust (epistemological rationality) and action (instrumental rationality) (Hanžek, 2012, p. 411).

constructed around the institutions and practices in which the antagonistic friend–enemy dynamic is transformed into "relationships of adversaries" (Mouffe, 2012, p. 632). Europeanisation as the reconstruction of the antagonistic Self–Other dialectics is—through European integrational identity—thereby achieved by constructing appropriate institutions. Hence, the Europeanisation via integration described above allows for an alternative interpretation of the collective nation-state identities—as Risse (2001) argued with regard to France, Germany and the United Kingdom, while Spohn and Eder (2005) to Central and Eastern Europe during the enlargement process, accordingly transforming the inherent antagonistic 'Us–Them' into 'We' (Mouffe, 2012, p. 633).

Nonetheless, such an idealistic view of European integration and Europeanisation, arising from the relative success of the reconciliation of Western European countries following the Second World War, neglects the structural and ideological consequences of the objectively different logic of EU membership for the Central and Eastern Europe (CEE) countries. This was also pointed out by Majstorović and Vučkovac (2016, p. 152) who argue that the post-Cold War Europeanisation process in all post-communist countries gave the impression of being "temporary and transitional" in the broader debate with a view to "making up for lost time". Accordingly, the rapprochement and integration of the 'East' (i.e., EU enlargement in 2004) is denoted as the integration of the "internal Other" and as a space that has to be filled with the material and symbolic efforts of (liberal) Western Europe (Todorova, 1997; Močnik, 1998; Dupcsik, 2001). Similarly, authors like Maier and Risse (2003), Nancheva (2017) and Juncos (2018) state that the Europeanisation of the twenty-first century could be understood as a strategy of self-representation aimed at relativising (ethnic) nationalisms with the argument of establishing a liberal political culture. In this context, the first point of departure made in this book lies in understanding the concept of Europeanisation to move away from it being an analytical (the transfer/projection/convergence of rules, interests, practices, policies and processes down from the EU level and vice versa) towards a normative concept. The latter means that we define Europeanisation as a context that, based on the "old Europe" narrative, "challenges" the classical elements of statehood with the political idea of homogenising "Europeanness" as a common civilisational, cultural, social and political referential frame of nation-states in Europe.

The newly established post-Yugoslav states are also subject to the process of Europeanisation. Most immediately identified EU membership as their principal foreign policy goal, with the EU in due course offering them a formal European perspective through the Stabilisation and Association process. One of the last post-Yugoslav states to formally expose itself to Europeanisation is BiH, which in 2005 began negotiations to sign the Stabilisation and Association Agreement (SAA). This process is deeply embedded in the political, social and economic reality of BiH, as defined by the Dayton Peace Agreement (DPA), which brought the Bosnian war to an end and underpins the contemporary post-conflict reality of BiH (Ker-Lindsay, 2016). BiH still functions today as a post-conflict country, with its material and social environment being vulnerable to various internal political demands arising from ethnic conflict, such as a greater degree of autonomy of the three constituent peoples—Bosnian Serbs, Bosnian Croats and Bosniaks (Kartsonaki, 2017, p. 503).[2] If the political elites wish to create the appropriate political climate to achieve stronger autonomy for their own constituent nation, they must (re)produce the 'metanarrative'. The latter could be defined as a coherent narrative about narratives and thus offers a framework for imagining one's own 'Self' with the aim of projecting the historical and cultural-political legitimacy of the 'Self' in "contemporary space and time" (Stojanović, 2003).

Given that BiH entails two political entities with a high degree of autonomy and District Brčko, inhabited by at least three constituent peoples (Bosniaks, Bosnian Croats and Bosnian Serbs), one may speak of the existence of at least three social and material environments in BiH. In each environment, the political elites attempt to (re)create metanarratives that—at the expense of legitimising their own 'Self'—'produce' both internal (Bosnian Croats, Bosnian Serbs and Bosniaks) and external 'Other' (EU). Following the Bosnian war, the creation of one's own 'Self' in relation to the 'Other' by (ethno-)political elites has occurred through a securitisation process—framing the Other as a security problem—to the extent that researchers began to talk about the securitisation of ethnic identities as a central axis of political discourse and action in BiH (e.g., Haynes, 2008; Becha & Visoka, 2010). The securitisation of ethnic identities in this way is vital because the nexus between identity and security

---

[2] Karlo Basta (2016) also discussed the importance of the instrumental and symbolic dimensions of the Bosnian–Herzegovinian institutional framework, which is based on ethno-federalist or ethno-consociational assumptions and demands for autonomy/centralisation by the three constituent nations. He concluded that any institutional deviation from civic (Bosniaks) or ethnic (Bosnian Serbs and Bosnian Croats) poses a threat to the collective identities of these constituent peoples (Basta, 2016, pp. 965–966).

cannot be understood without distinguishing ontological from physical security (Rumellili, 2013, pp. 12–13). Understanding that BiH is a post-conflict country currently devoid of major inter-ethnic physical violence, we consider this ethnic dilemma through the concept of ontological security. This form of security is defined as "trust in the continuity of one's own identity" of the chosen political entity (Giddens, 1991; Kinnvall, 2004; Mitzen, 2006; Steele, 2008; Ejdus, 2020).

The material and social environment of a political entity is crucial for determining the (sense) of ontological security. Both within and based on these two environments, the (ethno-)political elite creates a metanarrative for society by producing historical, cultural and political legitimacy of the 'Self'. Further, the aim of creating such a metanarrative is not solely to achieve legitimacy of the 'Self', but to consolidate separately the social and material environment of Republika Srpska (RS) from the one epitomising BiH, in that manner reflecting on the autonomous agency of RS as a (political) entity. We argue that the absence of ontological security of the metanarrative of the chosen political entity, which no longer makes sense of the collective (ethnic) identity and belongingness of an individual to this collectivity (Mitzen, 2006, p. 67) became more visible in RS after 2005[3] when BiH started negotiations on the SAA. This was reflected in the weak success of the police sector reform as a precondition for signing the SAA (Juncos, 2018), which we define as the first critical juncture; the failure of the Prud and Butmir process (constitutional reform—2009–2010) (Bieber, 2010), as the second critical juncture; and the referendum on the Day of RS (2015–2016), as the third critical juncture. In this respect, the instrumental rationality underlying the Europeanisation process in the first two critical junctures (police and constitutional reforms) was rejected by the political elites in RS who argued that the reforms were aiming for the centralisation and/or unitarisation of BiH, which in turn pose a 'threat' to the very existence of RS, its 'territorial integrity' and/or autonomous political institutions (e.g., Nezavisne novine, 2007, 2010). Namely, the instrumental rationality behind the Europeanisation process was framed as a "threat"

---

[3] This does not mean that the absence of ontological security may not have been even more visible in 1996 or 1998. I take such a position due to the Ontological security theory and for the purpose of the analysis of the EU's presence/involvement in the social and material environment of RS. Namely, for the first time, the EU became directly involved in RS' social and material environment in 2005 through reform initiatives.

to the social and material environment of RS (ontological security) as imagined by the (ethno-)political elite holding political power in this entity. Stemming from this, the third critical juncture is understood as the 'extraordinary measure' introduced by the political elite in RS aimed at not only assuring RS' continuity as an autonomous political entity but to further consolidate what Björkdahl (2018) portrays as a "state-making process" in RS. During all of these periods, only two political parties with a clear Bosnian Serb (ethno-)political programme were in power: the Serbian Democratic Party (*Srpska demokratska stranka*—SDS) and the Alliance of Independent Social Democrats (*Savez nezavisnih socijaldemokrata*—SNSD), which are also the only parties to have ruled the subnational RS since the Bosnian war came to an end (Kapidžić, 2017).

The problem described in the paragraphs above is the starting point for this book. In this context, the added value of linking the Europeanisation process and ontological (in)security is to understand how it is possible that Europeanisation, often uncritically viewed as holding considerable transformational potential to relativise (ethnic) nationalisms via desecuritisation at the expense of building a modern liberal political culture modelled on the EU (Noutcheva et al., 2004; Petritsch & Solioz, 2012; Milačić, 2020), can be understood as just the opposite—as a platform for further political reckoning, deepening the 'Self–Other' dialectic that adds to ethnic exclusion and/or even hatred. The subject of the study investigated in the book is both broader and narrower; if imagining the Bosnian Serb ethnic identity and the political identity of RS in the Europeanisation context is a *broader* subject of research, then understanding how the political elite in RS securitises Europeanisation is a *narrower* subject. The first research focus tackled in the book is to understand the historical elements that determine RS' material and social environment, that in turn enable imagining the ethnic identity of Bosnian Serbs and the autonomous agency of RS. At the heart of the research, I examine how it is possible that the expected effect of Europeanisation—transforming the antagonistic 'friend–enemy dialectic' into 'relationships of adversaries' through the institution and practices-building process (reform incentives)—has not been seen in the case of RS. We assume that the political elite in RS is using the EU's presence to securitise the internal and external 'Other', thereby hindering any transformation of the 'friend–enemy dialectic'. Consequently, the presented research reveals how the political elite of RS maintains a sense of ontological security of RS as an autonomous political agency at the expense of maintaining antagonisms between the ethnic groups in BiH in the setting of European integration.

The main research goal is to devise a conceptual model of the relationship between the concepts of Europeanisation, Securitisation and Ontological security. In *theoretical* and *conceptual* terms, there are four research objectives. The first is to determine how Europeanisation is defined by researchers as an attempt to transform (ethnic) identities, especially in relation to other dimensions of Europeanisation, where the logic of identity change in the exposed entities arises because of their identity-conditioned interests (*logic of appropriateness*). The second objective is to identify the place of Ontological (in)security in the context of European integration and Europeanisation, which is chiefly recognised as the EU's focal (transformational) potential in the process of post-conflict reconciliation, peacebuilding and relativisation of (national and ethnic) antagonisms. The third one is to understand the process of imagining ethnic identity via attempts to (re)produce and/or imagine ethnic homogeneity by the political elite; while the final objective is to identify where Europeanisation, Securitisation and Ontological security intersect.

Based on the mentioned objectives, the research questions are the following:

1. What is the context shaping the Bosnian Serb identity?
2. Do the political elites in RS construe EU integration as a threat to collective identity of Bosnian Serbs and political identity of RS?
3. How does the constructing of internal and external Others affect RS' integration with the rest of BiH and the EU?

The book is divided as follows. After the first chapter (introduction), the second chapter outlines the approach taken to the study of Ontological security, Securitisation and Europeanisation—the latter as a context for the potential transformation of ethnic identities. Here, we identify the conceptual nexus of these concepts to fill gaps in the literature. The third chapter analyses the historical emergence of the identity narratives in BiH, especially the ethnic ones, which were (re)imagined for the purpose of RS' contemporary material and social environment. The aim of this chapter is to explain the social and material environment of RS, whose ethnopolitical elite is trying to shape via the (re)produced metanarratives to project RS having autonomous agency. The three critical junctures are then put in the context of Europeanisation, which forms the basis for the empirical analysis. We employ critical junctures according to the theory of Ontological security—as shorter periods/events that allow analysis of whether there was a strengthening/weakening of a sense of ontological security. The (discursive) acts of the political elite in RS projected onto the social and material environment of RS to maintain a sense of ontological security are analysed. The fourth chapter is based on qualitative and quantitative analysis of the discourse where if and how the political elite in RS securitised Europeanisation is examined; as in, whether the EU's presence was securitised by the political elite of RS in the three mentioned critical junctures. Finally, the fifth chapter synthesises the findings and unravels the theoretical and policy implications of the study while outlining avenues for future research.

References

Basta, K. (2016). Imagined institutions: The symbolic power of formal rules in Bosnia and Herzegovina. *Slavic Review, 75*(4), 944–969.

Becha, A., & Visoka, G. (2010). Human security as 'ethnic security' in Kosovo. *Human Security Perspectives, 7*(1), 83–101.

Bieber, F. (2010). *Constitutional reform in Bosnia and Herzegovina: Preparing for EU accession (policy brief, 1)*. European Policy Centre. Available at https://www.files.ethz.ch/isn/115432/PB_04_10_Bosnia.pdf

Biermann, R. (2014). Coercive Europeanization: The EU's struggle to contain secessionism in the Balkans. *European Security, 23*(4), 484–508.

Björkdahl, A. (2018). Republika Srpska: Imaginary, performance and spatialization. *Political Geography, 66*, 34–43.

Björkdahl, A., Chaban, N., Leslie, J., & Masselot, A. (2015). *Importing EU norms: Conceptual framework and empirical findings*. Springer.

Bojinović Fenko, A., & Stahl, B. (2019). Chips off the old block: Europeanisation of the foreign policies of Western Balkan states. In J. Džankić, S. Keil, & M. Kmezić (Eds.), *The Europeanisation of the Western Balkans* (pp. 39–62). Palgrave Macmillan.

Dupcsik, C. (2001). The west, the east and the border-lining. In U. Becker & P. Tamás (Eds.), *The countries of Central and Eastern Europe and the EU: Attitudes and perceptions* (pp. 31–39). Informations Zentrum Sozialwissenschaften.

Ejdus, F. (2020). *Crisis and ontological insecurity: Serbia's anxiety over Kosovo's secession*. Palgrave Macmillan.

Finnemore, M. (1996). *National Interests in international society*. Cornell University Press.

Giddens, A. (1991). *Modernity and self-identity: Self and Society in the Late Modern age*. Stanford University Press.

Hanžek, L. (2012). Epistemička i instrumentalna racionalnost. *Filozofska istraživanja, 32*(3/4), 411–425.

Haynes, D. F. (2008). *Deconstructing the reconstruction: Human rights and rule of law in Postwar Bosnia and Herzegovina*. Ashgate Publishing Limited.

Johnston, A., & Acharya, A. (2007). *Crafting cooperation: Regional international institutions in comparative perspective*. Cambridge University Press.

Juncos, A. (2018). EU security sector reform in Bosnia and Herzegovina: Reform or resist? *Contemporary Security Policy, 39*(1), 95–118.

Kapidžić, D. (2017). Segmentirani stranački sustav Bosne i Hercegovine. *Političke perspektive: časopis za istraživanje politike, 7*(1/2), 7–23.

Kartsonaki, A. (2017). Twenty years after Dayton: Bosnia-Herzegovina (still) stable and explosive. *Civil Wars, 18*(4), 488–516.

Kaufmann, J.-C. (2009). *L'identité*. Available at https://www.cairn.info/identites%2D%2D9782749211121-page-55.htm

Ker-Lindsay, J. (2016). *The hollow threat of secession in Bosnia and Herzegovina: Legal and political impediments to a unilateral declaration of independence by Republika Srpska (working paper)*. LSEE – Research on South Eastern Europe. Available at http://eprints.lse.ac.uk/66259/1/__lse.ac.uk_storage_LIBRARY_Secondary_libfile_share d_repository_Content_Ker Lindsay_The%20Hollow%20Threat%20of%20secession_Ker_Lindsay_The_Hollow_Thr eat_of_secession.pdf

Kinnvall, C. (2004). Globalization and religious nationalism: Self, identity, and the search for ontological security. *Political Psychology, 25*(5), 741–767.

Lajh, D., & Kajnč Lange, S. (2009). *Evropska unija od A do Ž*. Uradni list Republike Slovenije.

Lavdas, K. A. (2018). Stalled Europeanization in post-sovereignty EU? Greek politics in hard times. *Uluslarasi Iliskiler, 58*(18), 35–46.

Maier, M. L., & Risse, T. (2003). *Europeanization*. Collective Identities and Public Discourses. Available at https://www.files.ethz.ch/isn/27144/07_Maier_Risse-03.pdf.

Majstorović, D., & Vučkovac, Z. (2016). Rethinking Bosnia and Herzegovina's post- coloniality challenges of Europeanization discourse. *Journal of Language and Politics, 15*(2), 147–172.

Manners, I., & Murray, P. (2016). The end of a Noble narrative? European integration narratives after the Nobel peace prize. *Journal of Common Market Studies, 54*(1), 185–202.

March, J. G., & Olsen, J. P. (1989). *Rediscovering institutions*. Free Press.

Marks, G., Hooghe, L. (2003). *National identity and support for European integration.* Available at https://www.ssoar.info/ssoar/bitstream/handle/document/11155/ssoar-2003-marks_et_al-national_identity_and_support_for.pdf ?sequence=1&isAllowed=y&lnkname=ssoar-2003-marks_et_al-national_identity_and_support_for.pdf

Milačić, F. (2020). Europeanization and the statehood problem: The case of Croatia and Serbia. *Nationalities Papers, 48*(5), 861–875.

Mitzen, J. (2006). Ontological security in world politics: State identity and the security dilemma. *European Journal of International Relations, 12*(3), 341–370.

Močnik, R. (1998). Balkan Orientalisms. V B. Baskar in B. Brumen (ur.), Mediterranean ethnological summer school (str. 129–158). : Inštitut za multikulturne raziskave.

Mouffe, C. (2012). An agonistic approach to the future of Europe. *New Literary History, 43*(4), 629–640.

Nancheva, N. (2012). *Transforming identities in Europe: Bulgaria and Macedonia between nationalism and Europeanization* (PhD Thesis). University of Westminster, School of Social Sciences, Humanities and Languages.

Nancheva, N. (2017). Securitisation reversed. *Does Europeanization improve minority/majority relations? Südosteuropa, 65*(1), 10–34.

Noutcheva, G., Tocci, N., Coppieters, B., Kovziridze, T., Emerson, M., & Huyysseune, M. (2004). Europeanization and seccessionist conflicts: Concepts and theories. *Journal on Ethnopolitics and minority issues in Europe, 1*(2), 1–35.

Petritsch, W., & Solioz, C. (2012). Europeanization at the crossroads. *Journal for Labour and Social Affairs in Eastern Europe, 15*(3), 413–420.

Recchia, S. (2007). *Beyond international trusteeship: EU peacebuilding in Bosnia and Herzegovina.* (Occasional Paper, 66). Institute for Security Studies. Available at https://www.iss.europa.eu/sites/default/files/EUISSFiles/occ66.pdf

Risse, T. (2001). *The euro and identity politics in Europe* (Research Paper, 6–8 December). Available at http://userpage.fu-berlin.de/~atasp/texte/021202_risse_euroidentity.pdf

Rumelili, B. (2013). Identity and desecuritisation: The pitfalls of conflating ontological and pyhsical security. *Journal of International Relations and Development, 18*(1), 52–74.

Sanders, D., Belluci, P., Toka, G., & Torcal, M. (2012). *The Europeanization of National Polities? Citizenship and support in a post-enlargement union.* Oxford University Press.

Spohn, W., & Eder, K. (2005). *Collective memory and european identity: The effects of integration and enlargement.* Routledge.

Stanley, P. (2013). *The construction of social reality.* Penguin Books.

Steele, B. J. (2008). *Ontological security in international relations: Self-identity and the IR state.* Routledge.

Stojanović, D. (2003). *Srbija i demokratija: 1903–1914*. Filozofska fakulteta.

Subotić, J. (2013). Stories states tell: Identity, narrative, and human rights in the Balkans. *Slavic Review, 72*(2), 306–326.

Tocci, N. (2007). *The EU and conflict resolution: Promoting peace in the backyard*. Routledge.

Todorova, M. (1997). *Imagining the Balkans*. Oxford University Press

Wiliams, M., & Kelstrup, M. (2000). *International relations theory and the politics of European integration: Power, security and community*. Routledge.

CHAPTER 2

Europeanisation, Securitisation and Ontological Insecurity

The theoretical chapter contains three subchapters and a conclusion. The first subchapter presents analysis of Europeanisation as a context that enables the transformation of (ethnic) identities. This is accomplished through the lens of social constructivism, which prescribes the importance of the 'ideational socialisation' via the enlargement process (i.e., reform incentives), enabling (ethnic) identities to be transformed. At the same time, the subchapter critically reflects on Europeanisation as a context that attempts to (re)configure the internal Other by integrating it into a common (EU-driven) economic, social, cultural and political framework. The second subchapter looks at key conceptual contours of securitisation in the field of critical security studies with an emphasis on the sociological approach to the theory to offer an appropriate operationalisation of the critical junctures identified. The third subchapter outlines the biggest elements of the ontological security theory by focusing on the explanatory potential held by ontological (in)security for ethnic identities and the material and social environment as a prerequisite for determining a sense of ontological (in)security. Finally, the conclusion considers the proposed conceptualisation of the interplay of Europeanisation, securitisation and ontological (in)security to grasp how the European integration—as a desecuritising mechanism—can function as a source of ontological insecurity.

© The Author(s), under exclusive license to Springer Nature   13
Switzerland AG 2023
F. Kočan, *Identity, Ontological Security and Europeanisation
in Republika Srpska*, Central and Eastern European Perspectives
on International Relations,
https://doi.org/10.1007/978-3-031-46169-9_2

2.1   Europeanisation as a Context
for the Transformation of (Ethnic) Identities

To understand Europeanisation as a setting that enables the transformation of (ethnic) identities, one must revert to the sociological contextualisation of Europeanisation, postulated on the social constructivism. Within the latter, the dominant questions touch upon how the (European) values and political paradigms, as internalised on the national levels, shape both the (political-driven) discourses and identities (Olsen, 2002, 935; Wendt, 1992). The contextual ambiguousness of these questions often leaves them prone to criticism (e.g., Radelli, 2000).[1] However, we ground Europeanisation in the field of social constructivism because the concept as such becomes—through sociological lens—'flexible' enough to take both historical and geographical determinants of Europeanisation into account (Flockhart, 2008, 3).

The second argument on which this book builds when highlighting the need for a broader sociological conceptualisation of Europeanisation is that the very same "conceptual ambiguity" has led to specific research agenda in the field. This then led—after researching intense political processes—to a research 'niche' that started to neglect other processes (e.g., cultural) inherently connected with Europeanisation (Subotić, 2019). This narrow research agenda hence inadvertently neglected the very own conceptual contours of Europeanisation. By this, we mean that Europeanisation became a phenomenon without a genesis and a codified culture from which Gellner and Smith (1996) gained attention by conceptualising it. Moreover, by neglecting the sociological (and historical) dimension and focusing on the processual nature of Europeanisation,[2] researchers of the Europeanisation agenda partly internalised the Eurocentric design of history, framing Europe as the most technically sophisticated, morally progressive and permanently superior in relation to the 'Other' (Flockhart, 2008, 6).

Such a (narrow) historical definition and simultaneous acceptance of a Eurocentric interpretation of history therefore formed a research agenda

---

[1] Radelli (2000, p. 145), for example, questioned if the Europeanisation can at once explain cultural changes, the development of new identities and policy changes. He went even further by arguing that Europeanisation—if it can explain all of this—will in the future become "everything and nothing" at the same time.

[2] For an extensive overview of the processual nature of Europeanisation in relation to the state-centric assumption, see Jordan (2002, 191–95).

with a limited number of research questions. The latter were largely concerned with explanations in the context of European integration and (eventual) EU membership (Hix & Goertz, 2000; Cowles et al., 2001; Börzel, 2002; Schimelfennig & Sedelmeier, 2005). Researchers in the field of International Relations and European studies mostly understand and define Europeanisation as either the effect of the EU on national political structures and policies and vice versa, or the combined influence of both approaches, known as 'uploading', 'downloading' or 'crossloading' (e.g., Börzel, 2002; Lajh & Kajnč Lange, 2009; Börzel & Risse, 2011; Tekin & Güney, 2015; Bojinović Fenko & Stahl, 2019). The focus in these cases is hence primarily on the process and the extent to which both member states and candidate countries adopt EU rules and implement EU policies and—through the logic of a feedback loop—influence EU institutions and policies. An important conceptual leap in this regard was made by Sedelmeier and Schimmelfennig (2005) who showed that adoption of the EU's rules and norms alone has an irreversible effect on the social learning process through socialisation as a mechanism that forms part of the Europeanisation process.

When Sedelmeier and Schimelfennig (2005) conceptualised the "logic of appropriateness"[3] and "logic of consequences",[4] they inevitably paved the way to a 'new kind' of understanding of Europeanisation premised on social constructivism. Among others, this prompted Flockhart (2008, pp. 5–7) to argue for the need to distinguish Europeanisation from EU-isation building on both the normative and conceptual leap in understanding Europeanisation. In so doing, Flockhart (2008) showed that such a distinction is important because EU-isation first and foremost reflects a political dimension,[5] while Europeanisation also entails a cultural dimension. While I do not opt for such a dividing line, my argument stems from the idea that Europeanisation continues to take account of cultural

---

[3] The logic of appropriateness is a perspective on the nature of the interpretation of human actions that inherently contains both cognitive and normative dimensions (March & Olsen 1995, 30–31). In this respect, the logic of appropriateness relies on the assumption that subjects follow the rules because they understand them as natural, fair, expected and legitimate.

[4] The logic of consequences is usually guided by action based on 'analysis' and involves weighing alternatives and expected outcomes (March & Simon 1993, 7). The logic of consequence is therefore an action based on weighing and calculating costs and benefits.

[5] Relations between the EU and member states and the transfer of organisational practices and policies.

processes, norms and patterns of behaviour that contribute to the forming of the EU's political identity and the European identity as such. This is additionally demonstrated by the social constructivist approach to Europeanisation (e.g., Kassim, 2000), which assumes that the identities of subjects are extremely unfixed due to the very nature of the changeability of (normative) structures (Hobson, 2002, p. 25). In this respect, one should not neglect the work of Bulmer (2007) who looked at the dual understanding of Europeanisation. This duality includes an understanding of Europeanisation not only as the transfer of institutional features, rules, beliefs and norms from E(U)rope, but also as a process of institutional capacity-building in E(U)rope. The underlying feature of such duality is that it is mainly ideas which lead to a change in the behaviour of subjects and institutions through the socialisation process.

In line with this, the ideas that trigger a change in the behaviour of subjects and institutions through the socialisation process are what Risse (2001, 203) understands as the "European collective nation-state identity", resonating with the modern Western concept of Europe as a liberal community. The latter builds on the idea that collective nation-state identity is constructed around the institutions and practices in which the socialisation may occur. But for such socialisation to occur, appropriate institutions (e.g., both social and political) should be constructed. By this alone, the idea that the European collective nation-state identity can transform the antagonistic 'friend–enemy relation' (Spohn & Eder, 2005) into what Mouffe (2012) views as relationships of adversaries.

Arising from this, to conceptualise Europeanisation as a context that enables the transformation of (ethnic) identities, one must consider the arguments made by Checkel (2005). He demonstrated that "subjects go beyond playing roles and accepting community or organisational norms as the only appropriate way, namely by changing their interest and their own identity so that they can become part of the community" (Checkel, 2005, 804). Such a definition is based on cognitive and social psychology, meaning that "individuals who are exposed to certain normative regulations transform their own interests" (Checkel, 2001, 58). They do this through social learning or ideational socialisation, which entails both active and reflexive internalisation of the logic of appropriateness that exists on the EU level (e.g., Carlson et al., 2018; Schimmelfennig, 2019). However, this cannot be done without constructing appropriate institutions, which then convey such socialisation, as was the case with France, Germany and the United Kingdom (Risse, 2001) or Eastern Europe (Spohn & Eder,

2005). The underlying feature in the mentioned cases is the idea of *stabilisation*, which—through the Stabilisation and Association process—is also at the forefront of the EU's approach to Southeast Europe (SEE). To grasp the idea of such stabilisation, one has to understand the ideational diffusion—'entrapped' in (re)creating institutions via reform incentives—in place to allow for the transformation of the antagonistic 'friend–enemy relation' to 'relationships of adversaries'.

2.1.1   From Institutional to Ideational Diffusion: Ideational Socialisation as an Enabler of the Transformation of (Ethnic) Identities

Tanil (2014, 487) provides a starting point for discussing ideational socialisation, framing the cooperation in/with EU institutions as "means to reshape the ideas, identity and interests via resocialization". European studies scholars engage with such argument with two approaches to Europeanisation: adaptation and learning. The difference between the two is shown by Rieker (2004, 372), postulated in questioning the values. If adaptation refers to behavioural changes without special questioning, i.e., activities are merely 'transferred to an own institutional structure', learning refers to questioning these activities in relation to the 'existing institutional structure' and the values on which the structure is based on. This difference is at the same time the central disparity between institutional and normative diffusion since the latter foresees deep socialisation effects on actors that adapt and internalise rules and norms during the process (Checkel, 2001, 58).

The mechanism through which EU norms are diffused (Manners, 2002; Björkdahl, 2005) in a certain national context with the aim of socialising subjects is defined as social learning within the theory of social constructivism. The latter, which Risse (2001, 12) defines as a "mechanism that affects the transformation of the subject's interest and identities", is what makes sense of Tanil's (2014) idea of single-loop vs. complex learning. In complex learning, subjects—largely the political elite—adopt norm-based rules and internalise them so that they become the basis for a shared (subjective) understanding of 'appropriate' behaviour (Finnemore & Sikkink, 1998, 895; Checkel, 2001, 57). This process therefore builds on the logic of "exposure to normative regulations with the aim of forming new interests and identities" (ibid.). Finally, complex social learning differs from single-loop learning since it is mainly about how the subject is acquiring new information and alternative strategies while still relying on the existing interests.

Such logic of socialisation is premised on two different types of social learning: Type I internalisation—acceptance of new roles—Type II internalisation, which presumes a change in values, interests and hence identities (Checkel, 2005, 804). In this respect, Type I internalisation presumes that subjects follow the logic of appropriateness as they are aware of what is supposed to be appropriate in a certain community. A good example of such internalisation is provided by Trondal (2007) who analysed changes in national political elites because of the intensity of their cooperation within the EU institutions. Similar conclusions were drawn by Beyers (2005) after analysing the co-influence of the domestic and EU environments in subjects' acceptance of new (supra-national) roles. On the other hand, the Type II internalisation assumes that subjects go 'beyond playing and accepting' the norms, interests and identity of a certain organisation because that would be 'appropriate', but because they believe that they are part of this community. In this respect, only the Type II internalisation can—as shown by Egeberg (1999)—have transformative effects on subjects, including how they perceive themselves (Self) and their interests in relation to the Other.

Building on this, I define ideational socialisation as a dynamic process where subjects are exposed to the norms and rules of a given community so that the socialiser (in our case, the EU) (re)socialises them through the learning and diffusion of norms. This means the subjects' ideas, interests and identities can change due to exposure to the EU, including perceptions of (in)appropriate behaviour. To properly understand in what way this socialisation with the goal of transforming identities within the Europeanisation framework occurs, we must discuss the 'ideational life cycle' (Marcussen, 2000). This is important as it helps—by way of stages— understand how subject develop, institutionalise and internalise new ideas over time. In this sense, the ideational life cycle begins with an ideational equilibrium defined by the phase in which domestic political elites share a set of unquestioned knowledge structures. At a certain point, such (consensual) knowledge is challenged by a radical change in the environment— alternatively, a critical juncture—which simultaneously challenges the dominant norms, ideas and identities. Such a situation, referred to by Marcussen (2000) as an external shock, may be seen as "a period of (political) delegitimization in which a window of opportunity opens, reflecting upon the outdated causal beliefs" (Goldstein & Keohane, 1993, 12).

For the purpose of methodological and conceptual consistency, I understand these external shocks as critical junctures. The latter are defined by Nabers (2015) and Ejdus (2017) as disruptive and radical processes that challenge the subject's ability to continue acting according to previous patterns. These critical junctures, therefore, due to the nature of the obsolescence of causal beliefs, which make it impossible to continue acting according to existing patterns, cause cognitive dissonance and a change in the subject's cognitive frameworks. This situation, which does not have a clearly prescribed model of behaviour given the large number of unknowns, causes an 'ideational vacuum'. During this phase, which Marcussen (2000, 15) defines as knowledge insecurity, political elites are supposed to be more receptive to new ideas beyond the existing ones, which would help them bridge the collectively felt cognitive dissonance. A thorough interpretation of the ideational vacuum is offered by Goldstein and Keohane (1993, 12) who argued that "ideas contribute to outcomes in the absence of a unique balance". This means that ideas can function as those points that define a common solution (between national and EU institutions and their policies), or actions, so that they become a connective 'glue' to promote the cohesion of specific groups (national decision-makers or decision-makers on the EU level).

The ideational vacuum is that crucial period in which one of many potential ideas is selected. The subject chooses an idea within the process of transferring ideational transfer mechanisms (Tanil, 2014, 489–492). The first ideational transfer mechanism is 'ideational modelling', which occurs in a time of ideational uncertainty when national decision-makers are looking for good practices beyond national borders to either legitimise the existing institutional structure or change their own institutional structure. This mechanism offers national decision-makers a particular level of cognitive stability and a set of immediate solutions to the problems they are supposed to be 'tormenting'. The second mechanism that occurs after ideational modelling is ideational socialisation, which takes place when national decision-makers begin to meet in international forums (Marcussen, 2000, 29). Namely, the process of ideational socialisation (transfer and internalisation) starts to unravel.

The third mechanism is ideational leadership, which happens through transnational political elites that hold important political positions and can promote (their) ideas during the decision-making process. Börzel and Risse (2003, 67) in their contribution to the topic of ideational leadership emphasised that such ideational leaders primarily are normative actors.

Accordingly, they derive from moral arguments and strategic constructs and can mobilise political elites in the domestic environment by transforming their interests and identities. When all three mechanisms are used, this leads to a certain decision being made and the process of institutional diffusion (full institutionalisation) commences (Miles, 2005, 29). The final stage of this process is therefore the creation of formal procedures, rules and norms, and the replacement of old structures with new ones that are built on new ideas (Marcussen, 2000, 22). In this respect, the (re) creation of such institutions does not simply offer a new ideational balance but also the potential to thereby transform (ethnic) identities, such that the old knowledge—premised on the antagonistic 'friend–enemy relationship'—is replaced by new ideas where the antagonistic dialectics (may) be converted to a relationship of adversaries (Fig. 2.1).

The logic of transformation of (ethnic) identities outlined above assumes that the structure is designed in such a way as to co-shape the subject's identity and interests, while the very same structure is also co-shaped by the subject's identity and interests. Finnemore (1996, 15) emphasised that socially formed rules, principles, norms, behaviour and identities are important because they offer subjects a framework of "importance" and legitimacy via expected behaviour in pursuit of their own interests. To be more concrete, these social structures strengthen subjects with both preferences and strategies that can be used to pursue their (own) interests. The latter—as Adler (1997, 324) underscores—can only be pursued with a certain identity which, like interest and behaviour, is socially

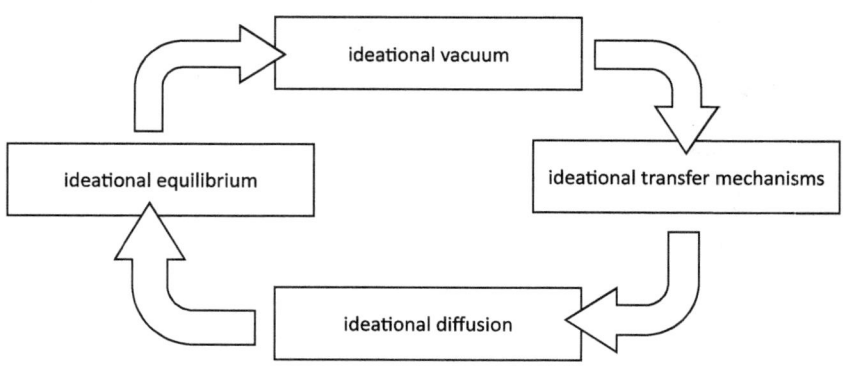

Fig. 2.1   Ideational life cycle. (Source: Marcussen 2000; Tanil 2014)

formed through collective meaning, interpretation and beliefs about the world. In this regard, the creation of such institutions, which offers a new ideational equilibrium where antagonistic dialectics (may) become a relationship of adversaries, builds on four (conceptual) assumptions (Tamil, 2014): (i) the structure consists of norms, comprehended as a (collective) reflection of how the logic of appropriateness is understood, (ii) the social structure is in a reciprocal relationship with the subject's identity and interests, (iii) the subject's interests are chiefly postulated on ideas and (iv) the subject's behaviour (political preferences) is determined by ideas and identities that have a reciprocal relationship with the structure's (normative) limitation.

To summarise, the aspect of the subject's (political) internalisation of ideas and norms is essential for understanding Europeanisation as a context enabling the transformation of (ethnic) identities. During the formation of interest and identity, it is thus an imperative to reflect upon the importance of ideas and identities that epitomise the (re)creation of the institutions which aim to transform the Self–Other dialectics. This is shown by the fact that, on the one hand, there are structural boundaries formed relative to the subject's identity and that become the legitimate basis for the subject's interests, and, on the other, interests that limit the legitimacy of ideas and norms (i.e., EU-driven reform incentives). Here, the influence of such (EU-driven) reform incentives with the aim to (re) create institutions somewhat exposes the domestic political elite for either accepting and internalising (with varying intensity, see Fig. 2.2) or rejecting these incentives that inherently pertain to (new) ideas and norms that influence identities. The process of ideational socialisation, which has a transformative effect on the normative and institutional environment of the political subject, accordingly works in a way that enables it to (re)shape the understanding of its own 'self' (Checkel, 2001).

Such a process of social learning through ideational diffusion with the goal of transforming (ethnic) identities was mainly applied to Western European countries after the Second World War. This process is significantly different from the Europeanisation process emerging after the end of the Cold War in post-socialist countries, including South-East Europe (SEE) where the latter is primarily understood through the "temporary and transitional" idea within the broader notion of "making up for lost time" (Majstorović & Vučkovac, 2016, 152). This expansion to the 'East' is characterised as the integration of the 'internal Other' in the EU, as a space that must be exposed to both the material and symbolic efforts of

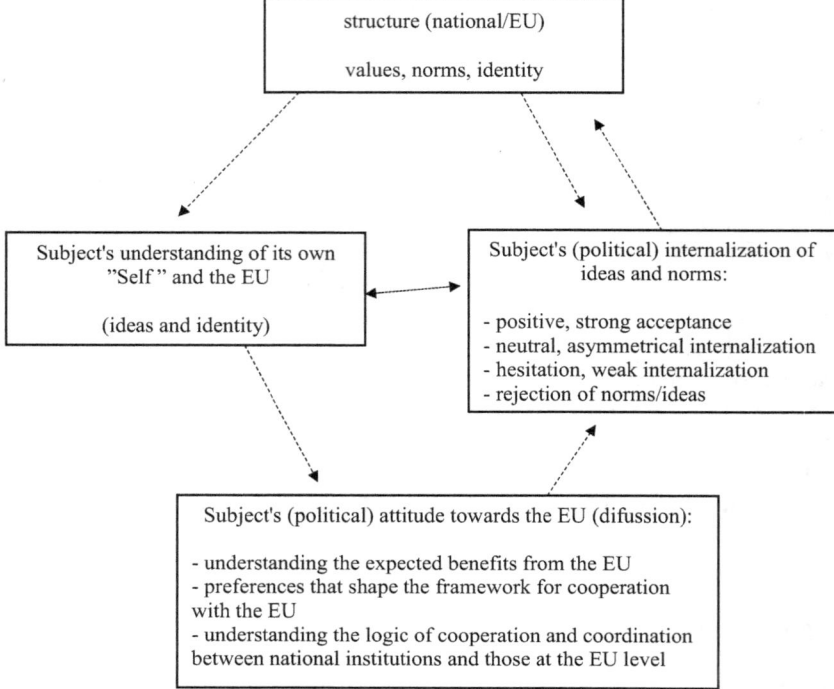

Fig. 2.2 Subject and structure vis-à-vis ideational diffusion. (Source: Author's own elaboration)

the (liberal) West via socialisation (ideational diffusion). This 'internal Otherness' of Europe is, among others, SEE, which 'needs to be stabilised and integrated' in order to become part of the common political, economic, social and cultural (reference) framework on which the EU is premised (Todorova, 1997; Močnik, 1999; Majstorović, 2007; Sarajlić, 2011). The next subchapter thus reflects on the contemporary content of the ideational framework of the EU, which—through socialisation—envisages "a path to normality" by way of the redefinition and integration of the 'Other' into what Subotić (2011) understands through the idea of Europe "as a state of mind".

2.1.2 *Europeanisation of the Internal Other in the EU's Common Political, Economic, Social and Cultural Framework*

To understand the Europeanisation of SEE as an 'internal Other' vis-à-vis the common referential framework of the EU, one must start with the work of Hériter (2005, 199–200). The author discusses the difference between the Europeanisation of the East and the West, which he substantiates with the metaphor of a one-way and two-way street (ibid.). In this way, he describes the Europeanisation of the West as a two-way street due to the feedback loop in terms of the EU's formulation of policies and its institutional structure, while the Europeanisation of the East has no such feedback loop. This was also considered by Hammond (2006) and Majstorović (2007) who justified the Europeanisation of the East through the discursive appearance of EU enlargement and found that—via the rhetoric of "civilisation" and "Europeanness"—the discourse is irreversibly directed to the (peripheral) societies of the Continent's East. Petrović (2009, 13) went even one step further and underlined that such discourses have created an enduring distinction between East and West (Europe/EU and 'still-not-Europe'), or old and new Europe, which in turn consolidated Western Europe as an (ideal) model of Europeanness.

This one-dimensionality is, of course, neither a modern phenomenon nor limited to the field of (political) discursiveness given that it relies significantly on the interpretation of historical processes. A good example is modernisation and democratisation within which countries of the East are merely the recipients of such (Western) models (e.g., Yurchak, 2006; Miškova, 2006). In the last two decades, interpretations of this type have attracted considerable criticism (e.g., Velikonja, 2009; Majstorović & Vučkovac, 2016). In this respect, Todorova (2009, 177) showed how such discourse and symbolic geographical imaginary of Europe is not a specific SEE issue, but an Eastern European phenomenon inherently connected to the socialist past. This is what then unites SEE and Eastern Europe after 1989 since they were discursively framed—as Petrović (2014) argues as being—"less European than the West". In a framework like this, socialism was understood as a non-European legacy preventing the societies of Eastern Europe from fully integrating into "democratic Europe". The socialist past of these societies is therefore a lever/mechanism to which both Eastern and South-East Europe are subjected to social learning and ideational socialisation through reform incentives.

However, this understanding of post-socialist/communist Europe is not only problematic for the production of knowledge and 'ways of knowing' (Todorova, 2004), but also for the political legitimacy and role of the political elite, both within their own societies and in international politics. In this sense, Buden (2009, 2013) importantly states that the imaginary of the "Eastern European" as a "child of communism" should not be understood as a metaphor, but as a symptom of the imaginary within which the need for the democratic transition of the East is created. A distinction along these lines was (in the most radical sense) used, among others, to support interpretations of the consequences of the Balkan wars during the 1990s and the post-war arrangement of the newly emerging states. Namely, the international community seemed to proceed from a logic of post-socialist transition whereby it was necessary to organise the states "completely anew" (Helms 2003). This logic produced an irreversible effect by erasing certain aspects of the socialist past and significantly contributed to the fact that the transition was not only necessary, but already had a precisely prescribed course and clear political consequences (projection and introjection of the Western liberal model). Miškova (2006) and Melegh (2006) also reflected on these consequences and noted that this democratic transition should not simply be understood in the context of mirroring the imaginary of the Western (hegemonic) discourse in Eastern Europe, but largely as an ideological mechanism for consolidating the liberal ideologies via reform incentives in this space with the aim to alter the 'self-narration' paradigm(s).

This (historically) entrenched belief about Eastern and South-East Europe as a semi-European periphery, as an area that needs to be directed—if not taught, was further reinforced after the end of the Cold War through the newly formed symbolic geography of Europe. The latter prescribed that the former socialist part of the continent was characterised by "violence, nationalism and backwardness", which can become part of Europe when it "gets rid of the socialist/communist past" and exposes itself to a one-way process of transformation through Europeanisation (Petrović, 2014, 19). This led, among others, to start debating the 'deprovincialisation' of Western Europe[6] (Todorova, 2012, 74). Along this path, not only could the integration of the Eastern and South-East Europe historiography into the broader European (historical) architecture be achieved

---

[6] The idea of deprovincialisation emerges from the assumption that the West is 'the sole owner' of the political and moral-philosophical development of Europe (Todorova, 2012).

(Debeljak, 2004, 21), but it would simultaneously lead to the complexity of the already established narratives premised on differentiation (Zahra, 2011, 787).

The aforementioned distinction hence stems from the basic assumption that Europeanisation, with its political, economic, social and cultural framework, holds the potential to "bridge a troubled past", be it socialist/communist or Ottoman (Todorova, 2004, 190). Here, it is worth considering the works of Kuus (2004) and Bôröcz (2001) who showed how the European integration of the East could be understood with regard to three arguments. First, colonisation as a strategy of alleged self-representation extends beyond intellectual debates in both Eastern and South-East Europe, which is visible in the presence of the international community in Kosovo and BiH. There, the discourse itself, the institutional structure and the political practices show clear signs of neocolonialism (Majstorović, 2007; Tatlić, 2008). The very idea that some form of (colonial) administration must be established in SEE with the aim of maintaining peace and enabling the development of the entire European continent could be found in the twentieth century in both academic and journalistic discussions (e.g., Kaplan, 1999; Carver, 1999; Hammond, 2006). Muršič (2007, 91) connected the idea of controlling SEE with the imaginary of the "crossroads" or "contact zones of great power". By doing this, Muršič (2007) showed the importance of such definitions, which preserved the discourse of hegemony. Since these countries existed at a crossroads or (undefined) contact zones, it was only sensible to insist on the "European way of organizing" (Muršič, 2007, 93).

The second argument, which is more general, stems from the understanding of SEE as a "European third world region", which made it possible to create a sense of the necessity for the EU's presence. Here, it is worth noting the argument of Petrović (2014, 8) who emphasised that the EU's presence should be seen as a step closer to "Europe" for the countries of Eastern and South-East Europe, but instead this closeness has only "pushed them into the European third world area" (ibid.). The EU is supposed to achieve this through a securitising discourse, such as by highlighting the level of organised crime, the corruption of political elites, drug trafficking, illegal immigration and even terrorism. The third and final argument that can be presented is to ensure economic control over Eastern and South-East Europe, which is inherently linked to global capitalism. In relation to this, the EU's external presence in controlling the markets of this part of Europe holds dual significance; the discourse on (development) aid and the discourse on administration/management (Petrović, 2014; Majstorović & Vučkovac, 2016).

The above arguments are summarised by arguing that the EU's common political, social, economic and cultural framework not only 'gives power' to the West vis-à-vis the East, but acts as a mechanism for integration of the East. This works in such a way that there is an (un)conscious erasure of the historical heritage of the East, which is looking for a legitimate place in the overall European (historical) architecture (Debeljak, 2004, 27). A series of historical events before, during and after the end of the Second World War in Europe led to the fact that the European idea and the archetype of "Europeanness" began to develop primarily through the unification of European countries on the 'right side' of the Iron Curtain (i.e., Western Europe). The further development of events, which aspired to the integration of Eastern Europe in the political, economic, social and cultural spheres, saw the European idea—due to the symbolic and material 'hijacking' of European institutions—begin to take on the face of exclusivity. While in the past Islam was the 'Other', over time—and especially after the end of the Second World War—Eastern and South-East Europe became 'Others'. The modern 'European idea' inevitably took shape under the pressure of the Cold War which forced Western Europe into 'homogenisation', following the idea of Europeanisation as a project of (political) unification (Olsen, 2002; Radelli, 2003).

Debeljak (2004, 28–29) argues that this idea developed in relation to the "necessity of resistance against the 'common enemy' on the other side of the Iron Curtain". The modern 'European idea', which is accordingly deeply rooted in the EU's institutional framework, and thus today still represents what Subotić (2011) sees in the idea of Europe "as a state of mind", remains significantly limiting vis-à-vis the Other. In this context, the (identity-driven) security paradigm, or what Petrović (2014) calls the rapprochement with Europe relative to the simultaneous push into the "third world area", was premised on the securitised discourse; the SEE as an area of "organised crime, corruption of the political elites, illegal migration" that must be "saved from itself". The solution, however, was the transfer of the liberal Western models through reform incentives with the aim of achieving ideological (re)socialisation. The latter would in turn offer a path to democratisation of the area, built on the rule of law and fundamental (human) rights. Such an interpretation calls for analysis of the theoretical paradigm of securitisation in the critical security studies field with a view to shedding light on the mechanisms of Europeanisation as a phenomenon that tends to project and introject the idea of the common political, social, economic and cultural framework upon which the EU is built (Fig. 2.3).

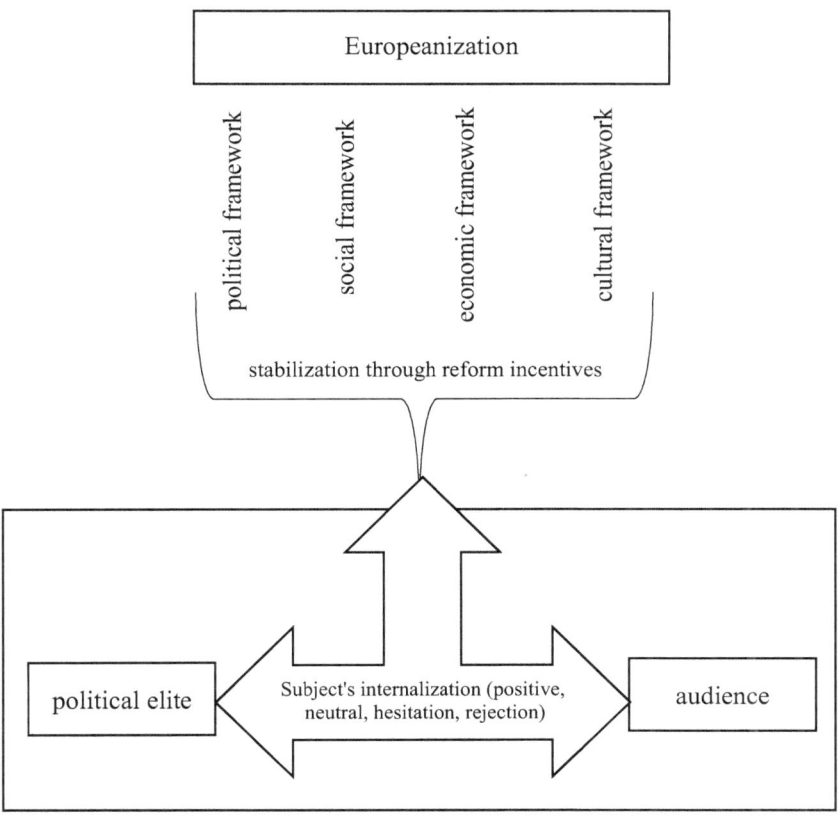

Europeanization

political framework

social framework

economic framework

cultural framework

stabilization through reform incentives

political elite

Subject's internalization (positive, neutral, hesitation, rejection)

audience

Political entity/state

Fig. 2.3 Europeanisation as a context for facilitating the transformation of (ethnic) identities. (Source: Author's own elaboration)

2.2   Securitisation Theory, Its Operationalisation and Points of Ruptures

The field of (critical) security studies contains rich discussions on 'competing' theoretical paradigms of securitisation theory, particularly on which perspective can better explain the process of securitisation. Expressed simply, securitisation should be understood as a process of framing a (social) phenomenon as a security problem that holds the potential to threaten the existence of a referent object. Discussions on securitisation are dominated by three schools: (i) Copenhagen (Wæver et al., 1993), (ii) Welsh (Booth, 1991, 2002; Jones, 1999, 2001) and (iii) Paris (Bigo, 2002; Balzacq, 2010; Ejdus & Božović, 2016). Moving beyond the most obvious (epistemological) differences between the approaches, the schools chiefly differ regarding questions like who or what is the referent object of security, whether security is positive or negative, whether the goal is securitisation or desecuritisation and whether the focus should be on normative or explanatory theory (Dagli, 2016). The central aim of this subchapter is therefore to present an overview of a philosophical approach to securitisation that deals with both discourse and speech act (Copenhagen School), and a sociological approach to securitisation (Paris School) more concerned with practices and governance that enables complex discourse analysis. While the Copenhagen School defends the basic argument that security challenges are the political outcomes of discursive actions (Buzan et al., 1998), the Paris School focuses more on security practices by emphasising the need for analysing beyond political agency through the integration of (political) institutions with the aim of comprehensively defining the risk (Bigo, 2002; Collective, 2006).

The analysis of ethnic identities and narratives in post-conflict BiH, where threat is strongly institutionalised in relation to the identity narratives of the 'Other' makes it necessary to first consider securitisation and only then contextualise the Paris School vis-à-vis the Copenhagen School. The starting point is that securitisation today (as both a process and a concept) is more flexible in its meaning and application to concrete cases (Coskun, 2011). While one could claim that the theory of securitisation has lost some of its analytical added value due to the increasing narrowing of research, one could also argue that it is precisely because of the greater narrowing and consequent looser framework that it has become a robust framework for the analysis of different realities; the latter vis-à-vis how to understand security challenges and the ways they 'translate' into political, emotional and performative reactions made by the political elites. In this book, I primarily rely on the Paris School, but from time to time consciously return to the Copenhagen School since the goal is not to follow (process-wise) the formation of the threat, but to analyse the role played by the critical junctures vis-à-vis the metanarrative used by members of the political elite as they attempt to (re)create the material and social environment of RS according to their (ethnopolitical) ideas.

The theory of securitisation has three elements at its heart: (i) a discursive act (speech act), (ii) the securitising actor and (iii) the audience. Wæver (2004, 13) emphasised that the central premise of securitisation theory is that it is not a given reality but instead a discursive act since merely marking something as a security challenge makes it become one. Namely, the securitising actor identifies a threat that in its view threatens the existence of a referent object (e.g., state, ethnic group, society, etc.). While aware that any broadening of the concept of security could bring incoherence and that it is necessary to limit oneself conceptually to prevent the creation of the logic that 'everything can be the subject of analysis', the Copenhagen School stresses that security must be defined as something more than just a problem (Buzan et al., 1998). When the Copenhagen School discusses security, it discusses "survival in the context of existential threats", and not everything bad that has the potential to occur (Buzan et al., 1998, 27). Framing something as an existential threat is therefore a central point of departure for the analysis of securitisation, yet this does not mean that every security threat which threatens the existence of something is automatically subject to successful securitisation. This requires three fundamental steps: (i) the identification of existential threats, (ii) extraordinary measures and (iii) the effect on relations within a certain community as a result of the end of clear rules.

If we convert these three steps into two more complex (and vivid) ones, in the first stage the securitising actor must possess (or create the illusion of possessing) the power to apply extraordinary measures to protect the existence of the referent object. Here, the second phase is probably even more important given that the securitising actor must convince the audience of the reality of the identified threat and mobilise them through support with the goal of legitimising extraordinary act(s). With this, the securitising actor de facto alienates—through discourse—certain phenomenon from the sphere of 'normality' (Tuareck, 2006). It is also worth pointing out that the Copenhagen School—influenced by Austin's (1975) conceptualisation of felicity condition—offers three conditions for successful securitisation (Ejdus & Božović, 2016): (i) the requirement that the discursive act follows the grammar of security, (ii) the 'capital' of the securitising actor and (iii) the historical association of the securitising act with the threat. Buzan et al. (1998, 33) argue that if there is no resonance with the audience and hence the establishment of certain security practices, we can hardly speak of a securitising act.

Such rigour in defining how a discursive act must be carried out to be successful among others sheds light on the fact that the decision to securitise something/someone is political. This was also shown by Wæver (2000) who stated that although historical conditions are important for securitisation, the latter should not be reduced to a condition of societal success because the decision to securitise is mostly political. This type of reasoning is criticised by Williams (2003, 521) who notes that such a narrow focus and search for a "securitizing act can lead to misunderstanding the process of securitisation" as the researcher can begin to focus only on the situation/context and consequently ignore the decision to securitise something/someone in the first place. Here, the greatest added value of the sociological approach to securitisation lies in the need to understand the audience in a more nuanced way. Therefore, this book's empirical focus on a post-conflict society makes it necessary to engage with the conceptual contours of the Paris School to understand the dynamics of security in such societies. Moreover, the fact BiH's post-conflict reality is prescribed by the DPA means that we need to understand the institutionalised securitisation 'entrapped' in the country's socio-political institutions.

In this respect, the process of securitisation in post-conflict environments, which is usually more susceptible to the institutionalisation of securitisation, is interesting for researchers because it can quickly experience a range of mutually exclusive securitisation practices. Certain security challenges in post-conflict environments can also be a 'historical fact' and, as such, part of 'normality'. This means the securitising actors do not need to (re)create discursive acts and seek legitimacy among the audience but must 'draw attention' to this threat, which already forms an integral part of their "political normality and reality" (Adamides, 2012). Contrary to the top-down approach envisaged by the Copenhagen School, the process of securitisation in post-conflict environments is more implicit and ambivalent because 'threats' and 'vulnerability' as such directly arise from the conflict itself. Built-in antagonisms, historical conflicts, myths, collective memories and (auto)narratives can be effectively reproduced by a large number of actors and practices since conflict is the first point of reference for evoking 'threat' and 'fear'. The result of this is that different actors enter the securitisation process (civil society, media outlets), which in turn blur the lines between the securitising actors and the audience. Stemming from this, the securitisation process can also take place 'bottom-up', even 'horizontally' (Adamides, 2012). In this respect, the following subsection broadens the theoretical perspective by engaging with the contours of the Paris School, which is usually understood as a sociological approach to securitisation.

2.2.1 Expanding the Securitisation Research Field: From a Philosophical to a Sociological Approach

The Copenhagen School distinguishes state security, which can be of a military, political, economic or environmental nature, and threatens territorial integrity through to societal security as such (Wæver et al., 1993). While state security deals chiefly with the organisational stability of states, systems of government and ideologies, societal security deals with the issue of "the ability of societies to maintain their character in the context of changed circumstances and potential threats" (Wæver et al., 1993, 23). Such a definition demands that we understand societal security through a situation in which societies define threat vis-à-vis their identity. Even if one tends to categorise security challenges into different levels (sectors) of analysis, it soon becomes clear that a certain level of security is always political, including the formulation of all threats and treatment options. Yet, it is worth emphasising that the Copenhagen School distinguishes between societal and political security. While the former deals with issues of identity and culture, the latter is focused on the non-military threats to territorial integrity and political threats in relation with the non-recognition of states' independence (Buzan et al., 1998). This distinction is important because it suggests that certain sectors exist as discrete domains of risk.

Huysmans (2006) supports such sectoral analysis of securitisation, arguing that 'vulnerability' varies by the nature of the threat and the referent object. This is, of course, nothing new and has also drawn considerable criticism (McSweeney, 1996, 1998; Williams, 1998). McSweeney (1996, 81), for example, questioned the Copenhagen School by arguing that the authors "understand society and identity as a given reality, instead of understanding communities and identities as fluid". Buzan and Wæver (1997) responded to this criticism, claiming that social constructivism itself never prescribes that the social world is unpredictable. In so doing, they stressed that when a security logic is formed, a significant number of societal practices, beliefs and institutions start to slowly take another form. Theiler (2003) agreed with this logic by arguing that the Copenhagen School uses social identity primarily as a conceptual tool with the aim of encompassing specific events in a given period. In this way, Thelier (2003, 256) argued that social constructs become stable at particular moments and points, which makes them relevant for the analysis. This was also empirically tested by Menéndzes et al. (2021) who showed how 'stable' the securitisation of immigration in the USA has become.

When it comes to criticism of reification, Williams (2003, 519) noted that researchers have missed the point of the concept of societal security as established by the Copenhagen School. This builds on the idea that behind the securitising act there is an attempt to (re)create a sense of homogeneity by unifying the understanding of oneself in relation to the threat. Wiliams (2003) concluded that the securitisation of identities challenges the flexibility and interrogative nature of identities, thereby directly referring to the Schmittian[7] logic of friends and enemies based on the politics of exclusion. Striztel (2007, 358) also faced similar questions within the societal security yet focused on the securitising actor–audience relationship, showing how the performative force of the articulated threat is a useful focus while seeking to understand the institutionalised securitisation. In this respect, he argued that the social side of securitisation must therefore focus on the audience's "psychological and cultural *dispositif*" (e.g., Balzaacq, 2005; Salter, 2008).

It is precisely at this point that the expansion of securitisation theory with the Paris School proves beneficial. This arises from the fact that securitisation is mostly an argumentative process instead of a discursive act since the discursive approach to securitisation offers an incomplete picture due to its inability to include other political instruments (Bigo, 2002; Balzacq, 2008). Bigo (2002) points out that at its core the process of securitisation refers more to the 'routinised practices of security' than to discursive acts. Based on this, Balzacq (2005) began to deal more with the political instruments that shed light on the process of securitisation,

---

[7] Ejdus (2009, 8) points out that although securitisation theory and Schmitt's theory share common narrative and thematic points, they differ significantly in an epistemological sense. Ejdus (2009, 10) hence argued that Wæver did not refer to Schmitt during the formation of the theory but studied his works in detail only after the publication of his scientific paper.

thereby paving the way for understanding both the scope and incidence of the process itself. With this, he tried to show that not only can the process of securitisation occur without a clearly identified audience and securitisation practices, but that securitisation can also be successful when there is a cognitive or behavioural change within the audience (Balzacq, 2005, 2008; Bello, 2020). Such conclusions suggest that where there is a cognitive and behavioural change in the audience, and thus an awareness that they must defend themselves against a certain threat, there may be a reproduction that calls for new/additional extraordinary measures to address the threat. In this case, desecuritisation is the 'only logical step'.

The Paris School builds its 'difference' compared to the Copenhagen School principally on the discursive act, which in its view is too broad relative to other practices of power (Bigo 2000; 2006). With this, the Parish School begins to conceptually justify the need to analyse the process of securitisation through the formation of networks of security that create the meaning of security and thereby power for their (security-wise) practices. The Paris School argues here that it is necessary to research the relationships between the security authorities, their status, role and the institutional environment. Bigo (2002, 65), for example, emphasises that the one who speaks—that is, creates—the discourse of security must also be able to establish a discourse about the enemy with the aim of introducing his own interpretation of the threat, whereby their success depends on his position and symbolic capital. Aradau (2004, 392) states that such a conceptualisation does not differ radically from the Copenhagen School, except that it gives greater emphasis to practices, audiences and contexts that enable the production of specific forms of governance; hence, the process itself moves securitisation from the level of political actors to the institutional level.

Here, it should be noted that the Paris School proposes a different definition of securitisation whereby security is not subjected to analysis itself as a central concept but is understood as a "technique of governance" (Bigo, 2000; Huysmans 2006). Despite the conceptual expansion and deepening of the discursive act, the process of securitisation is understood as a "top-down" process in which the performative process itself continues to be in the domain of government institutions. In post-conflict environments, actors reproduce historical narratives with the goal of maintaining a certain level of fear, which becomes part of identity narratives, routines and language itself. This argument is strongly related to Bigo's (2002, 65) where he stresses that "securitization is a technique of governance, used by both institutions and political elites". Bigo here (ibid.) builds on the basic assumption of securitisation upon which the Copenhagen School is premised, while partly overlapping with Schmitt's logic of sovereign exceptionalism. The idea behind it is that implementation of the discursive act is still in the domain of the executive power, possessed only by the political elites through (governmental) institutions (Doty, 1998; Hansen, 2012).

This exclusivity or exceptionality is based on the argument of the existence of a radical threat for which a certain political entity or society has neither an adequate legal basis nor other suitable political instrument(s) to address it (Baele and Thompson 2017). In institutional securitisation, this exclusivity or exceptionality can be transferred to the audience among whom there is already a general awareness of who the 'enemy' is, thereby rationalising the threat. At a particular point, the public may even become a securitising actor due to a fear for their own survival and demand extraordinary measures and policies to ensure a certain level of security for the exposed political entity and/or society. As a threat becomes visible, it is reproduced through daily routines and interactions. Illustrative examples of such a securitised public opinion that becomes part of the daily routine can be the moment one sees a woman with a headscarf in a shop or at a bus stop, or when we hear about an incident in a specific neighbourhood. Indeed, such events can arouse in people a sense of the legitimacy of the existence of a threat and a sense of threat to their own identity relative to the Other. Vouri (2010, 259) also argued along these lines, emphasising that the identification of threats can become institutionalised the 'master signifiers', which reduce the need for the additional illumination of arguments. In other words, a concept such as terrorism today "automatically carries a logic of security and prescribes a constant struggle that does not need to be questioned".

In (everyday) relations between Bosnian Serbs, Bosnian Croats and Bosniaks, there are quite a few examples, ranging from the use of words and phrases like "Turkish Serbs", "Balije", "Chetniks", "Ustashe", "Mujahedeens" and "genocide nation". By using such words on an everyday level, people create a context in which the institutionalisation of securitisation may occur. For the audience to internalise the feeling of a threat on a collective level, there must be a certain collective experience that makes all of this 'sticky' (Jeftić, 2019, 115). Such collective experiences, like social trauma resulting from the terrorist attack on the USA in 2001, establish reference points for securitisation to become 'sticky' and consequently institutionalised. Given that post-conflict environments are even more susceptible to the creation of the Self–Other dialectics, the institutional environment of such societies is exposed to the potential institutionalisation of securitisation.

The very concept of daily routine is not only important for both the Paris School and the needs of this book, but for the conceptualisation and operationalisation of 'critical junctures' as well, where the latter is understood as an 'exit' from the daily routines vis-à-vis the limits of the social and material environment (Bourbeau, 2014; Ejdus, 2020). Here, Bourbeau (2014, 14) notes that the political discourse itself can sometimes represent a critical juncture that accelerates the transformation of security practices as they are no longer the results of everyday routines and a non-reflection of a certain (new) phenomenon. Points of ruptures, defined as "points that force subjects in new and completely unknown circumstances" (Ikenberry, 2018), are becoming increasingly relevant. In this context, Mahoney and Thelen (2010) and Ejdus (2017, 2020) are especially important for achieving the goals of this book since they showed that critical junctures can be translated into a lasting legacy. This is where the logic of routine is extremely useful because routines as such are premised on established repetitive patterns that are never reflected upon. This leads us to assume that during the process of securitisation socialisation also takes place, whereby the subject 'transfers' the securitised practices to a new situation. This in step leads to the 'locking in of security practices' into the institutions of the (political) system and hence becomes part of the institutional structure of the selected political entity.

One of the biggest challenges facing institutional securitisation, as pointed out by Roe (2008), Balzacq (2011) and Bengtsson and Rhinard (2019), is that the securitisation process itself can have several directions (*loci*), meaning that one could search for "arbitrary discursive acts"; the latter would—in an analytical sense—be without any 'real added value'. At the same time, this is also one of the central divergences between the Copenhagen and Paris Schools, namely, with regard to understanding the audience–securitising actor relationship. In terms of operationalisation, the context, psychological-cultural *dispositif* [8] of the audience and the

---

[8] The psychological-cultural *dispositif* of the audience should be understood through the everyday discourses, practices, institutions, regulatory decisions and philosophical assumptions of a given society (Balzacq, 2010). What is even more important here is that every *dispositif* is determined—to a certain extent—by chosen (collective) traumas and memories.

power that both the securitising actor and the audience bring with their joint interaction is what is crucial for the Paris School (Bigo, 2000; Balzacq, 2011). For both theoretical schools, the logic of exclusivity or exceptionalism is very important as becomes most visible at the point when one analyses the challenges of societal security, where the Other is automatically translated into a threat. Buzan and Wæver (2009, 261) also discussed this and emphasised that we cannot talk about societal security without identifying the source of the threat—the Other, by which they stressed that securitisation is rooted in identity politics based on Self–Other dialectics. Huysmans (1998, 2006) also considered this and stated that "societal survival" is actually the survival of collective identities, which always occurs at the expense of the Other. This also explains why securitisation in the field of the societal is an attempt to consolidate group (ethnic/social) identity with the aim of identifying and excluding the (threatening) Other (Browning & Joenniemi, 2013, 2017).

In this respect, Adamides (2012) and Balzacq (2005) offer an operationalisation of security practices as a certain social context in which the identity, societal norms and (political) attitudes of both the securitising actor and the audience somehow align. Balzacq (2005, 172) understands this as the "psychological-cultural *dispositif*" of the audience. In post-conflict environments such as BiH, the psychological-cultural *dispositif* is usually determined by 'collective traumas' that are not necessarily centred around one historical event, but can become part of the 'stable' metanarrative of a selected social/ethnic group. In this way, such collective traumas and identity narratives become part of a wider institutional securitisation, which irreversibly reduces the need for the legitimacy of questioning the sense of framing the Other as an enemy or as one who threatens the existence of a selected social/ethnic group (Buzan et al., 1998, 27). Watson (2009, 23) conceptualises such a context as "episodic forms of securitization", referring to the importance of discursive practices that uphold institutionalised securitisation in post-conflict societies.

2.2.2   Conceptualising Desecuritisation in the Field of Identity Transformation

Despite the fact that securitisation entails desecuritisation, the very understanding of identity as an 'external factor' greatly limits this process (Wæver, 1998, 69). Still, identity is not the greatest challenge, as authors like Hansen (2000), Aradau (2004) and Austin and Beulie-Brossard

(2018) have already emphasised that the initial challenge lies in the actual concept of securitisation, which is conceptually underdeveloped. This gap is further addressed by Kay (2012), Lupovici (2012), Mitchell (2015), Rumelili (2015) and Ejdus (2020) who offer important insights into the relationship between reconciliation, recognition and desecuritisation. A common denominator among the authors when identifying a workable definition is that desecuritisation is a process within which the political community ceases to perceive someone/something as an existential threat; the latter is achieved by first advocating and then implementing extraordinary measures. By so doing, the authors showed that if a particular phenomenon can be securitised through discourse, then it can also be desecuritised and framed back within the field of 'normal politics'.

In previous subchapters, I established the argument that securitisation can take place on several levels, whereby a higher number of political, economic and societal challenges can be simultaneously securitised and presented as an existential threat to the survival of a referent object; the latter mainly being reflected as fear. Living in constant fear perpetuated by multiple sources is far from ideal. Moreover, the ideal state is the absence of security (asecurity), which is the opposite of security/threat as it envisages a state without fear and without existential threats. Considering that the ideal state of society does not exist and that securitisation is becoming an integral part of modern societies, the process of desecuritisation is extremely important for two aspects: (i) from the point of view of creating an inclusive environment for public debate and (ii) enabling the transformation of the Self–Other dialectics in a chosen society to 'shake off' the distinction between friends and enemies (Dagli, 2016, 90). Most likely, the initial problem while seeking to define desecuritisation is that both the Copenhagen and Paris Schools understand securitisation as a negative process per se because it leads to a state of emergency by creating dead spots in the system, inefficiency, non-transparency and fear. Desecuritisation, on the other hand, brings certain phenomena back into the field of 'normal politics' of transparency and public debate, which are actually some of the basic foundations of liberal democracies modelled by the West (ibid.). Securitisation needs desecuritisation as its constitutive and mirroring part to achieve analytical and political goals, as is also emphasised by Hansen (2012) who claims that the preference for desecuritisation is more technical and instrumental than political or ethical in nature.

Regardless, desecuritisation can be understood in the field of normativity and ethics. Among others, Hanrieder and Kreuder-Sonnen (2014) stressed this while conceptualising the 'emergency trap' since mobilisation and efficiency in an emergency (securitised) situation can be addictive. Based on the response of the World Health Organisation in 2003 to the SARS pandemic, the authors showed how the institutionalisation of the extraordinary power subsequently enabled the organisation having all the mechanisms to facilitate the securitisation of new (crisis) phenomena in the years to come (Hanrieder & Kreuder-Son, 2014, 342–344). Hence, this suggests that the legal and institutional consequences of securitisation are deeper than the actual concern with the inability to mobilise power and the necessary resources. This is because the question of an 'emergency' situation is not only a transitional part in the field of (political) decision-making, but becomes part of the transformational logic of the structure through the establishment of precedents. A situation like this is extremely undesirable in (liberal) democracies, especially if societal issues and identities are framed as a threat to the referent object. Desecuritisation is thus not only an alternative strategy in cases where emergency situations are not an effective way to face challenges, but part of a broader normative commitment when these challenges are related to societal issues and identities. All of this is inherently related to stabilisation vis-à-vis a socialisation process (Europeanisation).

If we understand securitisation as a 'top-down' process and define desecuritisation as the mirror image of securitisation, we must start from the same elements as in securitisation (securitising actor, discursive action, felicity conditions) for the conceptual definition of desecuritisation. Here, Hansen (2012, 533) provides a good starting point by showing how desecuritisation is a performative act. This means that one must first 'agree' that someone/something is no longer a threat, and as a result agree not to talk about it as a security problem anymore. In this respect, securitisation is both discursive and performative, making it possible for the institutionalisation to occur. Accordingly, one must take account of the cognitive and behavioural change as a consequence of the audience's psychological-cultural *dispositif*.

Starting with the Copenhagen School, three options are available for desecuritisation: (i) not addressing challenges as security problems, (ii) when a certain phenomenon is securitised, one must avoid creating security dilemmas and repeating cycles of these dilemmas and (iii) reframing and justifying the securitised phenomenon in the field of 'normal politics' (Buzan & Wæver, 2003, 253). Such a conceptualisation was soon criticised for its imprecision and looseness. One of the critics was Coskun

(2008, 393) who, by relying on the example of identities in a societal context, stressed that desecuritisation presupposes a certain degree of acceptance of the possibility of either coexistence or the legitimacy of the existence of two or more identities. In this respect, Coskun showed that securitisation does not necessarily 'escape normal politics', but leads to the redefinition of certain identities that become strongly linked to the question of existence. This is also why the process of desecuritisation is so difficult to achieve in post-conflict societies, even for the EU.

When talking about definitions of desecuritisation, Hansen (2012, 539) identifies four forms of it, namely: (i) replacement,; (ii) silencing, (iii) change through stabilisation and (iv) rearticulation. For the conceptualisation of desecuritisation in post-conflict societies, change through stabilisation is the most suitable, even though it is somewhat more complex than other forms. In this regard, it envisages a slow retreat outside the field of security discourse through a less aggressive, militaristic and politically (more) acceptable engagement. Gustafsson (2019, 5) also indirectly wrote about this and emphasised that the desecuritisation process is cumulative, which requires constant discursive repetition, with which the securitising actor shapes the "desecuritisation narrative". It should be highlighted that the strategy of desecuritisation through stabilisation (reform incentives via (re)constructing appropriate institutions) should become less and less interesting and used after the end of the Cold War (Hansen, 2017). Nevertheless, my argument is that change through stabilisation continues to be an important EU strategy implemented through the Europeanisation process. This takes place parallel to the strategy of rearticulation through (re)creating appropriate institutions, as indicated by the findings of Rumelili (2005, 2015). The mentioned author showed through a two-level analysis that the rearticulation of one's own Self in relation to the Other contains the dimension of ontological insecurity with the aim of managing existential anxieties. This then means that stabilisation is practically impossible without rearticulation (Çelik, 2015) (Fig. 2.4).

2.3   THE ONTOLOGY OF ONTOLOGICAL SECURITY

Although the theory of ontological security is not new in the disciplines of psychology (Laing, 1965; Erikson, 1968) and sociology (Giddens, 1984, 1990, 1991), its use in International Relations is relatively new, but increasingly present (Ejdus, 2017, 3). This is possible because the last two decades have seen the rapid development of critical approaches in security

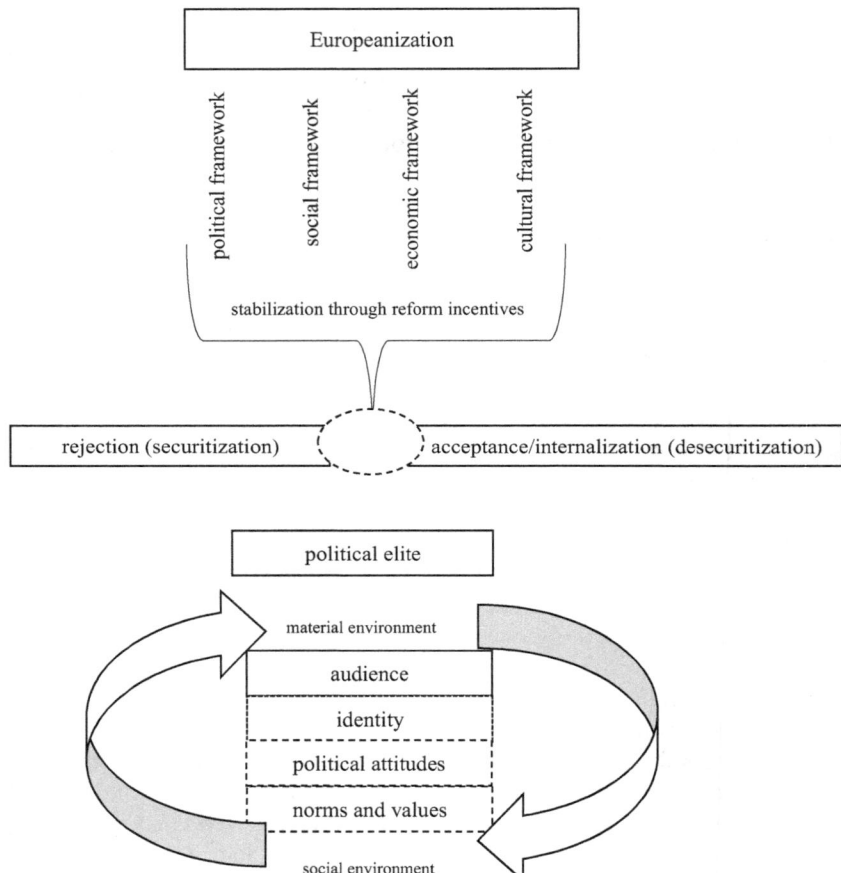

Fig. 2.4 Securitisation as a technique of governance in the context of Europeanisation. (Source: Authors' own elaboration)

studies in the context of the end of the Cold War. Indeed, these critical studies have begun to foreground economic, political, military, cyber, human and societal security. This also explains the need to establish a clear distinction at the beginning between the theory of ontological security and other critical (non-traditional) approaches to security, which understand the concept of security beyond states and military dimensions. The theory of ontological security does not have a normative commitment to emancipation, nor does it prioritise survival above all else. What ontological security offers in a conceptual sense, which thus distinguishes it from other approaches, is 'basic trust', which is located at the centre of the 'courage to be' with the goal of understanding security and one's own self-identity (Giddens, 1991). This means we should understand ontological security as "security of existence, a sense of courage and trust in the world as it is", and a "sense of basic trust in one's own biographical continuity" (Kinnvall, 2004, 30).

One of the epistemological challenges of security studies in the discipline of International Relations is that ontological security is understood in the context of physical security (security as survival) due to the dominant rationalist approach to security dictated above all by Hobbes' understanding of survival as the primary focus of actors. Indeed, a large number of researchers deal with the discourse and practices of security as survival where the very formation of identities depends on differentiation, which automatically leads to threat and endangerment (Wæver, 1998; Williams, 2003; Roe, 2004). Here, it is worth spotlighting the work of Roe (2006) who analysed the relationship between the preservation of identity distinction and securitisation, concluding that desecuritisation would lead to the disappearance of identity distinction. Accordingly, Roe (2006) understands the construction of identities through a "securitizing" lens whereby the Self–Other dichotomy becomes part of a securitising relationship based on survival. Such logic is criticised by Rumelili (2013) who noted that the desecuritisation of minority rights would not necessarily be the principle of their collective difference but would lead to the end of the reproduction of this difference through the presentation of this community as a threat to the majority. Behke (2006, 65) makes a similar observation while stressing that the principle of inclusion and community 'carries'—to some extent—the price of exclusion. This understanding of ontological security, i.e., of security as survival, reduces the issue of identities to the issue of the discourse of fear and threat, making desecuritisation itself practically impossible due to the mere "locking into the system".

Steele (2005), Mitzen (2006), Rumelili (2015) and Chernobov (2016) dealt with questions of this nature and when analysing identity narratives began to emphasise that the discourse on security is not necessarily indispensable for the (re)production of an identity narrative. They justified this by arguing that the subjects of international relations do not necessarily always strive for survival since they sometimes even strive for actions that could threaten their physical security with the goal of achieving ontological security. As a result, the Self–Other dialectics premised on the distinction of one's own identity relative to the Other is not necessarily automatic in a securitised relationship. For Browning (2016, 160), "nothing is natural or clear by itself when it comes to the prioritisation of physical security in international relations". In this respect, Rumelili (2015, 8) emphasised that it is possible in the societal sector "mainly because ontological security is different and cannot be reduced to physical security". Considering that identities in post-conflict environments usually cannot be imagined beyond a relationship based on survival, it is difficult to offer a robust theorisation for the formation of alternative identities that would enable desecuritisation according to the principle of normativity. The latter means that the coexistence of identities is either the norm or understood in a way that it is not a "zero-sum game" (Rumelili, 2015; Ejdus, 2020).

2.3.1   Ontological Security and Identity Challenges

While securitisation theory understands security as negative, where security and threat share the same security challenge and are not opposed through the classical binary logic, ontological security is positive security to which subjects strive. According to the definition provided by Wæver (1995), the state of security foresees a situation characterised by the presence of a security problem and requires a response, while the state of danger/endangerment envisages a situation without a response. With such a definition, the subjects of international relations do not want a situation that is defined through a security prism; in the absence of security (asecurity), the concept of security itself becomes an irrelevant concern. Unlike security as survival, ontological security is something that subjects strive for because it is a sense of security in knowing "who we were, who we are, and who we would like to be". When one senses ontological insecurity, one senses—at least on one level—the absence of security of his or her own identity.

The concept of ontological security was developed by the psychiatrist Ronald D. Laing (1971). He defined ontological security as "having a constant sense of presence in the world that is real and alive", while also pointing out that the absence of ontological security means "a sense of burden and anxiety of everyday life, consisted of immediate threats" (Laing, 1971, 32). A similar argument also appeared in the field of sociology about two decades later, namely with Giddens (1991, 46) who defined ontological security as "having confidence in the continuity of one's Self". For Giddens (1991), the feeling of ontological security means having—on the unconscious and practically conscious level—answers to fundamental existential questions that a person constantly addresses in some way during their life; this in turn serves as a precondition for managing the anxieties of everyday life (Giddens, 1991, 47). He emphasises that self-identity should be understood as the development of a consistent feeling about one's autobiography, particularly vis-à-vis the belief that one can maintain autobiographical continuity by establishing a system of basic trust in the (real) world and social relations with others.

Autobiography is thus a form of "discursive consciousness", which is manifested through self-narrative and gives meaning to the actions of the subjects narrating it (Giddens, 1984, 374). Self-narratives are hence those that offer meaning to the subject's own identity as they are primarily an expression of our "understanding and production of reality" (Steele, 2008, 11). Individuals possess several identities (e.g., sexual, ethnic, religious, national, professional), meaning that identities as such are created through multi-faceted identity narratives. The logical consequence of this is that one's own Self acquires a certain degree of coherence. Neumann (1999, 218) also discussed this and stressed that the creation of one's Self is chiefly a narrative process of identification where a large number of identities, already questioned during life, merge in a specific context and become part of the "dominant story". Even though there is no generally accepted consensus among scholars on who is mainly the one who strives for ontological security or creates it, the arguments of McSweeney (1998), Steele (2005) and Mitzen (2006) are sufficiently convincing for us to claim that collectives are those which strive for at least as much as the physical—if not more—ontological security.

Building on this, I continue with the already established argument that ontological security can be extrapolated to the collective or state level, while broadening it with a focus on subnational political entities. This is done even though one can find already existing works touching on ethnic groups vis-à-vis migration (e.g., Innes, 2017; Skey, 2010), internal Others (e.g., Kinnvall & Mitzen, 2017) and race (Turner & Steele, 2022; Newell, 2020). I adopt this position not only because it is quite common in the International Relations (IR) discipline to personify states, but because collectives (both states and subnational political entities) produce their own biographies and value their existence in making sense of their own selves (or sense of existence). The feeling of belonging to a certain country, ethnic group or other group is therefore created and consolidated based on a narrative that promises continuity; without the latter, mere 'membership' in this group would hold no meaning. From this comes the argument that collectives/states strive for actions that would reduce the challenges associated with their own narratives. A similar argument is made by Kinnvall (2004, 743) who states that history is interpreted and organised to recreate the dominant narrative for group identity. Steele (2008) goes a step further by emphasising that we can extrapolate individual feelings to the national level—and to the collective(s) and subnational level—since individuals are connected in one way or another to collectives and (sub)national political entities.

One's own identity is accordingly in a close relationship with group identities as there is a certain degree of 'attachment' of the narrative to collective/(sub)national entities that enable the development and preservation of one's own identity. In this sense, ontological security is equally centred on the past (memory and history) as it is on the future (continuity). It would probably not be erroneous to claim that collective identities and (sub)national political entities, which also (re)create their own narratives about the past, tend to ensure their own ontological security in the same way as individuals. Namely, collective identities and (sub)national political entities create a bond for individuals through the imaginary of common heritage and ancestors that goes beyond their lives, thus giving a certain group/formation even a sense of immortality when it comes to the question of existence or survival. It should be emphasised here that with such an argument I am not trying to offer an alternative reading of ontological security for understanding the behaviour of collectives and (sub) national political entities, but to offer a broader and more nuanced picture of the meaning and relevance of the theory within the wider field of security.

The concept of identity is relatively ambitious and at times even too complex. This view is shared by McSweeney (1996, 86) who stressed that the very human and moral connotation of identity, which is based on subjectivity, opens the way for 'everyone to be an identity expert'. Identity is almost always in the field of self-definition, which is not necessarily done on the conscious level. Even though the epistemology of identity itself is subjected to criticism, one can point out that there is a relatively established consensus that identity is not a social reality but is instead flexible and amorphous (Giddens, 1991; Hom & Steele, 2020). Collective identity is namely not out there waiting to be found. What is out there are identity discourses that illuminate the process of shaping, questioning and consolidating the need for a collective imaginary (McSweeney, 1996). Giddens (1991, 52–53) points out that the Self presupposes a reflexive awareness that a person makes sense of through his or her autobiography. Identity is thus not a property or a fact of a certain society and is instead a process of selection and formation that takes place with the engagement of individuals such as political elites and historians. Therefore, the question of who we are cannot be answered in a simple way only with public opinion polls, myths, folk traditions or historical records, but with a meaningful integration of all approaches, which I follow in this book. McSweeney (1998) also wrote about this and stressed that being English, Irish or Danish is the result of a political and social process, and not just the result of an (ethno)symbolic designation. In so doing, McSweeney (1998, 89) showed that one can also be "what he or she want to be", pointing out to the freedom and the potential of neglecting the social, material and political relations that are deemed important for the formation of identity politics.

Nevertheless, we cannot deny the need of individuals for a stable Self or the need to belong to a particular group, community or society. Nor can we deny that a certain measure of collective identity is a product of living together, or that national and ethnic identities cannot become a security problem (Stein, 2002). Moreover, social psychologists like Kelman (2007) note that identity is both a psychological need in itself and a mobilising force in fulfilling certain needs. Stein (2002, 23) makes a similar observation while arguing that "identity is what a person is, wants to be, or what he or she wants to be known for". Given that we have managed to establish that there is a consensus that identity is a social construct, we should still clarify that scholars are still quite divided on how they understand the process of identity formation. While authors such as Wendt (1999), Steele (2008) and Ejdus (2017) advocate an individual approach to creating a sense of ontological security and talk about endogeneity, authors like Rumelili (2004) and Mitzen (2006) advocate a social approach to ontological security or exogeneity. Individuality or endogeneity can be defined as the "internal dialectics of one's own Self", which dictates that we must first know our own Self before framing it in relation to another (Steele, 2008, 32). Wendt (1999, 224) makes a similar point while downplaying the importance of distinction in identity formation by arguing that collective identities are "formed as self-organized homeostatic structures", which makes them effectively—in a constitutive sense—"exogenous to the Other".

Mitzen (2006, 355–359) argues quite differently, emphasising that identities are formed exogenously and maintained in relation to the Other through (routinised) social relations. Researchers in the field of ontological security are also familiar with a third way, which Zarakol (2010) and Ejdus (2017) define as the middle-ground approach where the idea is that identity is both exogenously and endogenously formed. Such logic builds on the fact that it is difficult to determine whether (for identity) challenging interactions are those that act as a central source of ontological insecurity or whether threatening interactions are merely a symptom of the subject's uncertainty regarding his or her own identity. Even though at this point this appears to be a problem in establishing a causal relationship rather than a problem about the ontology of the identity formation process itself, one should consider the findings of Prozorov (2011). His view is that the internal and external processes of identity formation cannot be easily separated from each other as there is no clear dividing line between temporary (self-narratives) and spatial (relationship with others) identity formations (Prozorov, 2011, 1278). Nevertheless, my view is that the Self cannot exist without the existence of the Other or the distinction in relation to the Other. Nor can it be understood as independent of the Other or the social and material environment in which the Self is maintained. It should be noted here that this Other does not have to exist as an external Self, but can be an 'Other Self', which is established due to an internal dialectic through reflection (Rumelili, 2004; Gustafsson, 2019).

Rumelili (2004) used the example of creating the legacy of war and the bloody past as an 'internal Other' of the EU to substantiate a relationist ontology. She showed that it is not necessarily existential to one's own Self, which coincides with Steele's (2008) idea of "internal dialectics". Although ontological security requires differentiation, i.e., the Other, there are two extremes between this Other: (i) smaller differences that scholars recognise in the context of similarity, positive identification and friendship; along with (ii) larger differences that place the Self on the opposite side in relation to the Other (Rumelili, 2004; Browning & Joenniemi, 2013). Browning and Joenniemi (2013, 492) note that while subjects must distinguish themselves from each other to maintain their own existence, such differentiation is not necessarily always negative. Here, I follow a relational approach and—in line with the findings of Browning (2016, 169)—argue that the Self's interaction with the social and material environment cumulatively creates its own subjective biographical narrative that does not necessarily translate into a mutually exclusive or incompatible categorical apparatus of subjectivity. In this sense, the concept of friendship foresees alternative possibilities for ensuring ontological security, which already during friendship itself includes the active acceptance and even 'celebration' of differences. Such friendship, Browning argues (ibid.), is therefore a positive form of distinction based on equality, respect and solidarity.

To better understand how ontological security is at once related to and different from identity, we must return to Giddens (1991) who states that existence itself (being) presupposes ontological awareness. It should be stressed here that such awareness is not the same as awareness of one's own identity. Giddens (1991, p. 35) regards ontological security as the possession of confidence in the continuity of identity, for both the present and future. In a sociological and psychological sense, ontological security is therefore formed through one's own identity and trust based on the continuation of life, one's own Self and the existence of the real world.

Giddens (1991, p. 38)—relying on Erikson (1968) and Winnicott (1971)—points out that basic confidence in one's own identity arises from "an original interplay that presupposes an emotional and cognitive orientation towards the Other and the objective world". The very concept of basic trust is hence an integral part of the concept of "hope" and what Tilich (1962) defines as "the courage to be" since both of these elements act as a kind of shield protecting the individual from potential negative experiences in everyday life. For an individual, basic trust begins to develop in childhood, which (can) be translated into group identities (Dagli, 2016, p. 74). A child born into a world with a high level of anxiety because of the environment in which they exist needs to be protected by their parent/guardian who, alongside protection and socialisation, instils a sense of trust in them. Through this, the child begins to develop their own Self relative to the social and material context, which becomes important for the accumulation of experiences (Giddens, 1991, pp. 39–41). Here, Giddens (1991, p. 41) notes that the "constant struggle with being or not being" is inherent in every individual, who must not only accept reality but also create ontological reference points that become part of everyday life through routines. The latter thereby become an integral part of ontological security as they maintain trust in the social and material environment and manage anxieties. Mitzen (2006, p. 347) argues that it is necessary to understand ontological security as a 'vaccine' that prevents a deep sense of anxiety and chaos. Based on this, Browning and Joenniemi (2013, p. 485) emphasise that ontological security creates a mechanism for stability and predictability of the material and social environment, which is also a precondition for establishing ontological security (Giddens, 1991, p. 34).

Giddens (1991, p. 52) understands ontologically secure as meaning possessing answers to fundamental existential questions about life, which is translated through a sense of belonging. This also explains why "the actions of the Other are important for maintaining trust in the world" (ibid.), suggesting that ontological security cannot be separated from formation of the Self–Other dialectic. Goffman (2012) states that the Self always needs an audience because it is created for them, even if this audience is imaginary. Kinnvall (2004, p. 748) asserts that ontological security is about maintaining a stable narrative of one's Self on the assumption of "intersubjective relations", which refer to how either individuals or collectives define the Self relative to the Other. In this respect, issues of one's own identity and ontological security both depend on and also become part of the relationship with the Other, whereby basic trust in the relationship and recognition of the Other are key to reproducing and strengthening one's own identity and ontological security. Our basic trust in relation to the Other accordingly does not simply depend on how 'credible' or trustworthy the Other is, but mainly on how stable this relationship can be (Browning & Joenniemi, 2013). Hence, in its simplest form our relationship and experience of the social and material environment through reflection creates our own narratives and basic trust. This is enabled by a sense of one's own continuity, which is vital for understanding how ontological security is connected (and simultaneously separated) from one's identity.

2.3.2   The Weakness of Securitisation Theory for the Analysis of Ontological (In)security

The theory of ontological security builds on concepts like trust, hope, shame and anxiety, while the concepts of survival, power, risk and fear are ontologically more in the realm of psychology than political science. Distinctions of this nature are crucial for understanding the added value of ontological security in security studies. Including the concept of basic trust, namely, the central element of an individual's ontological security with the goal of managing their day-to-day life and anxiety, the key to understanding ontological security lies precisely in the concept of anxiety (as opposed to fear) and shame (as opposed to guilt). Indeed, Giddens (1991, p. 22) distinguishes anxiety from fear and shame from guilt, arguing that fear must be understood as a response to an identified threat. Giddens thus defines the referent object itself, while anxiety is a more general state of emotion that is not necessarily always on the conscious level and does not always have a clear referent object. A good example of this is the two-level approach to social security put forward by Rumelili (2011, 2013) through which she shows the need to distinguish between security as survival and security as existence, and consequently the difference between fear and anxiety.

Like anxiety, the concept of shame does not depend on identified rules and laws since it is realised at the point where there is a disconnect between the actions of the individual and their own narrative. Young (1999, p. 220) defines shame as "a self-directed judgment related to the idea that the individual is no longer what he or she expected/hoped/wanted to be". Shame is therefore an internal and intimate feeling of transgression since no rule has been broken (Steele, 2008, 57; Hagström, 2021, 3). Such emotional and conceptual distinctions between safety as existence and safety as survival can create a certain degree of dissonance when not intertwined through actions such as breaking the rules (guilt) with the goal of avoiding shame as we feel morally obliged to do something; or not breaking the rule to avoid guilt yet simultaneously feeling shame due to being unable to do anything, or staying in a toxic relationship (fear) because the anxiety about what we may become without that relationship is too great to actually end it.

Steele (2008, 59) explains that the constructivist paradigm sees identities and interests as interdependent. This means it is unnatural for an actor to identify as something and do the opposite since this would lead to shame and anxiety because the actor would not organise their behaviour around their own narrative. To simplify matters a little, we may argue that we feel shame when a clear conflict arises between our own identity (who we claim to be) and our actions, thereby failing to align our actions or decisions with our autobiographies that legitimise our behaviour. Steele (2008, 58) presents this lucidly by distinguishing between shame and guilt in subjects' responses to humanitarian crises. In his analysis, he shows that even if "liberal" regimes will not necessarily feel guilty about their inability to intervene in a humanitarian crisis, they may still feel shamed because their inaction is inconsistent with their sense of integrity and self-identity. In response to this shame, actors will be able to adjust their routines via reflexivity or start engaging in practices that 'mask' their sense of shame. Mitzen (2006, 364) and Steele (2008, 60) agree that it is rigid routines that prevent agents from the process of 'learning', in that way preventing the processes of adaptation, limiting subjectivity and introducing objectivity.

Using the example of the dilemma of shame and dissonance, Lupovici (2012, 817) went one step further and showed that identity and behavioural changes, whose function is supposed to be addressing a certain anxiety, can add a new dimension of ontological threat by creating "gaps between identity and expected final practices". He defines this as ontological dissonance, which—in contrast to cognitive dissonance, which is subject to analysis on the individual level—is framed on the collective level. At the same time, this is an objectively different understanding from 'identity conflict'. Namely, this defines the conflict between the identities possessed by collective actors and 'identity dissonance', which prescribes the understanding of the conflict between the identity and the actor's behaviour. The ontological dissonance in question presupposes a conflict between the actions an actor takes to address threats to a certain identity. Ontological dissonance hence refers to practices that try to preserve one of the identities in relation to the 'threatening Other', whereby the actor is supposed to possess both (Lupovici, 2012, 818–820).

It should be underlined here that anxiety does not necessarily translate into shame nor has a purely negative state. Even though Tilich (1962, 38) notes that anxiety must be understood as a slip into 'not being' in situations where our identity narratives and our own integrity are called into question to the point of triggering a sense of meaninglessness, anxiety itself is essential for reflection and 'authenticity of life' (Heidegger, 2002, 28). For Heidegger (2002), authentic life is not only about physically existing, but also about being aware of one's own mortality. What Heidegger calls "Dasein" is supposed to refer to the reflective awareness of one's own existence (being), which can lead to an authentic life and cannot be decontextualised relative to the world in which we actually live. Heidegger (2002) is referred to here because his arguments allow the possibility of projecting authentic life on the level of the community since members of the community are also supposed to be aware of their own mortality, acting as a lever for maintaining biographical continuity from a historical perspective.

A similar positive sign of anxiety is envisaged by Steele (2008, 61) who contends that everyday anxiety is positive because it serves as a reminder of humanism/humanity. While subjects try to eliminate the anxieties of everyday life, in their absence they would be left without reflection and leverage for everyday life since a certain level of anxiety enables the subject to live and not just exist. Anxiety is typically not understood as something positive as it soon becomes multifaceted, strongly connected to the question of existence and out of our control. Accordingly, if we have shown during this discussion that a certain amount of anxiety is (can be) 'positive', there are many aspects of anxiety that push the subject into the field of impossibility. This field of impossibility is important as it can lead to narratives being developed based on denial, or to securitisation itself with the aim of identifying the source of this anxiety. There is also a third way to deal with existential anxieties, which refers to the subject looking for quick solutions with the goal of distancing themself from any actions that would separate them from their own identity (adaptation). In this context, the reconfiguration of historical and institutional narratives is undesirable and unattractive to subjects since only distancing themselves from these narratives would lead them to lose their sense of Self (Steele, 2008). Laing (1971, 173–174) defines such a state as a disembodied or divorced self. At this stage, it is worth noting that Steele (2008, 62) argues that an excessive degree of reflexivity can lead to the self-denial of actions.

Steele (2008, 61) is crucial for my argument since he conceptualises anxiety on the (sub)national level by highlighting that "anxiety is felt not as a consequence of facts that exist outside our borders, but as a consequence of facts that are supposed to be within the limits of our subjectivity". Steele (ibid.) points out that complete/absolute emancipation can create "dizziness" and the inability to control anxiety, which causes subjects to create routines. These in turn reduce their freedom, yet they primarily function a mechanism for dealing with anxiety as they reduce the level of what we understand as a factor that creates anxiety. In line with this, Steele (2008) notes that the more power and capacity the subject possesses, the greater the level of anxiety they may feel due to the increased level of feeling of 'responsibility'. This was also discussed by Giddens (1991, 43–44) while stressing that the degree of anxiety subjects feel in a given situation "depends on the subject's knowledge and strength in relation to the outside world". At the same time, Giddens (1991) states that if the factor of reflexivity in relation to one's own social and material environment were lacking in the field of one's own Self, or if the subject did not understand its own change in the field of its own capabilities, it would not possess subjectivity either. The key to this debate is hence that if the subjectivity of the political elite diminishes, so too does the sense of shame or anxiety.

Ontological security is for that reason different from other non-traditional security concepts like societal security. Although the issue of identity is an integral and central element of both security, societal security is inherently linked to negativity based on threat and the issue of survival. This refers to the failure to face challenges in the field of 'normal' politics, which leads to securitisation with the aim of legitimising emergency measures (Buzan et al., 1998). When societal security is being discussed, we are talking about an articulated existential threat to the identity of a certain society, explaining why the societal security concept deals principally with the identification of threats and, hence, more with fear than anxiety. Ontological security, in contrast, based on basic trust in managing real-world anxieties and hard to identify as such, builds on a positive definition of safety that allows subjects to "be exactly who they are and continue on their own path" (Giddens, 1991, 32). McSweeney (1998) understands ontological security as "ownership of a relationship, as a lever for mutual security". For Rumelili (2013, 55), the concept of ontological security includes the distinction between positive and negative security by emphasising that what represents security to a certain Self can represent threats to its Other and vice versa. This leads to probably the most important conclusion; namely, that ontological security does not analyse threats to a certain identity, but mainly deals with its stability (Rumelili, 2013; Subotić, 2015; Zarakol, 2016; Ejdus, 2017). Moreover, identity is understood as an external variable in the field of societal security since it always refers to the process of ensuring the security of collective identity and so does not refer to the individual. It should be reiterated that the Copenhagen School does not envisage the unification of identities, such that they are objective or given, but instead envisages their actual stability and rigidity in certain periods, which are important for the analysis of the securitisation of a particular phenomenon (Buzan & Wæver, 1997; Thelier 2003). Wæver (1993, 23) defines societal security as "the ability of a given society to maintain its own nature in the context of changed conditions and potential or actual threats" In contrast, the theory of ontological security is not so much interested in the identification of a threat to a particular identity, but primarily in the question of maintaining a stable narrative.

A subject that feels ontologically secure should therefore possess fundamental existential answers and accordingly formulate their own actions later translated into routines aimed at consolidating their own identity and reproducing basic trust in the world and relationships with others. Giddens (1991, 39) describes how different forms of routines are important for the development of ontological security. In this respect, "routine acts as a lever for forming the framework of existence through the formation of a sense of existence (being) and its distinction from non-existence (not being), which is key to establishing ontological security". Ontological security is therefore based on a sense of predictability centred around the stability and routines that exist in each social and material environment (Browning & Joenniemi, 2013, 495). From this comes the critical difference between ontological and social security, that is, through the preservation of collective identities relative to an identified threat. This, in turn, reaffirms Giddens' (1991) conceptual difference between anxiety and fear, which thereby become an integral part of either social (fear) or ontological security (anxiety).

2.3.3   Introducing Points of Ruptures and the Social and Material Environment of a Political Entity into the Framework of Ontological (In)security

The literature in the field of ontological security is quite ambivalent about whether ontological security is understood as an (imaginary) search for a complete identity narrative with the goal of maximising security, or it is a given fact (state of being). Neither Laing's (1990) nor Giddens' (1991) conceptualisations can help in this respect in a holistic sense. Here it is worth noting that Giddens (1991, 62) emphasises that one's identity is not given in advance but created through routines and maintained through the reflective activities of individuals. This suggests that it is a changing spectrum of understanding of the concept of being, and ontological security is a personal quality rather than an ability. Nevertheless, it remains relatively unclear whether Laing (1990) views ontological security as something that one possesses or as a fluid sense that manifests as an ongoing search for fundamental questions on the conscious level. This ambiguity stems from the fact that the author alternately refers to ontological security as a "sense of existence" and a "basic existential position", which represents a person's "clear core of ontological security" (Laing, 1990, 4; 39; 42). While I argue that understanding the sense of ontological security might be more easily understood as an incomplete process, the conceptualisation of ontological security as an individual's basic existential starting point suggests that ontological security is an actual state that can be possessed.

According to authors like Steele (2005), Rumelili (2013), Subotić (2015) and Krickel-Choi (2021), ontologically secure subjects can either change or adapt their routines through reflective behaviour as an outcome of "critical junctures that create anxiety and challenge their own identity through a sense of basic trust". Ejdus (2017, 2) defines critical junctures as "circumstances of an unpredictable radical break, which, by creating anxiety, directly affects (collective) subjects and it acts as a threat to institutionalized routines". Here, Ejdus (2017, 18) goes a step further and operationalises critical junctures via four intertwining factors of ontological security: (i) existence, (ii) finitude, (iii) relations and (iv) autobiography. The subject is thus ontologically secure when they decide on a certain action that coincides with their sense of their own identity. If these points of ruptures become frequent or very intense, they can lead to existential anxieties due to their inability to integrate into the existing routines that exist in the material and social environment. For example, Kinnvall (2004), Steele (2005), Mitzen (2006) and Gustafsson and Krickel-Choi (2020) define such a state as ontological insecurity, referring to a 'break' where one's own Self has lost the central core of its own identity narrative. As a result, the individual loses the ability to maintain the coherence of their own identity narrative and to answer the fundamental questions regarding their own existence and functioning. Mitzen (2006), Zarakol (2010) and Ejdus (2017) underline that the consequence of uncertainty is deep existential anxiety. This happens because of a sudden change in the definition of one's own identity relative to the "objective material world" and the failure of both one's own identity consolidation and consolidation of the identity of the Other. Institutionalised routines that exist in the social and material environment are thus essential. To determine the feeling of ontological (in)security, I operationalise the latter according to Giddens (1991, 19–25). If the social environment is based on symbols, narratives, memories and myths, the material environment refers to spatialisation (e.g., erection or construction of specific religious buildings, museums, monuments and naming streets and squares after historical figures).

In a simplified way, one can stress that existential anxieties appear at the point when there is a change in the subject's own identity, whereby the subject who 'possesses' ontological security should be able to face these anxieties and adapt to the new situation through reflectivity (Giddens, 1991). Rumelili (2013, 8) emphasises that the Self, when talking about the feeling of ontological security, is stable and consistent in the context of one's own social existence. Similarly, Steele (2005, 52) also states that the feeling of ontological security is built through the subject's actions, which thus reflect the sense of one's own identity. It follows from this that "ontologically secure subjects" can manage everyday anxieties, adapt in the context of critical junctures and continue with their own 'existence'. This definition suggests that ontological security is accordingly something that subjects 'possess', or that it is a certain state, rather than at its core being a (never attainable) imaginary with the goal of maximising a sense of ontological security.

I proceed on the basis that ontological security is not a binary category or a given fact (*state of being*) within which one's own Self is either safe or threatened, or vice versa. Ontological security cannot be seen as a certain quality or something "that comes out", as Dagli (2016, 82) puts it. Identity as such is never really completed, it has no final goal or absolute state. The subject's own narratives are therefore always a work in progress, referring to interpretation, which originates from experience within a certain material and social environment. The identity of each subject is multi-layered, which means that their own narratives are also multi-layered and, in turn, so too are their anxieties. If we consider that ontological security is not external to one's own identity and cannot develop an independent own identity by itself, it must be understood through interdependence and co-formation in relation to 'being'. This leads to the argument that identity is always changing, with the outcome that all subjects are always "in search of a sense of ontological security" to maximise their sense of stable identity. Kinnvall (2004, 747) asserts that social constructivism is the only one able to explain collective identity as something more than a collection of individuals since identity formation is understood as a process, not a final goal. It needs to be emphasised here that the fact that individuals are looking for a stable identity does not mean that such (stable) identity actually exists (Kinnvall & Mitzen, 2020).

Giddens (1991, 53) emphasises that one's own identity is not a different trait or a set of different traits of an individual and instead one's own identity is designed and understood through reflexivity relative to one's own biography. The argument that ontological security is understood as an ongoing process rather than a quality that can be acquired arises from this. Giddens (1991, 54) also clarifies that both self-identities and routines are robust and fragile. One's own identity is fragile because of the biography of oneself, which is only 'one story' among many that could be told with the aim of making sense of oneself. On the other hand, it is robust because the sense of one's own identity is often guaranteed despite critical junctures. The same applies to routines, which are both rigid and sensitive given that, despite the reproduction of trust, they are sensitive precisely due to the very nature of the actor's own identity (Steele, 2005). Ontological security is therefore based on a cumulative narrative of oneself centred on routines and maintained through them. In this case, the autobiography is a set of experiences, attitudes and (dis)trust with respect to the material and social environment from which it originates. Every microparticle added to one's own narrative thus affects the assemblage itself through either solidification or challenge. Simultaneously, this means that every smallest addition with the goal of building an identity affects the feeling of ontological security.

Since eliminating all anxiety is impossible or even undesirable, achieving a holistic and comprehensive state of ontological security is also impossible or even undesirable. We try to maximise the feeling of ontological security by way of planning, creating routines, trust, consolidation, assurance or securitisation. Ontological security thus becomes something we strive for but are never truly able to achieve. Such a situation is neatly summarised by Wooley (2007, 184) when saying that the feeling of absolute ontological security would mean denying one's own status of existence 'for-itself' instead of 'in-itself', and also mean living and existing for the past, where all opportunities are already missed in advance. Derrida and Ewald (1995) made similar observations when underscoring that the state of our own Self is always open, which allows us to live. Absolute ontological security, in the case of Derrida and Ewald (1995, 276), means the closure of one's own narrative, which at its core is non-existent. This accordingly means that the complete securing of oneself within itself would mean a static state and, similar to the case of death, the entrapping of one's Self in the past. Of course, this does not mean that individuals and (sub)national political entities are not looking for a coherent and consistent narrative with the goal of securing their own self within themselves; quite the contrary. While Woolley (2007, pp. 183–185) conceptualises ontological security as a sense of one's own acceptance with the conditions enabled by the very experience of the authenticity of life, and defines this as "ontological quietude", I conceptualise ontological security as an incomplete process that straddles security and vulnerability (Dagli, 2016, 53–58; Bolton, 2020).

2.4   Instead of a Conclusion: Understanding Europeanisation as a Context Enabling the Transformation of (Ethnic) Identities, (De) Securitisation and Ontological (In)security

Post-conflict environments devoid of large-scale (physical) violence, like in BiH and RS, provide a good starting point for understanding spatial and temporal securitisation. This is particularly because the latter is becoming institutionalised following the establishment of exclusivist norms, rules, myths, narratives and institutions. At its centre, such institutionalisation predicts who is and who is not a 'member' of a certain group, whereby the mere articulation of the threat is no longer necessary. In environments where the institutionalisation of securitisation is present, the desecuritisation process itself is thus extremely demanding. The securitisation of identity in these environments becomes strongly determined by identity narratives, which—to make sense of the source of the (historical) threat to a given group directly (and selectively)—derives from specific traumas, victories or defeats. This means conflict in itself can function as a source of ontological security since a certain collective identity is constructed in relation to the 'threatening Other', and it is precisely the routines that are established in such a material and social environment which merely (re) produce these exclusivist identity narratives.

The securitisation process carried out by the political elite, which in the case of RS must be understood as a technique of governance, strives to unify identities by directly challenging their flexibility. In this way, it allows little room for the attitude to the Other to be transformed since the key is preservation of the *status quo*. In this case, the latter refers to the preservation of (societal-driven) antagonisms, which either uphold or even strengthen the actual legitimacy of RS' existence as a political entity. The transformation in question, which tends to be achieved by Europeanisation as a context of the (in)ability to transform identities through stabilisation, is extremely demanding. The exact logic of the EU's approach in practice (transferring the cultural, political, economic and social framework to a third country via reform incentives) means that this ideological socialisation does not offer a clear dividing line between how the political elite in a chosen political entity interprets the potential 'threat' that accompanies the (re)construction of institutions—it can be the concept of security as existence (securitisation) or the concept of security as survival (ontological security).

With this, Europeanisation itself—through the stabilisation and integration of the Other into the common (EU-driven) framework—is
becoming part of a broader desecuritisation strategy. Given that such a
context of Europeanisation only foresees differentiation through the addition of a new layer to existing (ethnic) identities and hence does not primarily strive for the stability of existing identities, the reaction to the
desecuritisation strategy can include the potential 'closure' of exposed
subjects. The latter do this through a self-narrative whereby they form
routines within their own social and material environment according to
patterns that led to the conflict in the first place. While the routines in
these cases do not have to be visible in everyday life, they can become a
wider part of (socio-political) practices which the political elite establishes
and reproduces through securitising acts (the language of security). It
should be noted here that ontological security and threat as survival or
ontological insecurity and the absence of security (asecurity) as survival are
not sustainable/permanent paradigms of security. This means that the
subject's need for survival can lead to the destabilisation of security-as-
being, which directly leads to a threat of non-existence. The latter (may)
create questions regarding the survival of the subject, which will turn to
securitisation with a view to consolidating their own identity narratives.
The latter will be achieved by identifying a threat to which they will direct
all of their existential anxieties to seek stability of their own identity. Within
such a framework, the ideal state of ontological (in)security prescribes the
security of one's own Self in terms of its biographical continuity and own
identity. This biographical continuity is important above all since it is
strongly linked to the very logic of the formation of ethnic identities,
which are not only preserved in the social and material environment of the
chosen political entity but become a legitimate part of a wider political
instrumentalisation, where one such governance technique is securitisation itself.

As shown in Fig. 2.5, the political elite in RS consciously strives to
strengthen the connection with the 'ethnic Self'. This should ensure identity security and thereby legitimise not only the '(re)created threat', but in
addition its own distinctiveness and consequent need for the existence of
RS, thus strengthening its ontological security. Namely, this is the only
path—in a discursive sense—to guarantee the existence of their own Self
(Bosnian Serbs). During these aspirations, which refer both to the preservation and consolidation of the collective Self, it may happen that these
groups propose political solutions that are firmly related to the values and

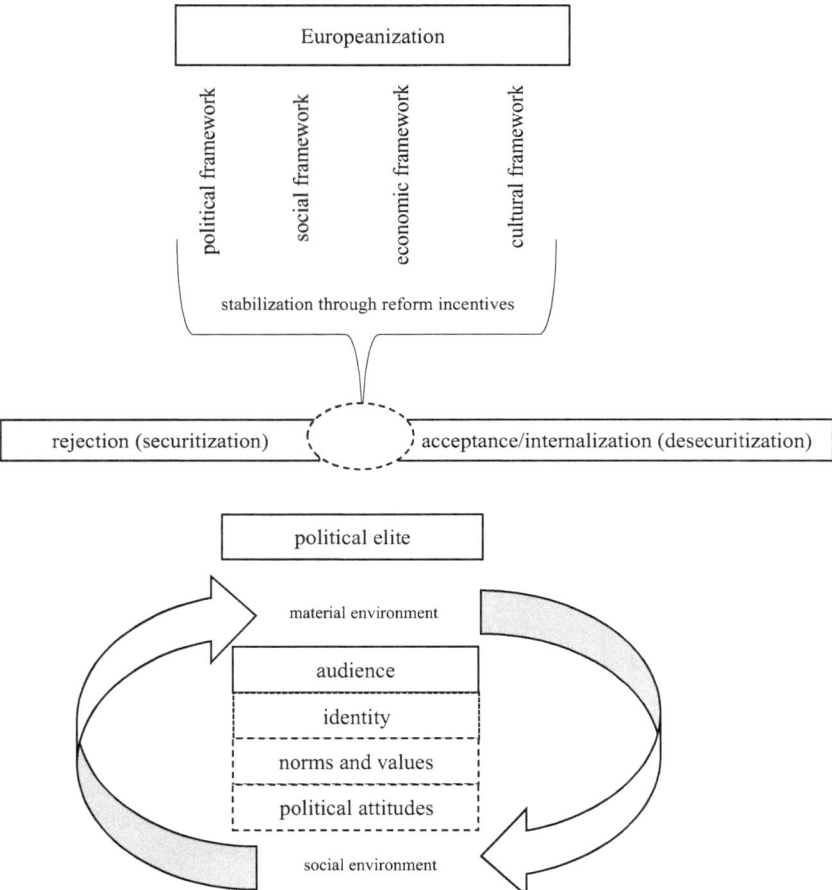

Fig. 2.5 Conceptual framework premised on Europeanisation, securitisation and ontological (in)security. (Source: Author's own elaboration)

norms that exist in their community (psychological-cultural *dispositif*). The result of this is that competing groups may come to see the other group as an obstacle to meeting their own goal—i.e., ensuring the stability of one's own identity, and thus begin to frame it as a threat. Within this process of securitisation, one's own Self begins to overlook the understanding that certain identity traits are subjectively created and hence the cultural markers of a particular group become an "objective reality". The securitisation of subjectivity with the aim of reaffirming one's own identity is directly involved in the way the objective stranger is understood as an 'enemy' where one's own Self is sacrificed with the goal of demonising the Other (Kinnvall, 2004). Put simply, one could argue that while establishing norms, routines and institutions communities already anticipate 'membership' and 'non-membership' in the pursuit of narrating their own identities and ensuring their own ontological security. Those on the 'threatening' side of the unfinished security/threat process are thus much more likely to establish inherently securitised relationships with Others, which are always understood as a threat to their own security. This Other is therefore both an 'external Other', such as the EU through the attempts to change the actual institutions that maintain such routines via reform incentives, and an 'internal Other' that lives and acts in the exact same material and social environment as the securitising actor(s).

In this manner, the importance of Europeanisation's potentially transformative effects as a context for transforming ethnic identity can be understood as an opportunity for desecuritisation via reform incentives that are understood as critical junctures. Instead of the goal, i.e., of diminishing "identity boundaries", these may even accelerate the rhetoric of exclusivism based on 'membership'/'non-membership'. 'Chosen traumas' and 'chosen victories' in such periods promote cohesion within one's own political entity and reduce the sense of ontological insecurity. In a period of the above-mentioned critical junctures, (ethnic) memories, traumas and narratives all form an integral part of the collective identity, which also function as a mechanism for 'closing' the space for reflexivity. This makes subjects less capable of reflecting on their actions, which is a consequence of historical narratives, a failed state-building process, a high level of existential threat or the institutional government system, structures and the political system itself. In circumstances like this, subjects may resort to xenophobia, fundamentalism, exclusivism and populism, ethnic nationalism and religion as a way of providing a sense of ontological security.

The fact that ontological security is interdependent, yet simultaneously objectively different from securitisation discourses, is precisely why securitisation is such a very attractive way to strengthen the feeling of ontological security, especially via the re-creation of routines that encourage and maintain conflict (Mitzen, 2006). Post-conflict environments are quite susceptible to such routines and a general tendency exists there to understand security-identity challenges as a "zero-sum game", where it is assumed that ensuring the identity security of one group is only possible at the expense of an identity threat to another. The result is the very process of peacebuilding in a post-conflict environment that does not anticipate the adaptation of its own narratives and routines is exposed to potential resecuritisation. Europeanisation as a context that enables the transformation of (ethnic) identities precisely anticipates this since stabilisation itself indicates that antagonistic and threatening relations in post-conflict environments are part and parcel of the existing (institutional) structure, which must be addressed primarily via reform incentives that inherently project the political, social, economic and cultural framework on which the EU is built. Ontological security is therefore key to sustainable and successful desecuritisation in reconfiguring the enemy-based dialectic of Self–Other.

There is an interdependence between identity and otherness that creates the 'paradox of distinction', making identity itself a threatening experience. This paradox of distinction emerging from the fact that identity depends on difference paves the way for arguing that the relationship between one's own Self and the Other is shaped so that the Other is a threat to the identity of one's own Self. These two levels of security are both interdependent and independent at once such that neither representations of Self and Other emerge from representations of threat and security, nor are social structures of knowledge, which means the latter shape identities so that they can be subject to either securitisation or desecuritisation. Although the potential for the transformation of difference, which is framed as a threat, continues to exist, it is the actual construction of (ethnic) identity that leads to the variability and unpredictability of the relationship between Self and Other.

Finally, it should be underscored that inclusivity/exclusivity, association/disassociation and/or recognition/resistance depend on the formation of Self–Other dialectics, which I have defined as acceptance/internalisation and/or rejection. The point here is that if the subject (the political elite) internalises/accepts the interests, ideas, norms and, thus, the identities that are a result of Europeanisation (stabilisation through reform incentives as a means to (re)construct institutions) can be transformed in a non-agonistic manner. However, if the subject (political elite) rejects all these ideas, norms and consequently identities, which are the outcome of Europeanisation, one can discuss the (maintenance of) exclusivity, separation and resistance vis-à-vis the Others, which occurs in an antagonistic way. All in all, it is exactly this dynamic of developing identities and imagining the Other, potential (de)securitisation and the search for ontological security in the Europeanisation context that is extremely challenging, especially because transformation through 'normality' (stabilisation via reform incentives as a means to (re)construct institutions) claims inclusivity where exclusivity has functioned as a key building block in forming of ethnic identities throughout history; namely, by way of the institutionalisation of such routines that are the product of conflict and the maximisation of the ontological security of one's own ethnic group.

References

Adamides, C. (2012). *Institutionalized, horizontal and bottom-up securitization in ethnic conflict environments: The case of Cyprus.* (PhD Thesis). University of Birmingham.

Adler, E. (1997). Imagined (security) communities: Cognitive regions in international relations. *Millennium: Journal of International Studies, 26*(2), 249–277.

Aradau, C. (2004). Security and the democratic scene: Desecuritisation and emancipation. *Journal of International Relations and Development, 7*(4), 388–413.

Austin, J. L. (1975). *How to do things with words.* Harvard University Press.

Austin, J. L., & Beaulieu-Brossard, P. (2018). (De)securitisation dilemmas: Theorising the simultaneous enaction of securitisation and desecuritisation. *Review of International Studies, 44*(2), 301–323.

Baele, S. J., & Thomson, C. P. (2017). An experimental agenda for securitization theory. *International Studies Review, 19*(4), 646–666.

Balzacq, T. (2005). The three faces of securitization: Political agency, audience and context. *European Journal of International Relations, 11*(2), 171–201.

Balzacq, T. (2008). The policy tools of securitization: Information exchange, EU foreign and interior policies. *Journal of Common Market Studies, 46*(1), 75–100.

Balzacq, T. (2010). *Securitization theory: How security problems emerge and dissolve.* Routledge.

Balzacq, T. (2011). Constructivism and securitization studies. In V. Mauer & M. D. Cavelty (Eds.), *Handbook of security studies* (pp. 56–72). Routledge.

Behke, A. (2006). No way out: Desecuritization, emancipation and the eternal return of the political – A reply to Aradau. *Journal of International Relations and Development, 9*(1), 62–69.

Bello, V. (2020). The spiralling of the securitisation of migration in the EU: From the management of a 'crisis' to a governance of human mobility? *Journal of Ethnic and Migration Studies, 48,* 1–18.

Bengtsson, L., & Rhinard, M. (2019). Securitisation across borders: The case of 'health security' cooperation in the European Union. *West European Politics, 42*(2), 346–368.

Beyers, J. (2005). Multiple embeddedness and socialization in Europe: The case of council officials. *International Organization, 59*(4), 899–936.

Bigo, D. (2000). When two become one: Internal and external securitisations in Europe. In M. Kelstrup & C. M. Williams (Eds.), *International relations theory and the politics of European integration* (pp. 171–204). Routledge.

Bigo, D. (2002). Security and immigration: Toward a critique of the governmentality of unease. *Alternatives: global, local, political, 27*(1), 63–92.

Bigo, D. (2006). Internal and external aspects of security. *European Security, 15*(4), 385–404.

Björkdahl, A. (2005). *Normative influence in world politics. Towards a theoretical framework for norm export and norm import* (Unpublished paper). Lund University. Available at https://lup.lub.lu.se/record/777217

Bojinović Fenko, A., & Stahl, B. (2019). Chips off the old block: Europeanisation of the foreign policies of Western Balkan states. In J. Džankić, S. Keil, & M. Kmezić (Eds.), *The Europeanisation of the Western Balkans* (pp. 39–62). Palgrave Macmillan.

Bolton, D. (2020). Targeting ontological security: Information warfare in the modern age. *Political Psychology, 42*(1), 127–142.

Booth, K. (1991). Security and emancipation. *Review of International Studies, 17*(4), 313–326.

Booth, K. (2002). Securitization in emerging markets, including government promotion of securitization: A comment on Hill and Arner. *Duke Journal of Comparative and International Law, 12*, 533–536.

Böröcz, J. (2001). Empire and Coloniality in the 'Eastern Enlargement' of the European Union. In J. Böröcz & M. Kovács (Eds.), *Empire's new clothes: Unveiling EU enlargement* (pp. 4–50). Central Europe Review.

Börzel, T. A. (2002). Member state responses to Europeanization. *Journal of Common Market Studies, 40*(2), 193–214.

Börzel, T. A., & Risse, T. (2003). Conceptualizing the domestic impact of Europe. In K. Featherstone & C. M. Radaelli (Eds.), *The politics of Europeanization* (pp. 57–80). Oxford University Press.

Börzel, T. A., & Risse, T. (2011). From Europeanisation to diffusion: Introduction. *West European Politics, 35*(1), 1–19.

Bourbeau, P. (2014). Moving forward together: Logics of the securitisation process. *Millennium: Journal of International Studies, 43*(1), 187–206.

Browning, C. S. (2016). Ethics and ontological security. In J. Nyman & A. Burke (Eds.), *Ethical security studies: A new research agenda* (pp. 160–173). Routledge.

Browning, J., & Joenniemi, P. (2013). From Fraticide to security community: Re-theorising difference in the constitution of Nordic peace. *Journal of International Relations and Development, 16*(4), 483–513.

Browning, C. S., & Joenniemi, P. (2017). Ontological security, self-articulation and the securitization of identity. *Cooperation and Conflict, 52*(1), 31–47.

Buden, B. (2009). *Children of postcommunism* (Research Paper, 159). Radical Philosophy. Available at https://www.radicalphilosophy.com/article/children-of-postcommunism.

Buden, B. (2013, 1 July). *Prevodenje s onu stranu Evrope*. Peščanik. Available at https://pescanik.net/prevodenje-s-onu-stranu-evrope/

Bulmer, S. (2007). Germany, Britain and the European Union: Convergence through policy transfer? *German Politics, 16*(1), 39–57.

Buzan, B., & Wæver, O. (1997). Slippery? Contradictory? Sociologically untenable? The Copenhagen school replies. *Review of International Studies, 23*(2), 241–250.

Buzan, B., & Wæver, O. (2003). *Regions and powers: The structure of international security*. Cambridge University Press.

Buzan, B., & Wæver, O. (2009). Macrosecuritisation and security constellations: Reconsidering scale in securitisation theory. *Review of International Studies, 35*(2), 253–276.

Buzan, B., Wæver, O., & Wilde, J. D. (1998). *Security: A new framework for analysis*. Lynne Rienner Publishers.

Carlson, S., Eigmüller, M., & Lueg, K. (2018). Education, Europeanization and Europe's social integration: An introduction. *Innovation: The European Journal of Social Science Research, 31*(4), 395–405.

Carver, R. (1999). *The Accursed Mountains: Journeys in Albania*. Harper Collins.

Çelik, A. B. (2015). Kurdish issue and levels of ontological security. In B. Rumelili (Ed.), *Conflict resolution and ontological security: Peace anxieties* (pp. 52–70). Routledge.

Checkel, J. T. (2001). Why comply? Social learning and European identity change. *International Organization, 55*(3), 553–588.

Checkel, J. T. (2005). International institutions and socialization in Europe: Introduction and framework. *International Organization, 59*(4), 801–826.

Chernobrov, D. (2016). Ontological security and public (mis)recognition of international crises: Uncertainty, political imagining, and the self. *Political Psychology, 37*(5), 581–596.

Collective, C. (2006). Critical approaches to security in Europe: A networked manifesto. *Security Dialogue, 37*(4), 443–487.

Coskun, B. B. (2008). Analysing Desecuritisations: Prospects and problems for Israeli-Palestinian reconciliation. *Global Change, Peace and Security, 20*(3), 393–408.

Coskun, B. B. (2011). *Analysing desecuritisation: The case of the Israeli-Palestinian peace education and water management.* Cambridge Scholars Publishing.

Cowles, M. G., Caporaso, J., & Risse, T. (2001). *Transforming Europe: Europeanization and domestic change.* Cornell University Press.

Dagli, I. (2016). *Identities in limbo: Securitisation of identities in conflict environments and its implications to ontological security: Prospects of desecuritisation for reconciliation in Cyprus (PhD Thesis).* Coventry: University of Warwick.

Debeljak, A. (2004). *Evropa brez Evropejcev.* Sophija.

Derrida, J. and Ewald, F. (1995). A Certain "Madness" Must Watch Over Thinking. Educational Theory, 45(3), 273–291.

Doty, R. L. (1998). Immigration and the politics of security. *Security Studies, 8*(2/3), 71–93.

Egeberg, M. (1999). The impact of bureaucratic structure on policy making. *Policy Administration, 77*(1), 155–170.

Ejdus, F. (2009). Dangerous liaisons: Securitization theory and Schmittian legacy. *Western Balkans Security Observer, 13,* 9–16.

Ejdus, F. (2017). Critical situations, fundamental questions and ontological insecurity in world politics. *Journal of International Relations and Development, 21,* 883–908.

Ejdus, F. (2020). *Crisis and ontological insecurity: Serbia's anxiety over Kosovo's secession.* Palgrave Macmillan.

Ejdus, F., & Božović, M. (2016). Grammar, context and power: Securitization of the 2010 Belgrade Pride Parade. *Southeast European and Black Sea Studies, 17*(1), 1–17.

Erikson, E. H. (1968). *Identity, youth and crisis.* W. W. Norton Company.

Finnemore, M. (1996). *National interests in international society.* Cornell University Press.

Finnemore, M., & Sikkink, K. (1998). International norm dynamics and political change. *International Organization, 52*(4), 887–917.

Flockhart, T. (2008). The Europeanization of Europe: The transfer of norms to Europe, *in Europe and from Europe* (DIIS working paper, 7). DIIS.

Gellner, E., & Smith, A. D. (1996). The nation: Real or imagined?: The Warwick debates on nationalism. *Nations and Nationalism, 2*(3), 357–370.

Giddens, A. (1984). *The constitution of society. Introduction of the theory of structuration.* University of California Press.

Giddens, A. (1991). *Modernity and self-identity: Self and society in the Late Modern Age.* Stanford University Press.

Goffman, E. (2012). The presentation of self in everyday life (1959). In C. Calhoun, J. Gerteis, J. Moody, S. Pfaff, & I. Virk (Eds.), *Contemporary sociological theory* (pp. 46–61). Blackwell Publishing.

Goldstein, J., & Keohane, R. O. (1993). *Ideas and foreign policy: Beliefs, institutions, and political change.* Cornell University Press.

Gustafsson, K. (2019). International reconciliation on the Internet? Ontological security, attribution and the construction of war memory narratives in Wikipedia. *International Relations, 34*(1), 3–24.

Gustafsson, K., & Krickel-Choi, N. C. (2020). Returning to the roots of ontological security: Insights from the existentialist literature. *European Journal of International Relations, 26*(3), 875–895.

Hagström, L. (2021). Great power narcissism and ontological (in)security: The narrative mediation of greatness and weakness in international politics. *International Studies Quarterly, 65*(2), 1–12.

Hammond, A. (2006). The danger zone of Europe: Balkanism between the cold war and 9/11. *Cultural Studies, 8*(2), 135–154.

Hanrieder, T., & Kreuder-Sonner, C. (2014). WHO decides on the exception? Securitization and emergency governance in global health. *Security Dialogue, 45*(4), 331–348.

Hansen, L. (2000). The little Mermaid's silent security dilemma and the absence of gender in the Copenhagen school. *Millenium. Journal of International Studies, 29*(2), 285–306.

Hansen, L. (2012). Reconstructing desecuritisation: The normative-political in the Copenhagen school and directions for how to apply it. *Review of International Studies, 38*(3), 525–546.

Hansen, L. (2017). Reading comics for the field of international relations: Theory, methods and the Bosnian War. *European Journal of International Relations, 23*(3), 581–608.

Heidegger, M. (2002). *On time and being*. University of Chicago Press.

Helms, E. (2003). Women as agents of ethnic reconciliation? Women's NGOs and international intervention in postwar Bosnia-Herzegovina. *Women's Studies International Forum, 26*(1), 15–33.

Héritier, A. (2005). Europeanization research east and west: A comparative assessment. In F. Schimmelfennig & U. Sedelmeier (Eds.), *The Europeanization of Central and Eastern Europe* (pp. 199–209). Cornell University Press.

Hix, S., & Goetz, K. H. (2000). Introduction: European integration and National Political Systems. *West European Politics, 23*(4), 1–26.

Hobson, J. M. (2002). What's at stake in Bringing historical sociology back into international relations? Transcending 'chronofetishism' and 'tempocentrism' in international relations. In S. Hobden & J. M. Hobson (Eds.), *Historical sociology in international relations* (pp. 3–41). Cambridge University Press.

Hom, A. R., & Steele, B. J. (2020). Anxiety, time, and ontological security's third-image potential. *International Theory, 12*, 322–336.

Huysmans, J. (1998). Security! What do you mean? From concept to thick signifier. *European Journal of International Relations, 4*(2), 226–255.

Huysmans, J. (2006). *The politics of insecurity: Fear, migration and asylum in the EU*. Routledge.

Ikenberry, J. G. (2018). The end of liberal international order? *International Affairs, 94*(1), 7–23.

Innes, A. J. (2017). Everyday ontological security: Emotion and migration in British soaps. *Intenrational Political Sociology, 11*(4), 380–397.

Jeftić, A. (2019). *Social aspects of memory: Stories of victims and perpetrators from Bosnia-Herzegovina*. Routledge.

Jones, W. R. (1999). *Security, strategy, and critical theory*. Lynne Rienner.

Jones, W. R. (Ed.). (2001). *Critical theory and world politics*. Lynne Rienner.

Jordan, A. J. (2002). *The Europeanisation of British environmental policy: A departmental Perspective*. Palgrave Macmillan.

Kaplan, R. (1999, 7 April). *In the Balkans, No Wars are Local*. New York Times. Available at https://www.nytimes.com/1999/04/07/opinion/in-the-balkans-no-wars-are-local.html.

Kassim, H. (2000). *The National co-ordination of EU policy*. Oxford University Press.

Kay, S. (2012). Ontological security and peace-building in Northern Ireland. *Contemporary Security Policy, 33*(2), 236–263.

Kelman, H. C. (2007). Social-psychological dimensions of international conflict. In I. W. Zartman (Ed.), *Peacemaking in international conflict: Methods and techniques* (pp. 61–107). United States Institute of Peace.

Kinnvall, C. (2004). Globalization and religious nationalism: Self, identity, and the search for ontological security. *Political Psychology, 25*(5), 741–767.

Kinnvall, C., & Mitzen, J. (2017). An introduction to the special issue: Ontological securities in world politics. *Cooperation and Conflict, 52*(1), 3–11.

Kinnvall, C., & Mitzen, J. (2020). Anxiety, fear and ontological security in world politics: Thinking with and beyond Giddens. *International Theory, 12*(2), 240–256.

Krickel-Choi, N. C. (2021). The embodied state: Why and how physical security matters for ontological security. *Journal of International Relations and Development*. https://doi.org/10.1057/s41268-021-00219-x

Kuus, M. (2004). Europe's eastern expansion and the reinscription of otherness in East-Central Europe. *Progress in Human Geography, 28*(4), 472–489.

Laing, R. D. (1965). *The divided self: An existential study in sanity and madness*. Penguin Books.

Laing, R. D. (1971). *Self and others*. Penguin Books.

Laing, R. D. (1990). *Politics of experience and the bird of paradise*. Penguin Books.

Lajh, D., & Kajnč Lange, S. (2009). *Evropska unija od A do Ž*. Uradni list Republike Slovenije.

Lupovici, A. (2012). Ontological dissonance, clashing identities and Israel's unilateral stepts towards the Palestinians. *Review of International Studies, 38*(4), 809–833.

Mahoney, J., & Thelen, K. (2010). *Ambiguity, agency, and power*. Cambridge University Press.

Majstorović, D. (2007). Construction of Europeanization in the high representative's discourse in Bosnia and Herzegovina. *Discourse and Society, 18*(5), 627–651.

Majstorović, D., & Vučkovac, Z. (2016). Rethinking Bosnia and Herzegovina's post-coloniality challenges of Europeanization discourse. *Journal of Language and Politics, 15*(2), 147–172.

Manners, I. (2002). Normative power Europe: A contradiction in terms? *Journal of Common Market Studies, 40*(2), 235–258.

March, J. G., & Olsen, J. P. (1995). *Democratic governance.* Free Press.

March, J. G., & Simon, H. A. (1993). *Organizations.* Blackwell Publishers.

Marcussen, M. (2000). *Ideas and elites: The social construction of economic and Monetary union.* Aalborg University Press.

McSweeney, B. (1996). Identity and security: Buzan and the Copenhagen school. *Review of International Studies, 22*(1), 81–94.

McSweeney, B. (1998). Durkheim and the Copenhagen school: A response to Buzan and Wæver. *Review of International Studies, 24*(1), 137–140.

Melegh, A. (2006). *On the east-west slope: Globalization, nationalism, racism and discourses on Central and Eastern Europe.* Central European University Press.

Menéndzes, D. C., Koops, J. A., & Weggemans, D. (2021). A country of immigrants no more? The securitisation of immigration in the National Security Strategies of The United States of America. *Global Affairs, 7*(1), 1–26.

Miles, L. (2005). *Fusing with Europe: Sweden in the European Union.* Routledge.

Miškova, D. (2006). U potrazi za balkanskim zapadnjaštvom. *Tokovi istorije, 2*(1), 29–62.

Mitchell, A. (2015). Ontological (in)security and violent peace in Northern Ireland. In V. Rumelili (Ed.), *Conflict resolution and ontological security: Peace anxieties* (pp. 99–116). Routledge.

Mitzen, J. (2006). Ontological security in world politics: State identity and the security dilemma. *European Journal of International Relations, 12*(3), 341–370.

Močnik, R. (1999). *3 teorije: Ideologija, nacija, institucija.* Založba/*cf.

Mouffe, C. (2012). An agonistic approach to the future of Europe. *New literary History, 43*(4), 629–640.

Muršič, R. (2007). The Balkans and ambivalence of its perception in Slovenia: The horror of 'Balkanism' and enthusiasm for its music. In B. Jezernik, R. Muršič, & A. Bartulović (Eds.), *Europe and its other* (pp. 87–105). Faculty of Arts.

Nabers, D. (2015). *A postcolonialist discourse theory of global politics.* Palgrave Macmillan.

Neumann, I. B. (1999). *Uses of the other: The "East" in European identity formation.* Manchester University Press.

Newell, M. (2020). Comparing American perceptions of post-Civil Ku Klux Klan and transnational violence. *Security Dialogue, 51*(4), 287–304.

Olsen, J. P. (2002). The many faces of Europeanization. *Journal of Common Market Studies, 40*(5), 921–952.

Petrović, T. (2009). *A long way home: Representation of the Western Balkan in media and political discourses.* Peace Institute.

Petrović, T. (2014). *Mirroring Europe: Ideas of Europe and Europeanization in Balkan societies.* Brill.

Prozorov, S. (2011). The other as past and present: Beyond the logic of 'temporal othering' in IR theory. *Review of International Studies, 37*(3), 1273–1293.

Radaelli, C. M. (2000). Policy transfer in the European Union: Institutional isomorphism as a source of legitimacy. *Governance: An International Journal of Policy Administration, and Institutions, 13*(1), 25–43.

Radaelli, C. M. (2003). Europeanisation: Solution or problem? *European Integration online Papers, 16*(8), 1–16.

Rieker, P. (2004). Europeanization of Nordic security: The European Union and the changing security identities of the Nordic states. *Cooperation and Conflict, 39*(4), 369–392.

Risse, T. (2001). *The euro and identity politics in Europe* (Research Paper, 6–8 December). Available at http://userpage.fu-berlin.de/~atasp/texte/021202_risse_euroidentity.pdf

Roe, P. (2004). Securitization and minority rights: Conditions of desecuritization. *Security Dialogue, 35*(3), 279–294.

Roe, P. (2006). Reconstructing identities or managing minorities? Desecuritizing minority rights: A response to Jutila. *Security Dialogue, 37*(3), 425–438.

Roe, P. (2008). The value of positive security. *Review of International Studies, 34*(4), 777–794.

Rumelili, B. (2004). Constructing identity and relating to difference: Understanding the EU's mode of differentiation. *Review of International Studies, 30*(1), 27–47.

Rumelili, B. (2005). The European Union and cultural change in Greek-Turkish relations. *The European Union and Border Conflicts, 17*, 1–31.

Rumelili, B. (2011). Identity and Desecuritization: Possibilities and limits. In *Paper presented at Norwegian Institute of International Affairs (NUPI) research seminar series.* NUPI. Available at https://citeseerx.ist.psu.edu/viewdoc/download?doi=10.1.1.461.4883&rep=rep1&type=pdf

Rumelili, B. (2013). Identity and desecuritisation: The pitfalls of conflating ontological and physical security. *Journal of International Relations and Development, 18*(1), 52–74.

Rumelili, B. (2015). *Conflict resolution and ontological security: Peace anxieties.* Routledge.

Salter, M. B. (2008). Securitization and desecuritization. A dramaturgical analysis of the Canadian air transport security authority. *Journal of International Relations and Development, 11*(4), 321–349.

Sarajlić, D. (2011). Bosnia and Herzegovina after the elections: A tale of disillusioned optimism, in the Western Balkans and the EU. In J. Rupnik (Ed.), *The hour of Europe* (pp. 47–58). EU Institute for Security Studies.

Schimmelfennig, F., & Sedelmeier, U. (2005). Introduction: Conceptualizing the Europeanization of Central and Eastern Europe. In F. Schimmelfennig & U. Sedelmeier (Eds.), *The Europeanization of Central and Eastern Europe* (pp. 1–28). Cornell University Press.

Schimmelfennig, F., & Sedelmeier, U. (2019). The Europeanization of Eastern Europe: The external incentives model revisited. *Journal of European Public Policy, 27*(6), 814–833.

Skey, M. (2010). 'A sense of where you belong in the world': National belonging, ontological security and the status of the ethnic majority in England. *Nations and Nationalism, 16*(4), 715–733.

Spohn, W., & Eder, K. (2005). *Collective memory and European identity: The effects of integration and enlargement.* Routledge.

Steele, B. J. (2005). Ontological security and the power of self-identity: British neutrality and the American civil war. *Review of International Studies, 31*(3), 519–540.

Steele, B. J. (2008). *Ontological security in international relations: Self-identity and the IR state.* Routledge.

Stein, J. G. (2002). Psychological explanations of international conflict. In B. A. Simmons, W. Carlsnaes, & T. Risse (Eds.), *Handbook of international relations* (pp. 195–219). SAGE.

Strizel, H. (2007). Towards a theory of securitization. Copenhagen and beyond. *European Journal of International Relations, 13*(3), 357–383.

Subotić, J. (2011). Europe is a state of mind: Identity and Europeanization of the Balkans. *International Studies Quarterly, 55*(2), 309–330.

Subotić, J. (2015). Out of Eastern Europe: Legacies of violence and the challenge of multiple transitions. *East European Politics and Societies, 29*(2), 409–419.

Subotić, J. (2019). *Yellow star, red star: Holocaust remembrance after communism.* Cornell University Press.

Tanil, G. (2014). The social constructivist fusion perspective: A theory for Europeanization. *Perspectives on European Politics and Society, 15*(4), 483–499.

Tatlić, Š. (2008). Mikrob u Evropi. *Reartikulacija, 2,* 9.

Taureck, R. (2006). Securitisation theory and securitisation studies. *Journal of International Relations and Development, 9,* 53–61.

Tekin, A., & Güney, A. (2015). *The Europeanization of Turkey: Polity and politics.* Routledge.

Theiler, T. (2003). Societal security and social psychology. *Review of International Studies, 29*(2), 249–268.

Tillich, P. (1962). *The courage to be.* Collins.

Todorova, M. (1997). *Imagining the Balkans.* Oxford University Press.

Todorova, M. (2004). *Balkan identities: Nation and memory.* New York University Press.

Todorova, M. (2009). Balkanism and postcolonialism or on the beauty of the Airplane view. In C. Bradatan & S. Oushakine (Eds.), *Marx's shadow: Knowledge, power, and intellectuals in Eastern Europe and Russia* (pp. 175–195). Rowman and Littlefield.

Todorova, M. (2012). Nostalgia – The reverse side of Balkanism. In W. Borodziej and J. con Puttkamer (Eds.), European un Sein Osten: *Geschichtskulturelle Herausforderungen* (pp. 61–74). : Oldenbourg Verlag.

Trondal, J. (2007). The public administration turn in integration research. *Journal of European Public Policy, 14*(6), 960–972.

Turner, C., & Steele, B. (2022). Race, religion, and the echoes of status insecurity in US foreign policy. *Alternatives: Global, Local, Political, 48*(1), 74–90.

Velikonja, M. (2009). Anatomija pcifernega uma. *Časopis za kritiko znanosti, 37*(235/236), 78–89.

Vuori, J. A. (2010). A timely prophet? The doomsday clock as a visualization of securitization moves with a global referent object. *Security Dialogue, 41*(3), 255–277.

Wæver, O. (1993). Securitization and Desecuritization. In R. Lipschutz (Ed.), *On security* (pp. 46–86). Columbia University Press.

Wæver, O. (1995). Securitization and Desecuritization. In R. Lipschutz (Ed.), *On security* (pp. 46–86). Columbia University Press.

Wæver, O. (1998). Insecurity, security, and Asecurity in the West European non-war community. In E. Adler & M. Barnett (Eds.), *Security communities* (pp. 69–118). Cambridge University Press.

Wæver, O. (2000). The EU as a security actor: Reflections from a pessimistic constructivist on post-sovereign security orders. In M. C. Williams & M. Kelstrup (Eds.), *International relations theory and European integration. Power, security and community* (pp. 250–294). Routledge.

Wæver, O. (2004). *Aberystwyth, Paris, Copenhagen: New "schools" in security theory and their origins between core and periphery.* Available at https://www.scribd.com/doc/40010349/Ole-Waever-Aberystwyth-Paris-en-New-Schools-in-Security-Theory-and-Their-Origins-Between-Core-and-Periphery

Wæver, O., Buzan, B., Kelstrup, M., & Lemaitre, P. (Eds.). (1993). *Identity, migration and the new security agenda in Europe.* St. Martin's Press.

Watson, S. D. (2009). *The securitization of humanitarian migration. Digging moats and sinking boats.* Routledge.

Wendt, A. (1992). Anarchy is what states make of it: The social construction of power politics. *International Organization, 46*(2), 391–425.

Wendt, A. (1999). *Social theory of international politics.* Cambridge University Press.

Wiliams, M. C. (2003). Words, images, enemies: Securitization and international politics. *International Studies Quarterly, 47*(4), 511–531.

Williams, M. C. (1998). Modernity, identity and security: A comment on the 'Copenhagen controversy'. *Review of International Studies, 24*(3), 435–439.

Winnicott, D. W. (1971). *Playing and reality.* Routledge.

Wooley, J. (2007). Is 'ontological security' possible? *British Journal of Undergraduate Philosophy, 2*(2), 176–185.

Young, J. (1999). *The exclusive society: Social exclusion, crime and difference in late modernity.* SAGE.

Yurchak, A. (2006). *Everything was forever, until it was no more: The last soviet generation.* Princeton University Press.

Zahra, T. (2011). Going west. *East European Politics and Societies, 25*(4), 785–791.

Zarakol, A. (2010). Ontological (In)security and state denial of historical crimes: Turkey and Japan. *International Relations, 24*(1), 3–23.

Zarakol, A. (2016). States and ontological security: A historical rethinking. *Cooperation and Conflict, 52*(1), 48–68.

CHAPTER 3

Imagining the Bosnian Serb Ethnic Identity: Historical Analysis

This chapter contains three parts. The first subchapter contextualises the history of Bosnia and Herzegovina from the perspective of the construction of the ethnic identity of (Bosnian) Serbs before the Bosnian War (1992–1995) and the establishment of Republika Srpska. The next subchapter analyses the ethnic identity of (Bosnian) Serbs in the period following the dissolution of the Socialist Federal Republic of Yugoslavia and before the referendum on the Day of Republika Srpska. Finally, the third subchapter offers an understanding of the social and material environment of Republika Srpska in the context of BiH's European integration, particularly with respect to how the Bosnian Serb political elite in Republika Srpska tends to shape it.

3.1   Bosnia and Herzegovina from the Arrival of the South Slavs Until the End of the Second World War (Second Half of the Sixth Century till 1945)

For the purposes of this book, the historical starting point of settlement in today's BiH is important. This dates to the sixth century when the South Slavs arrived on the Balkan Peninsula in search of new places to live. Before

© The Author(s), under exclusive license to Springer Nature   73
Switzerland AG 2023
F. Kočan, *Identity, Ontological Security and Europeanisation
in Republika Srpska*, Central and Eastern European Perspectives
on International Relations,
https://doi.org/10.1007/978-3-031-46169-9_3

long, the Byzantine influence penetrated South Slavic societies and brought several changes, including Christianity (Imamović, 2006, 18). The process of Christianisation was gradually conducted under the leadership of Cyril and Methodius, initially following the introduction of Old Church Slavonic as the language for communicating between people and consolidating religion (ibid.). The latter is important because the establishment of this language gave the Slavs "a sense of their historical identity" (Imamović, 2006, 19). The ethnogenesis and evolution of the 'state' of the South Slavs are therefore strongly linked to Christianisation (Croats in 879; Serbs in 891) and religious homogenisation in the following centuries (Velikonja, 2003, 22). The first mention of any state formation in today's BiH dates to the late eighth century, namely because of Constantine VII who in his work spoke about the area of Bosnia (*horion Bosona*) (Velikonja, 2003, 23). In this period, alongside the majority South Slavic nation, Avars, Romans and Illyrians were also present. The first form of government system in Serbia (*Rascia*) should be highlighted here, coinciding with the end of the eighth century and beginning of the ninth century and divided into administrative units called *župas* (Imamović, 2006, 38). The Byzantine Empire continued to have a great influence across the entire area, as reflected in the very Christianisation of the Serbs (ibid.). Thus, we start describing the latter as "Orthodox" only following the great schism in 1054, after which the Byzantine Empire accepted the Orthodox religion.

In the tenth century, the area of today's BiH endured many conquests—from Mihael Krešimir II (Croatia) to Prince Časlav (Raško) and King Bodin (Duklje). One outcome of this meant the Bosnian identity could only begin to develop in the late Middle Ages (Velikonja, 2003, 23). Certainly, religion was one of the most important sources of self-awareness in societies, as evidenced by the fact that political self-awareness in medieval Bosnia was the result of the religious distinction between the Bosnian Church (*Crkva Bosanska*) and the Eastern and Western forms of Christianity (ibid.). The Bosnian Church, which was the church of Bosnian and Huma (today's Herzegovina) Christians and heterogeneous in terms of liturgy, only became autonomous once Roman Catholic rule ended in the thirteenth century. A crucial period during the Middle Ages for Bosnia, which is today viewed as the golden period of Bosnian history, is the time of the reign of Banus Culinus (*banus Culinus dominus Bosnae*), namely between 1180 and 1204.

During this period, religiously diverse Bosnia faced constant threats from Byzantium and neighbouring Hungary. Emerik Ogrski and Vukan Nemanjić (Duklja) were especially important in this regard, having accused Ban Kulin of heresy in a letter sent to Pope Innocent III in 1199 (Velikonja, 2003, 24). Ban Kulin's period is important for the development of political ideas in what is today BiH largely due to the historical myth of 'godliness'.[1] This myth not only became a symbol of Bosnian sovereignty with respect to the invading neighbours but also became an obvious starting point for all three ethnic groups in BiH in the nineteenth and twentieth centuries, which justified the origin of their own identity through the Bogomil nature of religious autonomy. Velikonja (2003, 27–29) showed that Serbian authors (Petranović and Glušac) emphasised that the Bosnian Church was Orthodox, Bosniak authors (Handžić and Balić) connected the Bogomils with an Islamic and Bosniak identity, while Croatian nationalists believed the Bosnian Bogomils were ethnic Croats who later converted to Islam. For Serbian political thought, Ban Kulin's letter to Prince Krvaš of Dubrovnik in 1189, said to have been written in Cyrillic, not Bosnian, is especially important (Begenišić, 2019). This letter is claimed to be both a "monument of Serbian literacy", as Tanasić emphasised, and proof that "Bosnian script is nothing more than a quick script brought from the Serbian court to Bosnia by Tvrtko Kotromanić" (ibid.).

The Kotromanić dynasty is important for understanding the history of Bosnia because it became the last great medieval South Slavic state. In 1326, Stefan II Kotromanić, the son of Stefan Kotroman, subjugated Hum, which was under the control of the Serbian Nemanjić dynasty from 1168 onwards. Stefan Kotromanić maintained good relations with both neighbours, Hungary and Serbia, and it should be stressed that Bosnia continued to be formally part of the Hungarian kingdom (Velikonja, 2003, 33). At this stage, the Bosnian church during the time of Stefan II became ever more important since Bosnia had become the target of both Pope John XXII and Benedict XII, who underscored that the Bosnian bans accepted and protected heretics, which led to the engagement of the Croatian nobility who would 'take care' of Christianisation through the Franciscans (ibid.). This time period brought one of the most prominent tests for Bosnia. In 1350, Dušan Nemanjić (also the first Serbian emperor) attacked it with the aim of reconquering Hum, which was then taken by

---

[1] The myth of godliness only emerged in the nineteenth century when there was an enthusiastic revival of national(ist) history.

the Bosnian ban Stefan II Kotromanić. Kotromanić's successor was his nephew Ban Stefan Tvrtko I, King of Raška and Bosnia and Croatia and Dalmatia, then considered to be a religiously tolerant and politically extremely successful leader. Led by Ban Stefan Tvrtko I, Bosnia became one of the strongest powers in the Balkans, as shown by his victory over the Hungarians and the resistance army headed by his brother Vuk. Imamović (2006, 59) even hinted that in a way Tvrtko I was even the 'first Yugoslav king' due to their leadership of the country, which spread across the territory of today's Serbia, Bosnia and part of Croatia. After the death of Tvrtko I, Bosnia was subjected to decades of internal conflict, inter-dynasty wars, weak central authority and Hungarian interference, and the ever-present threat posed by the Ottoman Empire.

A clear indicator of Bosnia's 'fragility' was the renewed accusations of heresy by the Bosnian Church and the new wave of re-Catholicisation of the Bosnian population after 1430. This process, which King Tvrtko II was otherwise opposed to, coincided with the increasingly ambitious Ottoman Empire that had already defeated Stjepan Dabiša in 1395. In this regard, the events in Hum, which was basically part of the Serbian state and the Nemanjić dynasty and only later became a (semi-autonomous) part of Bosnia (Velikonja, 2003, 38), are probably even more important. Serbia was different from Hungary, which never really developed a 'terri-torial appetite' for Bosnia and never sent an army (ibid.). 'Orthodox' Hum, as Velikonja (2003, 38) notes, only came into conflict with the neighbouring Catholics in 1450, especially in the last years of the Bosnian kingdom's existence. It was then that the conflict between the Roman Catholic Church and the Serbian Orthodox Church over Bosnia officially commenced. The last Bosnian king before the official 'fall of Bosnia' under Ottoman rule in 1461 was Stefan Tomašević, who Pope Pius II crowned as the 'defender of Bosnia' and was beheaded in Jajce about 2 years later.

Before continuing the discussion on Bosnia during the Ottoman Empire, it is worth describing two crucial myths, or the 'myth of all myths', which managed to take shape at this time and have significantly determined Serbian political thought. The first myth is the cult of Stefan's brother Rastek who in 1190/1191 was given control of Zahumje, yet in 1192 fled from the Holy Mountain to the Russian monastery of Saint Panteleimon, where he was named Sava. Later, he not only mediated between Grand Mayor Štefan and Prince Vukan, but in 1219 even man-aged to convince the Patriarch of Constantinople and the Emperor of Nicaea to recognise the autocephaly of the Serbian Orthodox Church

(Ćorović, 2001). Sava thus became one of the 'fathers' of Serbian ethnic self-awareness and accordingly remains one of the central 'cultural heroes' for Serbs (Velikonja, 2003, 46). The second myth is the 'Vidovdan' myth connected with King Tvrtko I, who in 1389 fought together with the Serbian prince Lazar Hrebeljanović in a battle on *Kosovo polje* and survived, unlike Lazar, who was captured and beheaded. In so doing, Tvrtko I fought together with Prince Lazar Hrebeljanović against Sultan Murat I, who also lost his life in the battle. He was succeeded by his son Bayazid, who is noteworthy because he defeated Stjepan Dabiša in 1395 (Carmichael, 2015, 13).

The period after 1430 is important not only because the Ottoman Empire slowly began to conquer all of the Balkans but principally because the Serbs started to take refuge in Bosnia. The Ottoman Empire had captured Sarajevo by 1451, a large part of the rest of Bosnia in 1463 and then Herzegovina in 1481 (Filipović, 1997). Jajce and Bihać were the last to fall and it should be noted that after 1580, the Ottoman Empire controlled the entire area of present-day BiH, including Lika and Slavonia (Carmichael, 2015). The process of the 'Islamisation' of Bosnia and Herzegovina commenced systematically in the early sixteenth century when most religious buildings were converted into mosques (Lovrenović, 2015). Islam eventually became an extremely important factor in distinguishing people, best illustrated with the use of the word "raja" (*rayah*)— ordinary people—in relation to the Turks, which simultaneously legitimised the Janissary system. Between the sixteenth and eighteenth centuries, the Janissary system provided for over 100,000 'young and promising Christian boys' who, through the system of education and subsequent employment, would not only adopt the Islamic religion in military campaigns but above all be devoted and loyal to the Ottoman authorities (Carmichael, 2015). One of these was Mehmed Paša Sokolović, supposedly of Orthodox faith, whose exceptionally good knowledge of languages and pragmatic leadership skills meant he soon found himself among the sultan's most important and closest collaborators. Mehmed Paša Sokolović, who even became grand vizier in 1565 (de facto the first face of the empire after the sultan), is also important because he strove hard to restore the patriarchate of Peć. He succeeded with this in 1557 when his request was granted by Suleiman II the Magnificent. This was also important because it ended the decades-long dispute between the dioceses, the Patriarch of Constantinople, and the local Ottoman leaders (Samarčić, 1971, 14). Imamović (2006, 161) notes that Mehmed Paša did not do this due to "awareness of his own origin or attachment to Serbia", but such interpretations are a "national delusion of the Serbs with no objective basis". Among other things, Mehmed Paša also took care of the construction of five bridges, the most important of which is easily the bridge over the Drina in Višegrad, which not only is one of the greatest creations of Ottoman architecture in the territory of Bosnia and Herzegovina but also symbolises the intertwining of East and West or, as Andrić (1980, 6) describes, it symbolises "the only permanent crossing point that connects Bosnia with Serbia and through Serbia with other parts of the Turkish Empire up to Istanbul".

Even if Mehmed Pasha did not have 'ethnic/national self-awareness' in mind during the restoration of the patriarchate of Peć (since, compared to modern nations, these were only proto nations, which we talk about only from the nineteenth century onwards), the preservation and development of the ethnic/national identity of the Serbs occurred through the 'Millet system'. This came as a response to the efforts made by the Ottoman political elite with respect to objectively different ethno-religious communities and their integration into economic, administrative and political life in the Ottoman Empire. The paradox of the Millet system, Velikonja (2003, 73) states, was that it enabled the expansion and strengthening of the Serbian national identity (and others), as is further indicated by the restored Patriarchate of Peć which managed to preserve the Serbian political, religious and ethnic identity. The Ottoman Empire was in fact crucial to the Serbian political imaginary and ethnic identity as the Serb people were able—after being one of four mutually isolated religious communities within the Millet system—to start mythologising the Serbian medieval state, their leaders and national cults, with their leaders even becoming saints (Velikonja, 2003, 74). Malcolm (1996) shows that it was the policies of the Ottoman Empire that led to Sarajevo having its first Orthodox priest in 1489 and its first Orthodox church between 1520 and 1539, with the first Orthodox church being built as early as 1515 near Bihać.

The consolidation of the Orthodox Church's power was seen in the conflict with the Ottoman authorities in 1593 when Patriarch John I established relations with Russia, Austria, Spain, Poland and Venice with the intention of providing funds for the rebellion under the name "Saint Sava". Bougarel (1996) also wrote about this and underlined the fact that the Ottoman authorities did not tolerate such rebellions and hence Jovan I was brought to Istanbul and beheaded, and later even the remains of Saint Sava were transferred from Mileševo to Vračar (part of Belgrade) and publicly dispersed. He interpreted this event as a moment of "great shock" for the Serbs, especially when considering that the period under Sokolović was a time of relative peace and prosperity. From then on, the Serbian Orthodox Church lost all the privileges it had enjoyed during the Sokolović period. After 1699, when the Ottoman Empire suffered a severe defeat against Austria, the Church thus began to openly seek alliances with neighbouring Catholic countries and worry about any further development of Serbian political self-awareness (Velikonja, 2003, 75). At the same time, this coincided with the beginning of the decline of the empire, with the next two centuries marked by great oppression, competition and open hostility between the ethnic groups in Bosnia and Herzegovina (Bataković, 1996). Matters were not helped by the fact that Bosnia was one of the most autonomous provinces of the Ottoman Empire given that it was simultaneously one of the least developed in the empire. This period is also noteworthy because the Habsburg political elite sent contradictory information to the Muslim part of the population regarding the future of their religion if they were to rebel against the Ottoman Empire (Velikonja, 2003, 83). The Habsburg political elite was much more decisive in the period between 1737 and 1739 during the Austro-Turkish War when the Habsburg leadership threatened to 'expel' the Muslim part of the population if they did not convert to Christianity. This threat was fully realised in the Second War between 1788 and 1791 when Franz Joseph II promised freedom of religion in the event of Austrian occupation (ibid.).

It should be made clear here that the Bosnian elite was extremely conservative and from the very beginning of the reign of Sultan Selim III (1798–1807) and Mehmed II (1808–1839) resisted reforms, which later in 1831 was reflected in the rebellion of the Bosnian (Islamic) aristocracy (Velikonja, 2003, 84). The revolt was crushed and Sultan Abdülmecid's ideas were passed on to his successor, the Tanzimat, who in the post-1850 period through Omer Pasha Latas began to introduce unpopular reforms in Bosnia, including standardisation of the tax system, a secular school system, religious freedoms, and equality before the law (Imamović, 1977). Not all of these reforms were well received by the conservative Bosnian elite, who were soon joined by the Christian elite following the loss of connections with third countries and feudal privileges (Friedman, 1996). Through such a 'rebellion', Malcolm (1996) shows that the central hostility between the groups was not of an ethnic or religious nature, but an economic one, since Christians were mostly farmers, whereas Muslims were rulers/feudalists. Velikonja (2003, 87) shows how this economic hostility soon began to be translated via the prism of religion as the increasing pressures of the Muslim elite, on the other hand, created social frustrations and increased the influence of folk legends and the traditions of the Catholic and Orthodox churches, which started to 'idealise' the feudal society of their ancestors (ibid.). From here on, it was not far from the peasant revolts between 1852 and 1862 that were a result of the strengthening of the non-Muslim population's awareness that they were exploited, economically underprivileged, and oppressed by local leaders (Velikonja, 2003, 88). These rebellions held an important external dimension, referring to Serbia and Croatia in the first half of the nineteenth century, which led to the coexistence of ethnic and religious identities being seriously questioned. Velikonja (2003, 87) shows this by noting that the Millet system had become increasingly segmented and directly related to the differentiation between ethnic/religious groups (e.g., Serb-millet, Bosniak-kavmi and Bosniak taifesi). Bataković (n.d.) emphasises that the peasant uprisings held a deeper meaning, that is, the Serbs' centuries-long efforts to bring the Turkish provinces with the majority Serbian population together in the common state of Serbia.

However, even before continuing with the development of events in BiH under Austria-Hungary (A-H), it is worth highlighting the year 1826 when Serbia was given limited autonomy within the Ottoman Empire under the Akkerman Convention, and the year 1829 when Serbia gained independence under the Edirne Peace Agreement. This is how the first modern Serbian dynasty was formed and, consequently, a platform for the instrumentalisation of Serbian political thought through the 'imagining' of the Serbian nation. The first modern Serbian dynasty was led by Miloš Obrenović, a 'Montenegrin', who had migrated to Serbia. The Obrenović dynasty became important for Serbian political thought because it began to be compared to the Nemanjić dynasty. The key year was 1882, when Obrenović became king and Serbia became a kingdom (Velikonja, 2003, 97). With this, the perception of dreams having been fulfilled slowly started to be created, lasting for centuries and preserved in poetry, literature and the Church (ibid.). Here, two critical moments should be highlighted: (i) the beginning of the process of equating the Orthodox faith with Serbia, occurring mainly in the early nineteenth century (Banac, 1988); and (ii) the Kosovo myth became ever more present and important for the Serbian religious-national identity and the central feeling of a common origin, as reflected through both the ideological upgrading of the myth by Petar Petrović II Njegoš (1847) and by authors like Vuk Stefanović

Karadžić, Dositej Obradović, Ljubomir Kovačević, Lukijan Mušicki and Jovan Sterija Popović, who succeeded in elevating the "epic struggle and sacrifice of Prince Lazar" to the level of collective martyrdom. This (identity-wise) served as a reference point for the legitimate search for the right to Serbian national self-determination (Velikonja, 2003, 94–96).

A prime reason for the lack of success unifying the provinces in which the majority of Serbs lived with Serbia was the "Eastern Crisis" (1875–1878). The crisis commenced with Serbian revolts in Herzegovina and Bosnia, and ended with these two Ottoman provinces being occupied by the A-H. We must not forget the new dynamics that took place in those years, namely Montenegro and Prince Nikola, who tried to annex Herzegovina, and Serbia with Prince Milan Obrenović, who 'owned' Bosnia (Radušić, n.d., 111). The defeat of the movement for the annexation of Herzegovina to Montenegro and Bosnia to Serbia, which was decided at the Berlin Congress in 1878, is also important because it indirectly 'defeated' the spirit of *Načertanije*[2] of Ilija Garašanin (1844), a member of the Serbian political elite who envisioned the process of uniting all the Turkish provinces in which the Serbian population was living into a common and unified (Greater) Serbia. The very outcome of the Berlin Congress—which envisaged the annexation/joining of Bosnia and Herzegovina to A-H and not its independence—from the outset experienced a great rebellion among the inhabitants of BiH. In this respect, Muslims and Serbs prepared a joint rebellion against the A-H armies, in which approximately 150,000 people died (Bataković, 1996, 119). The defeat was primarily a blow to Serbia, with Prince Milan Obrenović being forced to sign the 'hidden convention' in Vienna in 1881, officially renouncing political engagement in BiH, which had been an integral part of Serbian foreign policy between 1804 and 1878 (Bataković, 1996, 77).

Bataković (1996, 121) emphasises that Serbia was politically absent from Bosnia and Herzegovina from that moment until the start of the twentieth century, reflected in the fact that the Bosnian Serbs could count

---

[2] Načertanije was the programme or booklet (no longer than 5000 words) of the national policy of the Principality of Serbia of the then Minister of Internal Affairs and later Minister of Foreign Affairs Ilija Garašanin, which was issued as a secret state document in 1844. Greater Serbia would be created, namely, a common state of all southern Slavs with the goal of restoring medieval Serbia. In addition to the Principality of Serbia, Greater Serbia is said to include the northern part of Albania, Herzegovina, Bosnia and Montenegro (Rastko, b.d.).

mainly on the support of the opposition parties (Serbian radicals and liberals) and clerical circles from Belgrade. This does not mean that the political elite was united in this, as Bataković (1996) makes clear when pointing out that the (allegedly) 'Austrophile' policy of Obrenović and subsequent policy of his successor, King Aleksander, were not popular among the Serbs, who 'didn't care' for his compatriots in BiH, including within his own progressive party (Bataković, 1996). We must not forget the Croats, who also counted on the occupation of BiH and its federalist future within Croatia-Slavonia (Ekmečić, 1982, 32). At that time, Croatian political thought on Bosnia and Herzegovina was mainly strengthened by Tadija Smičiklas with his 'scientific work' *Hrvatska istorija* (History of Croatia), significantly supplemented by Vjekoslav Klaić with his work *Atlas hrvatske istorije* (Atlas of Croatian History). This turbulent period was also considerably marked by the Hungarian aristocrat Benjamin Kallay, the Minister of Finance, considered to be an expert on Serbian affairs and who became the administrative head of Bosnia and Herzegovina in 1882. Kallay was important because while serving as consul in Belgrade (1869–1875) he noticed "that there is a strong connection between Serbia and Bosnia", which led to his efforts to ensure the further political isolation of BiH from Serbia (and Montenegro) (Bataković, 1996, 73). He did this by promoting the Hungarian concept of a 'political nation/citizen identity', thereby paving the way for the development of the idea of a 'Bosnian nation', which was believed to be unacceptable to Croats and Serbs (Bataković, 1996). For the needs of further distinguishing ethnic groups or nations with the goal of them peacefully coexisting, he even announced Bosnian as the official language, instead of Serbo-Croatian (Bataković, 1996, 125). Feldman (2017, 107–111) provides some insights in this respect. He showed that the Bosnian Serbs led by Kallay could only rely on religious and educational institutions to strengthen their own identity, and that the A-H authorities were constantly putting pressure on them.

The feeling the Bosnian Serbs were being oppressed was indicated a second time in 1896 when a movement of Serbian intellectuals from Croatia, Dalmatia, Vojvodina and Belgrade called for greater religious and educational autonomy for the Bosnian Serbs. Bataković (1996, 134) showed that Serbs sent three memoranda to Franc Jožef in 1896, 1897 and 1901 to demand the mentioned rights, including freedom of the media, assembly and constitutional protection. Kallay's time spent leading Bosnia and Herzegovina was crucial for inter-ethnic relations between

Muslims and Serbs, a point also noted by Male (1897, 339, in Bataković, 1996, 135) and Feldman (2017, 10–109) who claim that Kallay's favouring of the Roman Catholic Church encouraged the Serbian and Muslim political leadership in Slavonski Brod to enter into a political agreement in 1902 on together supporting an autonomous BiH. About 4 years after his death, the idea of a Bosnian nation faded away, including replacing the Bosnian language with Serbo-Croatian (Bataković, 1996, 135). The new administration in Bosnia and Herzegovina headed by Stefan von Burian, was also important for the Bosnian Serbs who became increasingly organised and supported by their 'compatriots' in Vojvodina, Belgrade and Croatia-Slavonia. A salient factor for this was the military coup in Serbia that led to the return of the Karađorđevićs to power, bringing with it a new foreign policy approach. The period between 1903 and 1914 was thus under the influence of Garašanin's Načertanije, whereby the new balance of power and circumstances in international relations meant that a certain recontextualisation and new alliances emerged. Bataković (1996, 137) describes how Serbia relied heavily on France and Great Britain in its foreign policy whose central goal was national unification, while reducing Germany's influence through Russia, which in Serbia's eyes was then a neutral ally and a traditional defender of Orthodox and Slavic interests in the Balkans. The increasingly present Serbian issue within the Habsburg Empire was responsible for an ever more visible conflict with A-H, where the issue of BiH did not top the agenda (Jerotijević et al., 2020, 96).

Over time, Serbia became more and more 'revolutionary' and a growing thorn in the heel of the Austrian court, which was increasingly at odds with the Hungarian court on the Serbian issue. Bataković (1996) showed that the Hungarian political elite—contrary to the Austrian idea of a war with Serbia—proposed establishing some form of protectorate for a formally independent yet territorially and politically completely neutralised Serbia. The answer to this was the annexation of Bosnia and Herzegovina on 6 October 1908, accordingly the result of the internal and external (Young Turk revolution) political needs of A-H. Moreover, Bataković (1996, 144) speculates that another factor in the annexation could be the alliance between Serbs and Croats in Dalmatia and Slavonia and a certain share of Muslims in Bosnia and Herzegovina. Bataković (1996, 140) highlighted that the annexation of Bosnia and Herzegovina meant the actual 'interruption of the dream' of Greater Serbia. The annexation itself, which otherwise led to a particular alliance between the Serbs from Serbia and the Croats, simultaneously revived the identity conflict in BiH, as shown by the publication of an essay by the Bosnian-Croatian historian Ferd Šišić (Bataković, 1996, 149). In the essay, he stressed that "the annexation of Herceg-Bosnia is historically completely unfounded and that in this respect Croatia has a much greater historical right to this territory" (ibid.).

This period is primarily important for marking the start of the institutionalisation of pro-Yugoslav and pro-Serbian political thinking when young people, following the example of Mazzini's Young Italy, established "Young Bosnia" in 1910 (Kalik, 2018). Aleksov (2014) notes that it was mostly Bosnian Serbs, yet also Muslims and Bosnian Croats, who believed in a common (Yugoslav) state, who gathered around Young Bosnia. The organisation's central goal was to accelerate the unification process, as part of which a branch of the organisation was quickly established in Belgrade in 1911 and began to cooperate with the Black Hand (*Crna ruka*). Mikić revealed how the pact between the Bosnian Croats and Muslims of Bosnia and Herzegovina concluded between 1911 and 1912 acted as an important homogenising moment for the Bosnian Serbs, as reflected in the speech given by Dr Sunarić in the BiH parliament just prior to the beginning of the Balkan wars. He declared that "as long as the Muslim-Croatian sword is directed against the Serbs, life in Bosnia and Herzegovina will be marked by constant crises". Such an inter-ethnic atmosphere (Muslim–Bosnian Croat cooperation) remained in place during the Balkan Wars and until the start of the First World War. The Balkan War (1912–1913) served as a prelude to the First World War, although the former was probably the most important. This not only led to the 'occupation' of Kosovo by Serbia and enabled Petar I to light a candle in Dečani in 1913 as a sign of "revenge for the Battle of Kosovo", but also a response from A-H. The latter became ever more determined to prevent Serbia from further territorial expansion and strengthening its influence in the Balkans. Becherelli (2015, 171) showed the Serbian public was extremely impatient due to the distinctly "weak position of Serbia in the international arena". Mutual accusations between Bulgaria and Serbia in the national media escalated and sparked the start of the Second Balkan War on the evening of 30 June 1913 when Bulgaria declared war on Serbia and Greece. Even following the Second Balkan War, 'Yugoslav unification' remained a core element of Serbian public opinion, which strengthened and legitimised the Young Bosnia movement. The latter was significantly helped by the October crisis of

1913 when the dispute between Serbia and A-H was taking on new dimensions in international politics since Germany was no longer so afraid of a potential worsening of the situation.

About 8 months later, on Vidovdan (28 June 1914), Gavrilo Princip, a member of Young Bosnia, "with a shot that echoed throughout Europe", killed the Austrian heir to the throne, Franz Ferdinand, and—as Becherelli states (2015, 20)—rounded off the transformation process of "Serbia as the Balkan Piedmont",[3] a reference point for the unification of the South Slavs. From then on, it was not long until the start of the Great War (First World War). Here, Hajdarpašić (2010, 205), Okey (2009, 184), Clark (2012, 22) and Malešević (2017, 17–18) should be highlighted for illuminating the role of the Bosnian Serbs beyond Young Bosnia and Gavrilo Princip at the beginning of the First World War. The Bosnian Serbs who were members of Young Bosnia came from the changing rural environment of Bosnia, which was largely unaware of the Serbian national project. As Hajdarpašić (2010) and Malešević (2017) describe, this is indicated by the fact that in 1910 up to 88% of the population in Bosnia was illiterate, and the majority of Bosnian Serbs, who were then farmers, were chiefly concerned with existential issues. The vast majority of Bosnian Serbs therefore did not want to hear anything about the national ideas of Serbian "enthusiasts" (Okey, 2009, 213).[4]

The period after the First World War was therefore extremely critical, especially for the Serbian political elites who used 'Serbian triumphalism' to recreate the myth of 'Serbs as saviours', about the 'creators of Yugoslavia' and generally about the Serbs' (overriding) importance in relation to the 'other brothers'. The Karađorđević dynasty hence tried to establish the myth of unifiers and saviours through Yugoslav integrism, whereby the cult of the Battle of Kosovo and peasant uprisings was joined in the early nineteenth century by the cult of Serbian victories, both in the two Balkan wars and in the First World War (ibid.). Bosnia and Herzegovina, which at

---

[3] The issue of Serbia as the "Balkan Piedmont" was dealt with in depth by Malešević (2017). He showed that the nationalist forces that were the godfathers of the consolidation of Serbian power in the Balkans were primarily of internal origin. The Serbian political elite took care of this because of the general state development.

[4] Malešević (2017, p. 18) showed that the Bosnian Serbs were distinctly sceptical. In so doing, he was even more vivid and, using an example of a report of the Bosnian district commissioner from Bijeljina in 1913, showed that they were more interested in whether "they will be able to provide enough corn for their own family and to sell at the market" than the Serbian national question.

the end of the war became part of the State of Slovenians, Croats and Serbs (later named the Kingdom of Serbs, Croats and Slovenians), was caught in the myth of the (finally) resolved Serbian issue since de facto almost every Balkan Serb was living under a common state (ibid.). This Yugoslav integrism—understood primarily as Greater Serbian hegemony—which King Aleksandar Karađorđević portrayed even more visibly from January 1929 by establishing the Kingdom of Yugoslavia, was questioned during the entire period up until the Second World War. This period was anything but peaceful for Muslims, as Banac (1996, 137) revealed while showing that the Bosnian Serbs in eastern Herzegovina constantly attacked Muslims, disparaging them as Asians or parasites. Croatian politicians also made plans for a future arrangement in BiH for the Muslims, who were declared to be ethnic Croats (Velikonja, 1998, 185).

Of course, the nationalistic imaginary described above about the Muslims of Bosnia and Herzegovina as ethnic Croats did not emerge from nowhere. This was mainly ensured by Ante Pavelić, who after 1933 paved the way for the development of the extreme Ustasha movement with his (nationalist) programme called *Načela Hrvatskog Ustaškog Pokreta* (Principles of the Ustasha Movement). This was based on the idea of Greater Croatia and hatred of Serbs and Jews (Velikonja, 1998, 191). One of Pavelić's first actions was to plan the assassination of King Aleksandar Karađorđević, which ended 'successfully' in 1934 in Marseille when the Macedonian nationalist Vlado Černozemski killed the king with the Ustasha movement's help. Another important event occurred in the same period when Aljozije Stepinac, who enjoyed the status of 'pro-Yugoslav' in Belgrade and a meritorious member of the Yugoslav Legion on the Thessaloniki front, became the Archbishop of Zagreb (Velikonja, 1998, 193). Alojzije Stepinac is considered one of the more controversial historical figures in modern Croatian history[5] and important for this discussion mostly for his ideas concerning the "re-Catholicisation of the Serbs" and his role in the fascist Independent State of Croatia (*Nezavisna država Hrvatska*, NDH), which I analyse in more detail below. At this point, it is worth highlighting another Catholic archbishop who was equally important for the further expansion of the fascist organisation of the NDH and

[5] One of such 'doubts' about Stepinac, which are becoming louder even on the floor of Croatian politics, is that Stepinac did support the Nazi regime of the Independent State of Croatia, but not the Ustashe as such, and he followed both the principles of anti-communism and anti-fascism.

Ustasha ideas: Ivan Šarić. The latter, who emigrated just before the end of the Second World War, declared in 1936 that "it is foolish to think that we can fight evil in a noble way and with gloves" (Velikonja, 1998, 200). The years following these events were fatal for BiH, which remained territorially circumscribed by the 'Turkish Constitution' of 1921 until the coronation (1921) of King Aleksandar Karađorđević. Probably the most important harbinger of the increasingly difficult life of the Muslims in BiH was the year 1939 when the 'Cvetković-Maček agreement' (hereinafter: the Agreement) was signed. The Agreement, with the "Croatian-Serbian" division of BiH, divided the latter into four *banovinas*, in which Muslims from BiH were in the minority (Velikonja, 1998, 181). Redžić (2005, 5) emphasises that the Agreement only deepened the crisis in the Kingdom of Yugoslavia. This was already strongly influenced by the general European geopolitical picture, which changed radically on 2 August 1934 when Adolf Hitler took advantage of Hindenburg's death and combined the position of chancellor of the country with that of president of Germany, in the process becoming the *Führer*. Indeed, Hitler's calls for the revision of the Treaty of Versailles had a direct impact on the Kingdom of Yugoslavia which, according to this logic, was understood as a typical example of the 'injustice' of the post-war Versailles arrangement. As Redžić (2005, 6) describes, this injustice enabled ethnic inequality, violence, and exploitation. Here, it should be emphasised that the Kingdom of Yugoslavia had established economic relations with Germany during the reign of Milan Stojadinović. Until the end, he followed the strategy of good economic relations with the aim of preventing a war with Italy since Germany was said to have no military interest in conquering the Kingdom of Yugoslavia (Lampe, 1996, 194). Still, Germany had other plans for this area, as made clear in Hitler's memorandum headed "Possibilities of great economic achievement under German leadership" in which the area of South-East Europe was seen as a "supplier of agricultural products and raw materials for Germany" (Redžić, 2005, 7).

In the period 1939–1941, the Kingdom of Yugoslavia had already become markedly economically subjugated to Germany. The respective economic ties with Germany led to a twist in the Kingdom of Yugoslavia's foreign policy approach, in which Germany played an important role (Redžić, 2005). The German minority (*Volksdeutsche*), which numbered 15,000 people in BiH and was most present in Zenica (Redžić, 2005), also played a role in this. The increased level of political contacts between the Kingdom of Yugoslavia and Germany therefore had a direct impact on the regime of Prince Pavle Karađorđević, who began to introduce discriminatory measures against Jewish people (approximately 14,500 in BiH and 82,000 in the Kingdom of Yugoslavia). The next step in strengthening political ties with Germany followed on 25 March 1941 when Yugoslav diplomats signed a protocol and joined the Tripartite Pact with Germany and Italy, under which the Kingdom of Yugoslavia was supposed to maintain its territorial integrity and avoid Italian and German soldiers on its own soil. This agreement was received extremely negatively in Belgrade, which formally cancelled the agreement with a military coup just 2 days after signing the Tripartite Pact. This forced Prince Pavel Karađorđević to flee, first to South Africa and then to Paris (Redžić, 2005). The military coup in question on 27 March 1941 is subject to many interpretations (and speculations) in the literature. For example, Redžić (2005, 37–38) states that for Prime Minister General Dušan Simović, who had led the coup, this represented a 'revolution' in relation to internal frictions, with Croatian separatism being the most important. Vauhnik (1972, 191–195), for example, emphasises that it was a national tragedy and catastrophe as the Tripartite Pact most likely prevented a war in the Kingdom of Yugoslavia. This caused the great suffering of the Serbs in NDH and hence the strengthening of the communist movement, which prevented the military-political pact. In so doing, Vauhnik (1972, 193) further emphasised that the Tripartite Pact was a complex diplomatic manoeuvre by Prince Pavel Karađorđević to prevent a Nazi attack on the Kingdom of Yugoslavia before Germany attacked the Soviet Union.

The military coup, which therefore annulled the concluded Tripartite Pact, led to the April War in which the German and Italian armies forced the Kingdom of Yugoslavia to capitulate within 10 days. The Kingdom of Yugoslavia, which formally surrendered on 17 April 1941, had suffered another blow 7 days before, namely, from retired general Slavko Kvaternik who declared a puppet state of NDH in Zagreb under the auspices of fascist Italy. This spread across the territory of the former Croatian Banovina (excluding central Dalmatia, some islands, and Istria) and BiH (part of the Drina and Zeta Banovina up to Zemun) (Velikonja, 1998, 203). In the first 2 months of its existence, NDH became an area of the systematic ethnic cleansing of Serbs, Jews and Roma, as well as opponents among Croats and Muslims. Ante Pavelić, the Croatian leader, who was trying to return Croatia "to its old borders", took care of this with fascist laws. He was supposed to achieve this by homogenising and racially purifying the Croats through ethnic engineering and systematically erasing the existence of Serb life. Anzulović (1999, 81) stresses that the repressive policies of NDH were implemented with the aim of preventing "Great Serbian resistance to Vidovdan", due to which many Bosnian Serbs were arrested from the very beginning in Sarajevo, Kalinovik, Srebrenica, Zvornik, Tuzla, Bijelina, Olov, Vlasenica, Bosanski Samac and other towns in BiH. All of this inspired Bosnian Serb resistance, the first of which was already seen in July 1941 in Drvar, before continuing in Sisak, Dubica, Prijedor, Banjluka, Jajce, Livno and Vrlika. An important role in the resistance was played by the Communist Party of Yugoslavia, which addressed the working people of BiH. The latter consequently became the central part of the operations of the entire national liberation Yugoslav partisan movement.

From this point onwards, we record the period of the first pronounced and comprehensive spiral of hatred (and violence) among the three ethnic communities in BiH, which in terms of cooperation, pacts and fighting on the ground was extremely complex, intertwining and at times even bewildering. Alongside the Ustasha movement, which was therefore primarily directed against Serbs and Jews and had institutional support in NDH, a movement with fascist tendencies emerged among Serbian extremists, namely the Chetniks, which were ideologically conceived by Dragiša Vasić and Dr Stevan Moljević, and in an operational sense relied on Dragoljub (Draža) Mihailović. Velikonja (1998, 205) notes that the Chetniks were characterised by anti-partisan, anti-Croatian and anti-Muslim, as well as Great Serbian propaganda and military activities. BiH's Muslims also sporadically joined both extreme movements, including direct involvement in the 'Handžar division'. Of course, one should not forget that a significant part of the Muslim population of BiH was involved in the multi-ethnic national liberation movement of Partisans led by the Communist Party of Yugoslavia (CPY) where, for example, the first Muslim partisan unit was formed in the liberated territory of Herzegovina in May 1942 (Velikonja, 1998, 223). The imaginary that encouraged the Chetnik and Ustasha movements and is key to understanding today's social environment in BiH in general and RS specifically should be stressed here. Banac (1996, 143) shows that Ustashe tended to solve the "Serbian problem" in three ways: (i) genocide and expulsions, (ii) Christianisation and (iii) creation of the Croatian Orthodox Church. In this regard, probably the most tragic and for the consolidation of Serbian imaginaries and narratives—beyond the process of Catholicising the Serbian population (200,000–300,000 by 1943)—was the establishment of the infamous concentration camp in Jasenovac at which between August 1941 and April 1945, some

77,000–100,000 people died (United States Holocaust Memorial Museum, 2020). We must also not forget the massacre in Drakulić (in the surroundings of Banjaluka) on 7 February 1942 when around 2300 Bosnian Serbs (mostly elderly and women) and 551 children were killed, and the massacres of the Bosnian Serb population in Bosnian Posavina (in villages around Modrići, Bosanski Samac and Odžak) at the end of 1944 and in early 1945 (ATV, 2020).

The fierce battles waged by the Partisans with the goal of victory over the occupier in Igman, Kozara, on the Neretva River and in Sutjeska, which are still important for the collective imaginary of the national liberation struggle, 'forced' Partisans of all ethnic and religious affiliations to fight against their compatriots on the other side, namely the Chetniks, the Ustashe and, in some places, the Muslims. The turning point during the war of 'everyone against everyone' in BiH was the liberation of Bihać, when the Central Committee of the CPY decided on 26 November 1942 that the military successes had made it possible to establish a political leadership, and hence the Anti-Fascist Council of the National Liberation of Yugoslavia (AFCNLY) was formed. Exactly 1 year later, the establishment of the Anti-Fascist Council of the National Liberation of BiH (AFCNLBiH) followed in Mrkonjić Grad, set up by Bosnian Serbs, Bosnian Croats, and Muslims. The AFCNLY meetings were important for BiH because they were shaping and defining national identities. For example, Malcolm (1996, 181) shows that the second session of the AFCNLY envisaged the creation of an autonomous province of BiH, but without clearly defining the Muslims of BiH as a nation. Bougarel (1996) and Velikonja (1997, 224) point out that the third AFCNLY meeting was crucial for understanding or making sense of the future of BiH, then defined as "the common and indivisible homeland of Serbs, Croats and Muslims".

The victory of the national liberation movement over the occupier, as portrayed by the Partisans and Josip Broz Tito, was therefore also important for the (Bosnian) Serbian issue Marko Attila Hoare (2013, 300–305) demonstrates in an interesting way. For instance, he argues that the Bosnian Serbs—who were increasingly present in Partisan units after the autumn of 1943 due to the destruction of the Chetnik movement in Bosnia and Herzegovina—were torn between the ideas of (Greater) Serbian unity and BiH's sovereignty, with the Partisans themselves playing an important role. The latter are supposed to 'play' with the aforementioned (Greater) Serbian imaginary, using the example of the three most important myths. Thus, to demonstrate, the 17th Division of the Bosnian

Partisans celebrated Vidovdan, the Battle of Kosovo and the Gavrilo Princip's assassination of Austrian Crown Prince Ferdinand as past 'patriotic' actions and connected them to the Partisans' current struggle against the occupiers and collaborators (Hoare, 2013, p. 301). Here, it is worth looking back at the third session of the AFCNLY when Serbia was already firmly in the hands of the Partisans. The session was attended by Siniša Stanković, President of the Serbian People's Assembly, with the aim of relativising the Chetnik narrative about the partisans as destroyers of Serbia. He said that "enemies and traitors are spreading lies about the disintegration of Serbia, because never before in history have Serbs been more united than in the union of free and equal Yugoslav nations" (ibid.). Moreover, Stanković even talked about Serbia's 'debt' to Bosnia and Herzegovina at the meeting, namely (Hoare, 2013, p. 302):

> Serbia will never forget what BiH did for Serbia, when it accepted countless fighters from Serbia during the difficult and painful moments of the occupation. Under the pressure of the enemy, they had to transfer their fight against the occupier in BiH. With this, Serbia is a debtor to BiH, and in fact all Yugoslav nations have become mutual debtors, with which a true legend of the 20th century can be created – the legend of the united and united southern Slavs, the legend of the noblest sons of our nations.

This speech is especially important for understanding the Serbian view of the Yugoslav equation given that such a Yugoslavia meant, on one hand, "brotherhood" based on the principle of separate federal units and, on the other, a place of "final unification of all Serbs". The most important role was played by Josip Broz Tito who had already achieved an important victory on 7 March 1945 with the Tito-Šubašić compromise agreement. With this agreement, he formed the first provisional government of the Democratic Federative Yugoslavia and introduced the "royal viceroyalty", securing international recognition. Indeed, on 12 May 1945, when the founding congress of the Communist Party of Serbia was held, Tito said the following in Belgrade (Hoare, 2013, 302):

> There are many who point out that Tito and the communists cut off Serbia. The latter is in Yugoslavia, and we have no intention of establishing countries within Yugoslavia that would fight each other. If BiH is an equal and independent federal unit, then it will be no different with Serbia. We have created contented and happy Serbs in BiH, and the same applies to Croats and Muslims. It is therefore a question of administrative division. I do not

want a Yugoslavia divided by borders – I have always emphasised that I want such borders that will unite our nations.

In this way, Tito created a climate—as Hoare (2013, 302) notes—that led to, for example, the mass gathering at Bijelina where BiH Prime Minister Rodoljub Čolaković and the President of the Presidency of the BiH National Assembly Vojislav Kecmanović instrumentalised the Kosovo myth with the aim of portraying the "Serbian national awakening" under the new government (Hoare, 2013, 303). Čolaković, who was probably one of the most conscious Serbs on the Bosnia and Herzegovina provincial committee, took the opportunity at one gathering attended by 530 delegates from all over BiH to strengthen the Serbian imaginary in BiH by talking about the victory of the Partisans as "Serbian victories". Čolaković pointed out that "Serbs in BiH are not only pioneers of armed resistance against the occupiers and collaborators in BiH, but also pioneers of democratic transformation or democratic revolution in BiH" (Hoare, 2013, 303). Rodoljub Čolaković went one step further and emphasised that the "federal arrangement is a sincere reflection of democracy, whereby the Serbs – not only in BiH but in the area of the entire Yugoslavia – are pioneers in solving the national question" (Hoare, 2013, 303).

The issue of the federalisation of Yugoslavia was hence extremely important for the Serbs who were supposed to realise their own unity most easily within Yugoslavia. Here, it is worth referring to Čolaković again, who said in August 1945 that "the enemies of the federation often like to use the argument that the federation raises questions about the security and fate of the Serbian nation in Yugoslavia", and underscored that "unity was of the Serbian nation according to the principle of centralisation known after the First World War, a false unity that actually turned all Yugoslav nations against the Serbs". The new federal system of Yugoslavia should thus be safer and more favourable for 'Serbian unity', which Rodoljub Čolaković further substantiated with a pamphlet entitled "On false and real Serbia" in which the true Serbia is said to have originated from the national liberation struggle, and the false one from Nedić's Serbia and the Chetniks (Hoare, 2013, 303). From this point on until 29 November 1945, it did not take long for the National Front to achieve complete victory, abolishing the monarchy and declaring the Federal People's Republic of Yugoslavia (FPRY) (Velikonja, 1998, 224). With this, BiH also became an equal federal republic within its borders from the times of A-H. In the next subchapter, I therefore pay special attention to the material and social environment in BiH, including the preservation, (re)creation and instrumentalisation of myths and narratives that led to the bloody Bosnian war between 1992 and 1995.

3.2   Imagining Bosnian Serb Ethnic Identity in Bosnia and Herzegovina After the Second World War (1945–1990)

The initial years following the end of the Second World War were extremely challenging for the winners who gathered around Josip Broz Tito, despite the optimism. Not only were the relations between religious communities and Yugoslavia difficult due to the policy of secularisation,[6] but also because of the way the national question was resolved in Yugoslavia. The latter is mainly discussed by Velikonja (1998), Ramet (2005), Troch (2010) and Gašić (2015) who show that modernisation, industrialisation and proletarian interests were primarily driven by two different (pro-moted) models of Yugoslavia: 'integral' and 'organic'. Integral Yugoslavia, whose underpinning logic was very much like the Soviet Union model—aspiring to develop a supranational (Yugoslav) identity—was mostly rele-vant until 1963 when the new Constitution was adopted. One of the biggest problems of integral Yugoslavia stemmed from the logic of politi-cal centralism, which aroused feelings of favouring the Serbs. It should be emphasised here that integral Yugoslavism was never understood as replac-ing the existing national/ethnic identities of the Yugoslav peoples, and as such was more like, for example, European identity. The second model of Yugoslavia, namely organic, followed the logic of a decentralised form of cultural and national homogeneity among the Yugoslav nations, whereby the federative community is understood as a framework for their coexis-tence (Velikonja, 1998, 231). In relation to this, it should be noted that both models of Yugoslavia stressed "brotherhood and unity" among nations (ibid.).

Both models held an extremely strong influence in BiH, whose political leadership was the most conservative in Yugoslavia. The core reasons for this are that it was multi-ethnic or multinational, explaining why in their engagements the political leadership always took care to ensure their

---

[6] Such secularisation on one hand promoted religious tolerance, yet on the other tried to marginalise the role of religion due to awareness of its power in relation to the construction of national/ethnic identities.

actions could not be interpreted as nationalistic (Maksić, 2017, 67). The policy of equal political representation, which followed the logic of the 'ethnic key' along with the principle of BiH's unity, helped them in this (Donia & Fine, 1994). One should note in this regard that the effects of integral and organic Yugoslavia in BiH were more present or internalised in urban environments since in rural environments, which were relatively 'mono-ethnic', there was still an anti-discourse about "brotherhood and unity" due to massacres following the Second World War (Maksić, 2017, 67). The latter, which was said to be given legitimacy primarily by certain religious leaders, could even be observed on the level of reported offences between 1959 and 1962, as the BiH authorities during this period were said to be dealing with at least eight infringements per year on average, standing in contrast with "brotherhood and unity" (Bergholz, 2013, 691). Stemming from this, Maksić (2017, 68) emphasised that it was the rural environment in BiH that maintained ethnic differentiation according to the principle of creation of the Other. Here, while talking about religious leaders or religion as such, it should also be noted that the Serbian Orthodox Church (SOC) continued to play an important role in building the (Bosnian) Serbian ethnic identity. Although prohibited by the leadership, the SOC as such highlighted the connection between the history of Serbia and Orthodoxy (Velikonja, 1998, 263). Velikonja (1998, 263) offers several examples, ranging from the ritual cremation of the remains of Tsar Dušan in 1968 in Belgrade to the call to protect Serbs and their holy places in Kosovo in 1982.

It is necessary to state at this point that neither 'model' of Yugoslavia could exist without the two central mythologies that drove the formation and processes of the Yugoslav reality: (i) the cult of Josip Broz Tito and (ii) the mythology of the national liberation struggle. Josip Broz Tito, who was supposed to be the embodiment of the unity of the Yugoslav nations and "a man who is equally great for everyone and whom everyone loves equally", was then understood as the creator of the new Yugoslavia (Velikonja, 1998, 233–234). The second metanarrative, or the 'myth of all myths', was therefore the national liberation struggle, characterised as an "unequal, continuous and fierce struggle with a hundred times stronger enemy" (Velikonja, 1998, 235). Both metanarratives encouraged the accelerated development of the Yugoslav idea in politics, culture and society, which coincided with Yugoslavia's strong industrialisation and modernisation to serve the even development of all federal units.

In the paradigm of industrialisation and urbanisation, BiH was understood as a federative unit that took care of the production of raw materials. This is shown by the fact that the predominantly agrarian economy of BiH, which in 1948 was still 72% based on agricultural production, reduced its dependence on agriculture by half by 1971, namely to 36.6% (Anđelić, 2003, 29). BiH's industrialisation and modernisation was important not only for economic diversification but also mainly because of the development of factories that became a venue for inter-ethnic interaction and cultural exchange. Maksić (2017, 69) stresses that urbanisation led to multiethnicity and multiculturalism, which not only irreversibly reduced stereotypes of the (ethnic) Other in urban settlements, but also became present in the rural environment. Ethnic diversity and coexistence in brotherhood and unity became an important social norm even in the villages, where it was mainly ensured by schools and the media that promoted pro-Yugoslav narratives as well as military service in the Yugoslav army (ibid.). Still, it should be emphasised that inter-ethnic marriages in the rural environment continued to be an exception rather than the rule (Bringa, 1995). It is also worth highlighting the findings of Gagnon (2006, 42) here, who points out that in this period of socialist Yugoslavia, the distinction between Bosnian Serb and Muslim families was only apparent "through their own names".

Yet the enthusiasm for the outlined economic development with industrialisation and modernisation did not last long since it did not consider the equal socio-political representation of the nations of the federative units in Yugoslavia. The first hints of dissatisfaction started to appear in the 1960s. At that time, for example, the Bosnian Croats had already begun to point out the underrepresentation in the main governmental bodies in BiH and increased their demands considerably with the Croatian Spring between 1969 and 1971. This period, which coincided with the removal of Ranković, was especially important for the Muslims of BiH as the Central Committee of the Union of Communists of BiH (CUCBiH) declared Muslims to be the sixth constituent nation (and no longer a special ethnic group) in January 1969 (Velikonja, 1998, 271). The fact that Muslims became the sixth constituent nation in Yugoslavia was not popular among certain nationalist and conservative circles in either Croatia or Serbia (Velikonja, 1998, 272). The time that followed the Croatian Spring and the recognition of Muslims as the sixth constituent nation coincided with a period of great socio-political changes in Yugoslavia. These movements reached their peak in 1971 with certain constitutional amendments, and in 1974 when a new Constitution was introduced that provided for six republics and the two autonomous provinces of Vojvodina and Kosovo. These reforms were opposed by intellectuals like Vojislav Koštunica, Kosta Čavoski and Dobrica Ćošić. In fact, Koštunica and Čavoski were even dismissed from the Faculty of Law in Belgrade due to their criticism of the "fragmentation of the Serbian nation" (Biserko, 2006, 19). Since the Constitution was reformed in 1974, we therefore encounter a period of weakening of the hegemonic metanarrative about the coexistence of the Yugoslav nations and the cult of Josip Broz Tito because there was a major deviation from the proposed economic guidelines, planned through a vision of self-governing relations. All of this started to arouse distrust, anger, frustration and doubt in people following a sudden drop in living standards (Lorenčič, 2010, 268; Maksić, 2017, 60). Still, Yugoslavia would probably also have survived this had the death of Josip Broz Tito (4 May 1980) not occurred during this period. This moment shed light on the serious economic crisis facing Yugoslavia, which then added to the frictions between the federal units.

In these circumstances, there was also increased friction in BiH, more specifically in the relationship between the Yugoslav authorities and the Muslim socio-political elite, which had allegedly become more and more 'pan-Islamist' and were seeking to change the national identity of Muslims into an exclusively religious one (Velikonja, 1998, 275). Amid this tense atmosphere, Branko Mikulić, a member of the federal presidency of the CUCBiH, attacked the "clerofascists of all religions", including Muslims (ibid.). Mikulić was extremely important because he acted like some kind of antipode of (Greater) Serbian political thinking. Even Serbian national-ist circles viewed him with deep mistrust, as he was said to be mostly con-cerned with loosening the historical ties of the Bosnian Serbs with the 'Serbian motherland'. A good example on the other side of the (Greater Serbia) equation is Dr Vojislav Šešelj, who was dismissed from the Sarajevo faculty in 1984 due to an unpublished work in which he promoted the idea of a greater Serbia and understood Muslims as a nation as Serbs and Croats (Kamberović, 2011; Pirjevec, 1995; Velikonja, 1998).

This period was also significant for political thought and the construc-tion of the identity of Muslims in BiH because in 1983 there was the trial of the 'thirteen'. The individuals included the first accused, Alija Izetbegović, who in 1970 had written the Islamic Declaration with which he tried to solve the question of Muslims in Yugoslavia. Pirjevec (1995) and Velikonja (1998) also wrote about this and stressed that Alija

Izetbegović, otherwise accused of trying to create a Muslim republic, was collateral damage to the political intrigues at the time since the convictions of the most prominent pan-Islamists were supposed to offer satisfaction to the Serbs within and beyond the borders of BiH. Bosnian Croats also showed a similar form of (religious) rebellion with the aim of relativising the Yugoslav regime, namely through the apparitions of the Virgin Mary on 24 June 1981 in Medjugorje, Herzegovina. This was, as Velikonja (1998, 255) notes, one of the "quiet forms of rebellion against the social-ist government", and one should add that, according to the Bosnian Croats, the Herzegovinian government was distinctly pro-Serbian (ibid.). All this and more—in an ethnopolitical sense—was expressed in the mem-orandum of the Serbian Academy of Science and Art (*Srpska akademija nauka i umjetnosti*—SANU) in September 1986 that challenged the exist-ing constitutional order and connected Yugoslav socio-economic condi-tions with ethnopolitical ideas (Maksić, 2017, 61). SANU blamed the new Constitution for the fragmentation of the Serbian nation, and Slovenia and Croatia for Serbia's economic problems. The greater public reach of the memorandum was mainly ensured through *Večernje novosti*, then con-sidered to be one of the most widely read newspapers in Serbia (Maksić, 2017, 62). SANU, which enjoyed a good reputation in the Serbian public sphere, therefore represented a legitimate point of reference for the subse-quent political instrumentalisation of the (Greater) Serbian narrative and victimisation, especially exploited by Slobodan Milošević (Dizdarević, 1999, 185).

Slobodan Milošević was hence the one who interpreted the SANU memorandum in such a way that he introduced elements of nationalism into the Yugoslav—and especially Serbian—landscape, and used his own political success and increasingly stable support for the 'anti-bureaucratic revolution' with which he tried to amend the 1974 Constitution, and thus there was renewed centralism and the abolition of the autonomy of Kosovo and Vojvodina and the change of power in Montenegro. With this step, Milošević de facto held four out of eight seats in the federal presidency, dangerously disturbing the balance between the republics. This was the critical turning point in the ethnicisation of Yugoslav politics, including the increasingly present debate on the right to self-determination. Maksić (2017, 65–66) states that economic issues were then also subject to the logic of nationalism, as particularly evident in Milošević's attitude towards Slovenia when the political conflict led to the announcement of a boycott on Slovenian products. Here, it is necessary to highlight the fact that Milosevic's popularity in Serbia cannot be reduced to an element of nationalism since quite a few protesters were mobilised at that time due to the non-transparency of officials, industrial relations and the general rise in active citizenship reflected mainly in 'proto-political' groups like environmentalists, pacifists and public debating clubs (Maksić, 2017, 66).

The spiral of nationalism, which tried in every way to delegitimise the Yugoslav regime, was also strongly present in BiH, notably after 1987 when there was a high-profile corruption scandal in the extremely important agricultural conglomerate Agrokomerc in Velika Kladuša. This scandal led to the resignation of BiH's most important political officials, including Hamdija Pozderac. An important political vacuum was thus created, leading Neven Anđelić (2003, 20) to even hint that the Agrokomerc affair significantly determined the results of the first democratic elections in BiH in 1990. Maksić (2017, 70) also came to similar answers through interviews with high-ranking officials at the time. In this regard, it is worth noting the interview with a Bosnian Serb official who emphasised that had this scandal not occurred, 'third-rate' and 'inexperienced' nationalists would not have come to power. This period is also important because in September 1987 the first serious confrontation with the politics of socialist Yugoslavia occurred in Sarajevo, namely in the form of student protests, and the increased level of liberalisation of the media landscape due to the growing activity of youth organisations. Although words like "prosperity", "equality", "working class" and "democracy" became increasingly present in the public sphere, they still did not have a clear nationalist connotation.

However, the general picture of then socialist Yugoslavia indicated that nationalism would become an ever more important factor. This was mainly ensured by Milošević's logic of nationalist leadership based on national victimisation. With his rhetoric and actions, Milošević successfully 'expanded' the field of antagonism since, on top of the Kosovar Albanians and the Slovenians, the Croats also became enemies. In light of the increasingly harsh instrumentalisation of the Croatian Serbs by Milošević, in 1989, Croatian Serbs established the Croatian Democratic Union (*Hrvatska demokratska zajednica*—HDZ) led by Franjo Tuđman. Milošević thereby de facto contained a source of legitimisation for nationalist politics and in fact a 'partner' in the further ethnicisation of Yugoslavia. The growing antagonism between Croatia and Serbia (as well as Slovenia), principally reflected at the 14th CUCY held in January 1990, had an irreversible impact on the increasingly uncertain situation in BiH. During this inter-federal conflict, BiH was a more passive observer in the political sense, but the very multinational nature and presence of Croats and Serbs in BiH meant the state experienced the radicalisation of 'ethnopolitics' the most in the following years.

The period that followed the 14th CUCY was considered the start of the period of political pluralism, including the rise of ethno-political parties. One of the first of these was the Serbian Democratic Party of Croatia established on 17 February 1990 in Knin that enjoyed strong political support among the political and intellectual elite of Serbia, including Dobrica Ćošić (Maksić, 2017, 70). Soon after, its 'sister' party in BiH also emerged and played a key role in the Bosnian War and later in post-Dayton BiH. Still, political pluralism in BiH came relatively late as the first official political organisation in BiH was the Democratic Party originally from Montenegro that only had a 'branch' in Mostar after 12 March 1990.

By the end of March 1990, seven political organisations were present in BiH, only three of which were originally from BiH. By comparison, for example, in the same period, there were already 17 such organisations in Serbia and up to 20 in Croatia (Maksić, 2017, 70). The first party with clear ethno-political potential was established soon after, on 26 March 1990, when 38 Muslim dissidents and religious leaders established the Party of Democratic Action (*Stranka demokratske akcije*—SDA). Alija Izetbegović was appointed president of the SDA. This period is also of note for the development of various civil organisations holding clear ethno-political potential, among which the Forum for the Protection of Muslims, led by one of the most insightful intellectuals, Dr Muhamed Filipović, and the Serbian cultural society *Prosvjeta*, which was established by Serbian academics under the leadership of Dr Vojislav Maksimović.

It did not take long from this point until August 1990 when the Bosnian Parliament officially allowed ethno-political parties to be established. This led to the legal and formal legitimation of the political parties of all three ethnic groups, namely, the Serbian Democratic Party (*Srbska demokratska stranka*—SDS) (established in July 1990), SDA (established in March 1990) and HDZ BiH (established in August 1990). Maksić (2017, 74) emphasises that SDS was the only party not to enter the Bosnian-Herzegovina public sphere as a political player that would build its position on resistance to the hegemonic socialist regime in BiH, but as one of the political alternatives in an ever more competitive political environment. However, even at its core, it indicated the increasingly nationalist atmosphere that dominated the social and political environment of Bosnia and Herzegovina. Roughly speaking, we can identify five central reasons for the ethnicisation of the political space in BiH: (i) Milosevic's anti-bureaucratic revolution as a lever for ethnic differentiation, (ii) the presence of Serbian and Croatian ethno-nationalist discourse in Bosnia and Herzegovina, (iii) the impact of HDZ's victory in Croatia, (iv) the rise of SDA in Bosnia and Herzegovina and (v) the first cases of nationalist excesses and violence.

The anti-bureaucratic revolution was important because before 1990, ethno-nationalism in BiH was undesirable and as such would have been strongly condemned by all three ethnic groups (Maksić, 2017, 75). Slobodan Milošević was also aware of this, explaining why he maintained his discourse before 1990 in such a way that it did not yet have a clear nationalist charge, and he managed to create this in two ways. First, Milošević's Serbian nationalism was extremely intertwined with the cognitive framework of Yugoslavia, which he successfully created mainly through 'truth rallies' accompanied by Yugoslav symbols and "in the name of defending Yugoslavia" (Maksić, 2017, 74). Maksić (2017, 75) states that Milošević understood himself as an alternative to nationalism. Such logic was successful mainly with the help of the media, which primarily showed the antagonism between Franjo Tuđman and Vuk Drašković. Second, Serbian nationalism was primarily centred around the Kosovo issue and the desire to "protect the threatened Serbs in Kosovo". In this regard, the pro-Yugoslav political elite in BiH was also extremely important and, by emphasising Albanian separatism, it gave legitimacy to Milošević's rhetoric and actions (ibid.).

The Kosovo issue became important for BiH as well, namely, in September 1988 when the Kosovo Serbs tried to organise a 'truth rally' in Jajce, but UCBiH successfully prevented it on the argument of the inadmissibility of unapproved gatherings. Yet, serious problems for BiH began mainly after the 14th CUCY, providing a real dilemma for the presidency of the UCBiH—if they were to continue cooperating within UCY, they would be recognising the supremacy of Milošević but, if they were to leave him, they would be following in the footsteps of Slovenia and Croatia and be participating in the disintegration of socialist Yugoslavia. Paradoxically, Milošević himself took care of this since the BiH delegation did not agree with the 14th CUCY continuing, although was outvoted. In the following, the BiH representatives also presented several proposals about the future of UCY, but they were 'outvoted' on all points. This led to the chairman of the UCBiH Nijaz Duraković and five other members of the delegation leaving the 14th Congress, thereby incurring the 'anger' of the Bosnian Serbs who even started protesting in local committees in cities that had a clear majority (Maksić, 2017, 76). Duraković's action—like the Agrokomerc affair—weakened the position of CPBiH prior to the first democratic elections in 1990. This was also clearly evident in the transfer of certain Bosnian Serb officials to SDS, which was completely in line with Milošević's policies (Maksić, 2017, 77).

These events coincided with the increasingly present (Greater) Serbian propaganda, which became an ever more important part of BiH's political sphere. Cigar (2000), for example, points out that the Serbian victimisation narrative became more and more apparent in the media, especially the weeklies *Intervju* and *Duga*, which devoted greater space to the Bosnian Serb 'Orientalists'. The latter emphasised that the desire for domination is part of the 'Muslim character', while 'radical Islam' was presented as the greatest threat to non-Muslims in BiH (Cigar, 2000, 43–48). Maksić (2017, 77) showed, for example, that the Serbian discourse soon became present on the day-to-day level where the daily newspaper *Politika* began intensively reporting on the growing splits within UCBiH, whereby most space was devoted to critics of Duraković. It is also interesting that the Serbian agitation against the 'green transversal' or the 'global Islamist agenda on Islam from Indonesia to BiH' ensured that "general anxiety due to insecurity was getting an increasingly clear face of the ethnic Other", namely, Islam and Muslims as a threat (Maksić, 2017, 78). Daily media coverage soon gained a strong reputation in academic circles. One of these academics was Dr Vojislav Lubarda, who in his book *Svilena vrvica* (Silk Cord) described the status of the Bosnian Serbs in BiH as an ethnic group that were experiencing silent torture by the ever more apparent desire for Islamic domination (Maksić, 2017, 79). Even the political elite of the Serbian state apparatus joined in this, as BiH's member of the Presidency of UCBiH Bogić Bogičević learned in November 1990 in eastern BiH that the Serbian state apparatus had prepared a secret report of the Serbian state security that the Bosnian Serbs were to migrate from eastern BiH because of the growing "Muslim threat" (ibid.). While it also became a first-rate scandal, which soon became part of the media reality, it is worth noting that it was never really known whether this report existed or not. It is clear, however, that reporting on this had an impact on the public sphere since the public (mainly Bosnian Serbs) began to think about the ethnic challenges, with this slowly beginning to create a clear distinction between the (Bosnian Serb) Self and the Other(s).

The internal Other, portrayed by SDA and Alija Izetbegović as a rising Islamic threat, was before long joined by the Bosnian Croats following events in Croatia where HDZ won the Croatian elections in April 1990. This gave Serbian nationalists a powerful resource for creating the perception of 'Croats as a threat'. Maksić (2017, 80) states that HDZ officials began to emphasise that BiH is Croatian land, which in turn led to the establishment of 40 local committees in Herzegovina, which reportedly had as many as 50,000 HDZ members. When the latter came to power, there was an increase in ethnic differentiation in BiH as well since for Bosnian Croats, for example, the newly established Croatian flag is said to be a strong reminder of the feeling of a common origin and a continuation of Croatia's history (Maksić, 2017, 80). Yet, the Croatian 'red-and-white chessboard' did not symbolise something positive for the (Bosnian) Serbs, who started to strongly associate it with the Second World War and NDH. Such connections were made by Tuđman himself in February 1990 when declaring that "NDH was not only a Quisling creation, but also an expression of the thousand-year desire of the Croatian nation for independence" (Maksić, 2017, 81). The Serbian media landscape commenced portraying HDZ as the new Ustashe, while the Belgrade weekly *NIN*, for example, also began to visually connect HDZ with NDH (Maksić, 2017, 81). HDZ is important for BiH mainly because immediately after HDZ's victory in the Croatian parliament, Šime Dodan (a member of parliament) declared that "BiH is Croatian land, where the Croatian flag should fly on top of Romanija" (Žanić, 2007, 215). His statement succeeded to provoke the population of Romanija, which was then multi-ethnic, with the fewest Bosnian Croats living there (Maksić, 2017, 81).

As the penultimate factor in the ethnicisation of the area of BiH, one should consider ethnically motivated incidents that at once functioned as political opportunities and political limitations. BiH was relatively isolated in this context until 1989 when the first minor incident with a clear ethnopolitical connotation occurred—a dead pig was left in front of the mosque in Trebinje (Anđelić, 2003, 71). The first serious incident came on 5 January 1990 at an ecological protest held in Duvno (today's Tomislavgrad), which was mostly inhabited by Bosnian Croats. The rally had a clear Croatian nationalist dimension as the crowd was protesting against the arrival of the BiH special police unit using slogans like "this is not Kosovo, this is Croatia" and "long live Croatia!" (Maksić, 2017, 80). The next

incident occurred on 2 July 1990 in eastern Herzegovina when fans celebrated Yugoslavia's World Cup victory by driving through the multi-ethnic Čapljina to the majority Bosnian-Croatian town of Ljubuški. They
reportedly faced the anger of around 500 individuals, which led to a physical confrontation and the burning of Yugoslav flags (ibid.). The first incident in a multi-ethnic urban environment appeared on 2 March 1990 in
Foča when employees of the local transport company Fočatrans started a
strike, demanding the resignation of the director due to alleged nepotism
and arrogance (Maksić, 2017, 81). On the same day, Muslims allegedly
stopped the protest due to a rumour that Bosnian Serb workers wanted
the director to resign because of his ethnic origin (ibid.).

Maksić (2017, 84) states that during this period there were many minor
incidents in multi-ethnic environments. Such cases included, for example,
Skelani when 72 Muslims wrote a letter to all governments of the six
republics about ethnically motivated verbal and physical attacks made by
Bosnian Serbs against Muslims (Maksić, 2017, 82). Another example was
an incident in Vlasenica when rumours spread about the presence of
Serbian Chetnik formations (Maksić, 2017, 82). A third example was an
event in Sarajevo when someone wrote graffiti "Serbs, out of Bosnia"
(Maksić, 2017, 82). A fourth such case was Brčko when a student painted
over the monument of a partisan hero with Muslim nationalist messages
because this partisan was allegedly of Serbian ethnic origin (Maksić, 2017,
83). As a last example, we may mention an event at Janje when Orthodox
tombstones were desecrated (Maksić, 2017, 83). Maksić (2017) nevertheless points out that such isolated incidents did not excessively affect the
general relations between voters of the three ethnic groups, which he justified by the fact that Radovan Karadžić argued before the ICTY that there
were practically no problems between the three ethnic groups until
November 1990.

The only serious incident before the November elections managed
'from bottom-up' was the one in Fočatrans. The described events must
thus be seen primarily as part of particular micro-dynamics that emerged
mainly in eastern Herzegovina and eastern Bosnia, that is, areas during the
Second World War where there were the most war actions of NDH and
Ustasha. Namely, there was still great awareness that this was a very taboo
topic, or a topic censored by the socialist regime (Maksić, 2017, 83). Yet
it would be generally wrong to claim that the cases functioned as a political opportunity for ethno-political elites, as demonstrated, for example, by
the Institute for the Study of Inter-Ethnic Relations, which showed on a

sample of 1100 residents that as many as 88% of them believed that the situation was beyond doubt the fault of the political elite, and just 16% predicted that ethno-political parties could have a great influence in this period (Maksić, 2017, 83). An even more detailed breakdown was provided by the Institute in April 1990 when, based on a sample of 842 residents, it showed that only 23.6% of Muslims and 19.8% of Bosnian Serbs believed that religion was an important factor in choosing a partner (Maksić, 2017, 83). More interesting are the data regarding support for the idea of a joint BiH state, which was believed in by 11.4% of Bosnian Serbs, 14.1% of Bosnian Croats and 20.7% of Muslims at the time, and the question of support for the dissolution of all nations, which 27% of Bosnian Serbs supported, 24.5% of Muslims and 19.3% of Bosnian Croats (Maksić, 2017, 83). These numbers reveal the clear discrepancy between the feelings of the majority population of BiH and the discursive framework of ethno-political elites. Maksić (2017, 84) emphasises that the first serious signs of a change in the discursive framework were visible only after July 1990 when SDS was established, which strove to homogenise Bosnian Serbs by uniting them within a common political party.

Establishment of the ethno-political SDS is therefore the last factor in the ethnicisation of Bosnia-Herzegovina, which was driven by Serbian activism with a clear political ambition in Belgrade and later also in Knin. The ideological leadership of SDS was centred around Serbian academics and SANU, which already in the winter of 1990 had started talking about forming a Serbian ethno-political party in Croatia. Đukić (2001, 1150) notes that among the 'academics' there were not only Ćošić and Rašković, but also Ljuba Radić and Dejan Medaković. In the early period of SDS in BiH, the Serbian cultural association *Zora* was also important, which in terms of organisation was primarily active in Croatia. In the following, the central political figures of the Croatian SDS were important for the rise of ethno-nationalism in BiH. Maksić (2017, 174), for example, points out that party leader Jovan Rašković has publicly emphasised that the aim of the Croatian SDS is to expand into BiH as soon as possible.

Before describing the period after the breakup of Yugoslavia and the Bosnian war between 1992–1995, it is necessary to explain the metanarrative (successfully) created by the ethno-political SDS in BiH that relied on the central interpretation of the political crisis in socialist Yugoslavia and BiH. Maksić (2017, 175) identifies at least two different directions of interpretation. The first is Markovic centred in the 'Serbian ethnogenesis' with the aim of addressing Serbian self-awareness. The emphasis here is

therefore on treating an imaginary ethnic group as the object of the narrative. The other interpretation goes in the direction of the integrity of the
'Serbian ethnogenesis', whereby the Serbian nation or the Serbian ethnic
group is the subject of the narrative of the conflict between the Yugoslav
nations. When SDS entered the political scene in 1990, its first goal was to
address the clear discrepancy between the primordial understanding of
ethnic identities and the actual state of Serbian ethnic solidarity in BiH. In
the process, they tried to instrumentalise mostly the ethnic feelings of the
Bosnian Serbs, where they primarily relied on the Yugoslav socialist regime,
which was supposed to be opposed to the ethno-national nature of nations.
They succeeded in this by talking about the fact that the Serbs were "victims of delusion" or the illusion of Yugoslavia, which stigmatised national
self-awareness (Maksić, 2017, 176). For example, Karadžić highlighted
the following (Maksić, 2017, ibid.):

> For the sake of false and illusory peace in the house, we sacrificed our great-
> est values, abandoned our own traditions and national culture, denied our
> own churches and left them. Everywhere, but especially in BiH, we were
> most loyal to the system, which was more than obviously established with
> the goal of destroying our nation.

The 45-year period of relative peace in the common Yugoslav space was
therefore framed as an illusion, in response to which a 'national awakening'
was offered as a 'solution'. Maksić (2017, 177) showed that this was what
Karadžić depicted with his party that was intended to "teach Serbs how to
be Serbs". SDS hence offered itself as the saviour of 'sleeping Serbia'. Yet,
Karadžić had a problem because a large swathe of the socialist political elite
in Yugoslavia belonged to Serbs in an ethnic sense. Karadžić addressed this
by presenting them as being alienated from their own nature, their descen-
dants, and their own being (Maksić, 2017, 177). Ljuba Tadić labelled such
Serbs "masochists", while Karadžić described them as people "who have
certain problems with being Serbs" (Maksić, 2017, 177). Maksić (2017,
178) also wrote about this and showed that a few Serbian newspapers, such
as *Javnost*, began to write about Serbs and 'Serbs' in their texts, with use of
the single quotation marks intended to portray those Serbs as being 'false
ones'. SDS in BiH, for instance, described them as 'Brankovići', which
started to connect them with Vuk Branković, who in Serbian mythology is
viewed as a traitor. What is even more interesting is that SDS defined those

Bosnian Serbs in BiH who supported BiH statehood as Janissaries or Islamised Orthodox (Maksić, 2017, 177). It was also important in all of this that SDS constantly talked about "mother Serbia", which not only paved the way for a similar discourse of victimisation to be used by the political elite under the leadership of Slobodan Milošević, although Milošević created the idea that 'Mother Serbia' would protect them (Maksić, 2017, 179). In this way, SDS managed to first create a clear dividing line between the 'real' and 'false' Serbs, and only then did it begin to frame the internal Others, namely Muslims and Bosnian Croats.

(Bosnian) Croats have been 'a problem' of SDS since the very beginning, presenting the Croatian nation and especially Tuđman's HDZ as an existential threat to the Serbian nation. Both Tuđman and HDZ were portrayed as a reflection of the "Croatian Self", with SDS linking HDZ with Ustasha as such (Maksić, 2017, 180). Moreover, Maksić (2017, 181) states that SDS used the words "Ustasha" and "Croats" interchangeably with the aim of equating them. It should also be emphasised that SDS did not allow much space in the first multi-party elections in 1990 to avoid connecting the victory of Franjo Tuđman and HDZ in 1990 with the period of the Second World War (ibid.). A slightly more fluid situation concerned the 'Muslim/Bosniak Other' as SDS perceived SDA as completely benign at the time when they were defending a federal Yugoslavia. This changed especially after 1991 when SDA started advocating the independence of BiH and the Muslims thereby became a 'threat' to the Bosnian Serbs (Maksić, 2017, 182). From 1991 onwards, SDS began relatively coordinated and uncompromising actions to create internal Others: Bosnian Croats and Muslims/Bosniaks. While the memory of the crimes of Ustasha and NDH during the Second World War may still have been relatively fresh, it was somewhat more difficult for the Muslims/Bosniaks. In so doing, SDS started to refer to the period of the Ottoman Empire when Muslims became 'Turks' and 'Ottomans' against whom the Serbian hajduks "heroically" defended themselves. Maksić (2017, 182) notes that in both cases the SDS political leadership began to use mythical images and heroes, where the most prominent was the "ideal Serb who fought in the battle of Kosovo".

However, Maksić (2017, 195) adds that the 'Ustasha threat' was the most visible, making it easier to connect the political moment of 1990 with the year 1941. With this, SDS emphasised that anyone with Serbian ethnic origins could be a potential target, regardless of their ideological background. Even Karadžić stated this when emphasising that "Serbs could even thank Tuđman, because he helped them form their own selves" (ibid.). Finally, it is worth highlighting Loza (1990) who highlighted that even the first SDS political programme was based on the idea that the well-being of the Bosnian Serbs could only be ensured by their own ethnic party, which considers the cultural, religious and political diversity of the Serbian nation.

3.3   IMAGINING BOSNIAN SERB ETHNIC IDENTITY IN BOSNIA AND HERZEGOVINA FROM THE FIRST MULTI-PARTY ELECTIONS UNTIL THE END OF THE BOSNIAN WAR (1990–1995)

The convincing victory of three ethno-political parties in November 1990 heralded an increasingly tense and nationalistic atmosphere that led to war in BiH about 2 years later. SDA, SDS and HDZ BiH therefore occupied all seats in the presidency and more than 4/5 of all seats in the BiH Parliament (Maksić, 2017, 219). Even though UCBiH and the Union of Reform Forces of Yugoslavia together won over 20% of all votes, they did not obtain a single position in the new political structure of BiH. SDS, HDZ BiH and SDA divided local self-governance in addition to the national one, namely according to the 'ethnic key'. In this way, the ethno-political parties in BiH ensured the de-individualisation of the inhabitants of BiH, which helped to recreate the logic of community and homogeneity within all three ethnic groups (Maksić, 2017, 221). The promotion of fair and equal representation of all three ethnic groups in socio-political life caused the first serious problems. SDS, for example, began to emphasise that TV Sarajevo did not equally represent the interests of Bosnian Serbs, and thus it proposed the idea of establishing three television channels (Maksić, 2017, 213). Karadžić also complained about the alleged underrepresentation of Bosnian Serbs in the Ministry of the Interior; for example, in Doboj, he pointed out that there was not enough Cyrillic, and in Zvornik that Muslim villages had five times more paved roads than Bosnian Serb ones (Maksić, 2017, 214).

During this time, extremely important changes also occurred in the social environment of BiH. In February 1991, SDA proposed the Declaration on the Independence of BiH. This marks the start of the (Bosnian) Serb framing of Muslims as an "Islamic threat" no different from the "Croatian threat". SDS, which blocked the Declaration, began to emphasise Alija Izetbegović's desire to establish an "Islamic Republic" (Maksić, 2017, 215). The most active in this regard was the local SDS committee in Banjaluka, which framed Izetbegović as a "Serbophobe", even a potential "eater of Serbs" (Maksić, 2017, 216). From this point on, the Muslims/Bosniaks were viewed as being the same threat as the Croats, which led to an article in the newspaper *Javnost*, for example, which stressed that SDA's real desire was to unite BiH with NDH (Maksić, 2017, 217). In April 1991, barely 1 month after the 'Karadjordjevo agreement', under which Milošević and Tuđman are said to have devised a plan for the "dismemberment of BiH", the thesis about the "Muslim Ustashe" led by an imam started to spread in the public discourse (Maksić, 2017, 217). This kind of discourse did not remain on the local level, as Radovan Karadžić and Biljana Plavšić began to emphasise it more and more, while talking about the fact that if an independent BiH were to happen, it would be a "Muslim state" (Maksić, 2017, 217). It is also interesting that the protest in Fočatrans, which was relatively suppressed or censored by SDS until March 1991, obtained a new context. Blagojević and Kisić report that SDS understood this protest as an event at which Bosnian Serbs were physically attacked. Between March and June 1991, two more important events took place, which the public blamed on Izetbegović; namely, a punctured tyre of a journalist in Sarajevo and a physical attack on the Minister of Information, Velibor Ostojić (Maksić, 2017, 219). While, in the case of the punctured tyre, the public wrote the next day that "Izetbegović will be billed for the punctured tire", the attack on Ostojić became somewhat more historically contextualised. The public began to emphasise that the attack was similar to the one in 1804 when the Ottoman Janissaries killed the Serbian princes (Maksić, 2017, 217).

This period is also important because it marks the start of changes in the material environment in BiH when ethno-political parties began to alter the names of streets and schools that bore the names of socialist heroes to ones that clearly indicated ethnic exclusivism (Maksić, 2017, 215). In April, for example, the local SDS erected a monument to King Peter Karađorđević in Mrkonjić Grad. SDS continued this practice, for instance, in Srbac, where a local school was named Sveti Sava, and in Titov Drvar, where they removed the words of Tito, including his signature, which were present on one of the hills there (Maksić, 2017, 219). Probably even more important than this was that they started erecting monuments to the Bosnian Serb victims of the Ustasha massacres. One of the first of such acts was the establishing of a memorial church near Loparov and a monument in Bileći, as well as making changes to the inscription on the monument in Bugojno that previous read "to the victims of fascist terror" to "to the Serbian, Jewish and Roma victims of fascist terror" (Maksić, 2017, 219). The key change was probably in the village of Drakulići where the generic inscription "victims of fascist terror" was replaced by the inscription "genocide of Serbs" (Maksić, 2017, 220).

Another important moment for the material environment of BiH was 'spatialisation' as SDS began to create in the 30 municipalities in which it held a majority (Maksić, 2017, 218). In so doing, even the constitutional regulation of BiH, which provided for the right of municipalities to unite, came into their hands. This also explains why the local SDS in Banjaluka planned to establish the Union of Municipalities of the Bosanska Krajina (*Zajednica opština Bosanske Krajine*—ZOBK) (ibid.). When ZOBK was established, SDS emphasised above all the economic side of such regionalisation. Maksić (2017, 225) notes that in this way SDS started to create the imaginary of the Bosnian Serb ethnic territory, which continued in September with 'regionalisation', meaning that the Communities of Municipalities of Eastern and Old Herzegovina would become part of the joint Serbian Autonomous Region of Herzegovina. About 4 days later, ZOBK also upgraded its status and became the Autonomous Region of Krajina (ARK), and the Community of Municipalities of Romanija (SOR) was established as well. Later, SDS merged the northeastern municipalities into the Community of Municipalities of Northeastern Bosnia and the Community of Municipalities of Northern Bosnia (ibid.). With such ethno-political regionalisation within BiH came Karadžić's argument that "at this moment BiH is divided according to cultural, spiritual and economic key" (Maksić, 2017, 225). The legitimacy that Karadžić gave to the creation of such an ethnopolitical imaginary encouraged Nikola Koljević, who commenced by relativising the BiH spirit of neighbourliness (*komšiluk*) with the statement that "there is no return for neighboring Bosnia, where one would kindly ask another about his health, but then work against him behind his back". Later, Koljević even said that the potential partition of BiH "must not be understood as hostile".

Soon after, SDA and HDZ BiH responded on 15 October 1991 by adopting the Memorandum on the Sovereignty of BiH, which triggered a sharp reaction from SDS. The SDS leadership started talking about political violence committed by HDZ BiH and SDA, and 3 days later Karadžić even declared a state of emergency in all municipalities (Irwin, 2011).

Karadžić and Milošević met in this respect towards the end of October 1991, and Karadžić is said to have presented Milošević with the idea of a separate Serbian parliament, which Milošević did not take well (Maksić, 2017, 227), saying that such moves are non-Serbian and the population in BiH would not accept it well, with Karadžić replying that you cannot "mobilise people with mineral water" (ibid.). On the same day, the Parliamentary Assembly of the Serbian Nation in BiH was established, existing parallel to the Parliament of BiH (Maksić, 2017, 228). The (para) institution in question immediately proclaimed itself the supreme representative body of the Serbian nation in BiH, which was above the republican institutions in BiH (ibid.). Between 9 and 10 November 1991, a plebiscite was held in 101 municipalities at which Bosnian Serbs could reorganise whether they supported the newly established Parliamentary Assembly of the Serbian nation in BiH remaining in the shrunken Yugoslav community. According to the responses of the plebiscite organisers, 1,162,030 Bosnian Serbs voted, among whom 99% voted for the idea of remaining in Yugoslavia (ibid.). In this way, the results became a legitimising tool in the hands of SDS to promote the idea that all local communities in which at least 50% of Bosnian Serbs live would remain in Yugoslavia (Maksić, 2017, 229).

The BiH Memorandum and the 'Bosnian Serb Plebiscite' coincided with the growing Yugoslav crisis and war, which saw to the establishment of the Badinteri Commission that provided a series of different legal interpretations and solutions, including the statement that "Yugoslavia is a state in disintegration" (Pellet, 1992). Karadžić took the call seriously and immediately quoted Njegoš in public on 12 December, calling for "unity and responsiveness" (Maksić, 2017, 235). He thereby began to emphasise the possibility of forming a confederation in BiH, where the Bosnian Serbs would remain in "Serbian areas" and in a federation with Serbia (Maksić, 2017, 235). However, the Presidency of BiH decided otherwise and on 20 December 1991 submitted a request to the European Community (EC) for the recognition of BiH as an independent and sovereign state. This encouraged Karadžić to organise a meeting in the Sarajevo Holiday Inn at which over 200 of the highest Bosnian Serb political officials were present (Maksić, 2017, 235). The meeting was crucial because of the agreement on the establishment of Republika Srpska in BiH (RSBiH), which was supposed to take place on 14 January 1992 on the Serbian New Year, and bring together all the autonomous Serbian provinces created by

SDS during this period under a single Bosnian Serb framework (ibid.). This was later established on 9 January 1992, but—in addition to the legal formalities—encountered a problem with the use of symbols. For example, in the parallel institutions of the Bosnian Serbs, the Yugoslav flag was displayed next to the Serbian flag (ibid.). This was interrupted by the political leadership only later, for which, among other things, the speech of the President of the Parliamentary Assembly of the Serbian Nation in BiH, Momčilo Krajišnik, during the seventh session of the Parliamentary Assembly of the Serbian Nation in BiH was also credited. He said that "symbols are what make people die and why people go to war" (ibid.). He was also assisted by the fact that there were major changes on the Bosnian Croat side as well since on 18 November 1991, Mate Boban, Dario Kordić, Jadranko Prlić, Ignac Koštroman and Gojko Šušak set up the Croatian Community of Herceg-Bosna as a cultural, economic and social area for Croats in BiH.

Karadžić's SDS was not satisfied with this and continued to instrumentalise the social and material environment of BiH as it tried to 'maximise the Bosnian Serb territory'. SDS did this in two ways. First, with the argument of ownership, he stressed that 64% of all BiH belonged to Bosnian Serbs due to their ownership of land and real estate. However, such an argument was completely wrong, with Golić showing that absolutely no state agency possessed ownership data broken down by ethnicity, including the fact that approximately 53% of all ownership was in state hands. Second, SDS started promoting "Bosnian Serb areas" by mobilising past injustices. Emphasising these strengthened the legitimation of ethno-territorial engineering as a policy for eliminating these injustices. For example, Maksić (2017, 238) shows that SDS began to highlight that the current demarcation lines were the result of Ustasha crimes committed half a century ago. One of these areas was Bosanska Krupa, for which SDS started to emphasise that it was perfectly legitimate to annex Muslim villages to the Serbian municipality as these villages grew on land upon which Serbs were killed during the Second World War (ibid.). Another good example of this is the establishment of a separate municipality near Čapljina, in which the majority Bosnian Croat population lived, using the argument that it was land that historically belonged to the Serbs (Maksić, 2017, p. 238).

In this atmosphere, it was hard to expect that because of the mediation of the EC between the three ethno-political parties, the Carrington-Cutileiro plan (hereinafter: the Plan) would succeed given that SDS had practically already achieved its political goals. A large part of the territory, including the population that identified themselves as Bosnian Serbs, had already been united within the RSBiH framework, which is why the Plan also envisaged the 'cantonisation of BiH' according to the ethnic principle, which SDA did not agree with. It should be emphasised that even SDS could not fully agree with the Plan because it had envisaged a clear border between the Bosnian Serbs in BiH and the Serbs in Serbia. Therefore, on 25 February 1992, Karadžić began to emphasise that it was only a "temporary sacrifice", connecting this with the policy of the Serbian king Miloš Obrenović who between 1830 and 1833 had been given an opportunity to consolidate the Serbian state (Maksić, 2017, 239). When it became clear that there would be a referendum on the independence of BiH, a period of anxiety among the SDS leadership commenced (ibid.). The SDS leadership was not convinced the Bosnian Serbs living in multi-ethnic cities would not vote for the independence of BiH and thus started to disseminate exactly this message through letters among the local committees of the municipalities where SDS was still present (Maksić, 2017, 240). This was also a period of change in the SDS rhetoric in relation to the Croats since not only did HDZ BiH and SDS work as partners during the negotiations on preparing the Plan, but Karadžić also emphasised, for example, in an interview for the Slovenian newspaper *Delo*, that the Serbs and Croats had enjoyed good relations before the establishment of Yugoslavia (Maksić, 2017, 241). He even added that Izetbegović is the one who "hopes that the Serbs and Croats in BiH will always be on opposite sides" (Maksić, 2017, 240). Certainly one reason for such a discursive turn was the meeting between the SDS delegation led by Nikola Koljević and Croatian President Franjo Tuđman held on 8 January 1992 where they discussed a common strategy in BiH with the aim of ethnic demarcation (Maksić, 2017, 241). The latter was even to have included the exchange of residents.

When BiH's referendum for independence was being held, SDS activists exerted all their powers to prevent the Bosnian Serbs from participating in those municipalities where they formed the majority. A good example of this was the area of Bosnian Krajina where SDS started a campaign to frame any Bosnian Serb who would vote in the referendum as a traitor (Maksić, 2017, 242). Grubić showed that SDS activists began distributing leaflets with the message that anyone voting at the referendum would be betraying Tsar Lazar's struggle. Maksić (2017, 243) showed that the local SDS committees explained to every Bosnian Serb of legal age why they could not participate in the referendum or be part of the electoral commission. This also happened because the local political elites of SDS in those municipalities in which Bosnian Serbs represented the majority population refused both ballots and to set up polling stations (Maksić, 2017, 243). Drvar, for instance, had no polling station at all, and in Prnjavorje, the electoral commission even operated "illegally" (ibid.). When BiH's referendum succeeded (63%), a period of wider mobilisation of the Bosnian Serb population followed. Karadžić, who immediately after the outcome of the referendum stressed that "not a single (Bosnian) Serb will accept an independent BiH", started organising events that would be interpreted by the public as "spontaneous reactions" of Bosnian Serbs (Maksić, 2017, 243). A good demonstration of this was Karadžić's decision to erect barricades in Sarajevo because of the murder of the father of the groom at a Bosnian Serb wedding in Baščaršija, only for them to be removed within 48 hours (ibid.). Maksić (2017, 244) showed, for example, that here SDS tried to send a clear signal to both the internal (Bosnian Serbs, Bosnian Croats, Muslims/Bosniaks) and external (international community) publics that the Bosnian Serbs were against the independence of BiH and also ready for war. The local SDS committee in Prijedor, for example, characterised this murder as a crime "against the Serbian national essence, which is not only a consequence of Muslim-majority politics, but also a clear sign of what awaits the (Bosnian) Serbs in independent BiH" (ibid.). Just before the war erupted, Karadžić started talking about civilisational topics on a global level for the external public and began to connect them with the increasingly uncertain domestic situation. In one of his last high-profile speeches just prior to the war, he even announced that "he thinks that they cannot avoid an inter-ethnic and inter-religious war, such as the war between India and Pakistan" and "that the situation in Northern Ireland would look like a summer holiday in comparison with BiH" (Maksić, 2017, 242). The war also officially began when Alija Izetbegović rejected the principles of the Plan given that the Minister of Internal Affairs, Momčilo Mandžić, had started to establish a parallel Serbian police unit which, together with the Army of the Republic of Srpska (ARS) under the later leadership of Ratko Mladić, served in the Yugoslav People's Army (YLA) and Serbian paramilitary units.

Even though Björkdahl (2018, 41) emphasises that the "Drina campaign" with its starting point in Zvornik marks the beginning of the Bosnian war, the ICTY's verdict against Momčilo Krajišnik in 2006 showed that Bijelina was the "first municipality in BiH" to have been captured by the Bosnian Serbs in 1992 (ICTY, 2006). Both views are correct since Bijelina was indeed the first municipality in BiH in which organised and systematic aggression against the non-Serb population took place but, unlike the one in Zvornik, it was primarily led by a paramilitary unit led by Željko (Arkan) Ražnatović and Mirko Blagojević's local paramilitary unit. During the paramilitary takeover of Bijelina, at least 48 civilians were killed, and by September 1992, with the help of Duško Malović, the local SDS had succeeded in persecuting the vast majority of Muslims/Bosniaks and Bosnian Croats who, due to a fear of being sent to the Batković camp, were looking for ways to leave Bijelina. During the massacre of the non-Serb population in Bijelina, in which 1078 people are said to have lost their lives, including 250 civilians, all seven mosques were also demolished (Human Rights Watch, 2000, 4; Prometheus, 2013). The social and material environment of Bijelina changed during and after the war to such an extent that immediately after the end of the war in BiH, fewer than 2700 Muslims remained in Bijelina (before the war, there were approximately 19,000), and by the end of 2012, only 5000 Muslims (Bosniaks) had returned to the city (Karabegović, 2012). It should also be mentioned that the local Bosnian Serb population celebrates 1 April as the "Day of the Defending the City", with one of the streets there being named after the Serbian Volunteer Guard.

With the help of the YLA and paramilitary units, The ARS managed to secure approximately two-thirds of the entire territory of BiH by the end of 1992 and ensured the consolidation of the perception of ethno-political communities in BiH (Gow, 1997). Maček (2009) believes the most important strategy was probably the siege of Sarajevo (5 April 1992) as the capital of BiH, with which the ARS and YLA created a sense of threat and fear among their 'own' population. In 1992, at least 36 massacres took place—in addition to the one in Bijeljina—in Doboj, Foča, Prijedor, Zvornik, Višegrad and Bijeli Potok. Seeking to establish an ethnically homogeneous (Bosnian Serb) space, violent reorganisation of the space with ethnic engineering and cleansing, began to take on stronger outlines in the east, west and north of BiH, where Bosnian Serbs represented most of the population. An analysis of the ICTY judgment (2006, 110–163), for example, shows the Bosnian Serbs had tried to seize power through violence in at least 37 municipalities out of 109 in BiH, home to a total of almost 1.7 million people (including 675,657 Muslims, 742,100 Bosnian Serbs, 128,275 Bosnian Croats, 242,682 Yugoslavs and 104,439 'Others') (ICTY, 2006, 123).

Björkdahl and Kappler (2017) state that the 'Bosnian Serb' space was created using the 'housing policy', which had become part of the visible material environment. This entailed the Bosnian Serb political elite either occupying non-Serb houses or destroying them while, immediately after the war, passing legislation preventing Bosniaks and Bosnian Croats from returning to them. Another way of creating a 'Bosnian Serb' space was through name changes and the destruction of cultural and religious buildings that marked the existence of the Other in this territory. Feldman (2005) and Mannergren Selimović (2013), for example, show that in 1992 Mostar became Serbian Mostar. A similar act happened with Foča, which was ethnically 'cleansed' by April 1992 and renamed by the Serbs. Finally, it is worth mentioning the towns of Divić where a local mosque was demolished and an Orthodox church was built on the same site, and Banjaluka where all 16 mosques were destroyed (Stjepanović, 2015). The very beginning of the Bosnian war was relatively confusing, including events on the ground. An obvious reason for this—beyond the interpretation of who started the war—was the role of the YLA that was supposed to leave BiH in May 1992. The next municipality after Bijeljina, where the RS army under the leadership of SDS, together with the YLA, continued the policy of ethnic cleansing was the Municipality of Prijedor where on the night of 29–30 April 1992, the local political elite of the SDS started to make clear on the radio station that the Bosnian Serbs would be taking over the municipality. Thus, all those employed in the security structures and police units in Prijedor were called to a sit-in in Cirkinovo polje (part of Prijedor), where they were divided into 5 groups of approximately 20 men and tasked with taking over certain buildings like the police station, town hall, banks, post offices and courts. The local Bosnian Serb political elite quickly began setting up concentration camps, certainly the most infamous being the Keraterm and Omarska factories, in which 3197 Bosniaks and 125 Bosnian Croats were allegedly imprisoned between 27 May and 16 August 1992.

During this period, the war became even more complicated at the expense of the Graz Agreement that caused the Army of BiH (*Armija Republike Bosne i Hercegovine*—ABiH), led by Sefer Halilović and largely (70% Bosniaks, 18% Bosnian Croats and 12% Bosnian Serbs) composed of Bosniaks, was threatened by the Croatian Defence Council (*Hrvatsko Vijeće Obrane*—HVO). Around this time, HVO had already begun to take over central BiH, especially the areas still under ABiH control (then understood to be Bosniak territory). In fact, the Graz agreement of May

1992 had already caused a split within HVO at the outset of the war since HVO leader Blaž Kraljević strongly supported cooperation with the Bosniaks, not with the Bosnian Serbs. It is worth highlighting three more massacres committed against the Bosnian Serbs in Bradina, Čemerne and Zalužje. Members of HVO and the ABiH killed 48 Bosnian Serb civilians in Bradina, and in Čemerne (Ilijaš) the ABiH captured and killed 21 members of the ARS, including 9 Bosnian Serb civilians, while in Zalužje (Bratunac), Bosniak soldiers led by Naser Orić killed 69 members of the ARS and civilians.

Much of what happened in BiH in 1993 may be characterised as military clashes between Bosniaks and Bosnian Croats, even though at the beginning of the year the ARS killed Deputy Prime Minister of Bosnia and Herzegovina Hakija Turajlić (LeBor, 2006). This period is simultaneously known for at least four important milestones in the international presence in Bosnia and Herzegovina. First, in early 1993, the Security Council of the United Nations Organisation (UNSC) adopted Resolution no. 808 leading to the ICTY being established on 25 May 1993. Second, UN Special Envoy Cyrus Vance and European Community (EC) representative Lord Owen started negotiating a peace agreement with representatives of all three ethnic groups. The failed plan to divide BiH into three ethnic parts by the principle of ten cantons, which was rejected by 96% of Bosnian Serbs in a referendum between 15 and 16 May 1993, is said to have only exacerbated the conflicts between Bosniaks and Croats within 30% of the territory, which they still had control of (Macqueen & Mitchell, 1995). The following year, 1994, was important for the social environment in BiH mainly due to the intense and direct involvement of the international community in the war, with NATO and the UN taking the lead. The role of NATO grew especially after February 1994, when until the downing of four Bosnian Serb planes in the vicinity of Banjaluka due to a violation of the UN's no-fly zone policy over BiH, and continued after April 1994 when military planes began shelling Bosnian Serb positions around Goražde. On the other hand, the UN's role started to be considerably strengthened in April 1994 when a Danish contingent (Nordbat 2) survived an ARS ambush in the village of Kalesija near Tuzla (Bethlehem & Weller, 1997, 17). Even as the war continued in Bosnia and Herzegovina during 1994, the UN and NATO were working hand in hand, and it is worth noting the operation in August 1994 when NATO air units began shelling the ARS in Sarajevo and continued in September with an attack on an ARS tank in Sarajevo. However, the ARS was able to settle the score with NATO and at the end of November 1994 attacked two of its military aircraft south of Otok (northwestern BiH) (ibid.).

While the war in BiH continued in 1995, the circumstances had completely changed following the Bosniak-Bosnian Croat agreement and coordinated cooperation, which was especially important at the very end of the war in Bosnia and Herzegovina. The Bosniaks and Bosnian Croats captured a large part of western Bosnia with Operation Storm, and even reached Banjaluka with Operations Maestral and Sana, yet were later stopped due to the framework agreement on a peace agreement drawn up by the foreign ministers of Croatia, Yugoslavia, and Bosnia and Herzegovina in New York. This year was a turning point not simply because the war in BiH came to an end, but chiefly because of the ARS' continuation of the policy of ethnic cleansing that began on 25 May (Tito's birthday) in Tuzla when it bombed Kapija and 71 people died, before continuing in Srebrenica. The latter, which was subjected to the worst form of ethnic cleansing between 6 and 11 July 1995—genocide—is becoming a (meta) symbol of the war in BiH today, along with Sarajevo. In the first days of the attack on Srebrenica, around 2000 members of the ARS managed to break through the defensive ring of about 6000 ABiH members and commenced enforcing a policy of ethnic cleansing in the southern part of the Srebrenica enclave (ICTY, 2001). The ARS, which faced no major resistance in the face of the majority demilitarised Bosniak population and the international community's relative passivity, was ordered by Karadžić to occupy Srebrenica on 9 July 1995 (ICTY, 2001, 65). When some 1500 members of the Drina unit of the ARS began to besiege Srebrenica, Karremans asked NATO to defend Srebrenica. The latter agreed to the request and attacked Bosnian Serb military positions in the vicinity of Srebrenica on 11 July. Yet, the relative lack of transparency on the ground, especially the threat of the ARS with a bomb attack on the UN base in Potočari and an attack on the surrounding areas, where between 20,000 and 30,000 refugees were located, forced the military operation to come to an end (ICTY, 2001, 64).

Just before the beginning of the genocide in Srebrenica in which 8372 Bosniaks died, accompanied by the forced expelling and abuse of between 25,000 and 30,000 Bosniak women, children and elderly, Ratko Mladić allegedly warned Karadžić and Krajišnik that their plan in Srebrenica could not be carried out without genocide. Bečirević (2006, 43) thus highlights the following words of Mladić:

People are not like small pebbles or keys in one of the pockets so that they can be moved from one place to another just like that [...]. This is also why we cannot ensure that only (Bosnian) Serbs remain in this area, while others are moved to another part of Bosnia in a painless way. I don't know how Mr. Krajišnik and Mr. Karadžić will explain this to the world. This is genocide.

The period between 13 and 22 July thus marks a period of systematic cleansing of Bosniaks in the vicinity of the Jadarska River, Cerska dolina, Kravica, Tišća, Grbavac, Orahovac, Petkovići, Branjevo, Kozluka, the road between Bratunec and Konjević polje, Mecesa as well as Nezuk-Baljković (ICTY, 2001, 64–82). The genocide at Srebrenica is hence becoming one of the most important factors for the Bosnian Serb ethno-political elite, which is still trying to build an (imaginary and homogenous) genocide denial policy by searching for reasons for the attack on Srebrenica, relativising the number of victims and delegitimising the credibility of the international community, the ICTY and the Court of BiH and the ethnic identity of the Bosnian Serbs. I present this in greater detail in the next subsection where I deal with the material and social environment of RS after once the Bosnian war ended. The Bosnian war ended relatively quickly after the genocide in Srebrenica, with the last military operation being recorded on 28 August 1995, again in Sarajevo's Markale by the ARS, when 43 people died. This event is of note because the ethno-political elite of SDS had begun talking about their readiness to accept Richard Holbrooke's peace plan just a few hours before the attack (Burg & Shoup, 1999). This also explains why the ARS later tried to accuse the BiH government of having organised an attack on its own population. Still, the UNPROFOR investigation showed the attack had been launched from Trebević, then occupied by Bosnian Serb military forces, which led NATO to launch an air campaign against the ARS in Operation Deliberate Force. The latter, which lasted between 30 August and 20 September 1995, unofficially signalled the beginning of the end of the Bosnian war. Six days later, this looked more and more official as the foreign ministers of BiH, Yugoslavia and Croatia reached an agreement on principles in New York that would form the peace agreement (Europa Publications, 2003, 803).

On 2 October 1995, a 60-day ceasefire was implemented, while approximately 2 weeks later peace negotiations began in Dayton (Ohio). The Bosnian War officially ended on 21 November 1995 upon the signing of the Dayton Peace Agreement (DPA), the final version of which was signed on 14 December 1995, in Paris. Yet already, the period between the cessation of hostilities and signing of the DPA indicated that both the social and material environments of the post-Dayton BiH would be greatly affected by the consequences of the long and bloody war in BiH, in which around 100,000 people died, more than 2.2 million people were either internally or externally displaced, and 12,000–25,000 women were raped. It was in this period that the ICTY first indicted Karadžić and Mladić for the genocide in Srebrenica, which—as I show in the subsection below— significantly strengthens the metanarrative about the Bosnian War with the aim of homogenising the (imagined) identity of the Bosnian Serbs that the Bosnian Serb ethno-political elite is today trying to recreate.

3.4   IMAGINING BOSNIAN SERB ETHNIC IDENTITY IN BOSNIA AND HERZEGOVINA IN THE CONTEXT OF EUROPEANISATION (1995–)

The period after signing and implementing the DPA was seen as a new beginning for BiH, which the DPA institutionally frames as an asymmetric consociational federation, yet already right after the war ended, it faced at least three central challenges concerning the social environment. First, the conflict between the three ethnic groups in BiH had a secessionist nature as BiH first seceded from the SFRY, and immediately after BiH, RS and the Croatian Republic of Herceg-Bosna attempted to secede (Biermann, 2014, 495). While later during the war the Bosnian Croats reached a compromise with the Bosniaks and became part of the Federation of Bosniak-Bosnian Croats (the FBiH), the Bosnian Serb ethno-political elite was first defeated militarily and only then accepted the DPA. At the same time, approximately 2.5 years after BiH's de facto statehoods, both RS and the Croatian Republic of Herceg-Bosna were reintegrated into BiH (Biermann, 2014). Second, official Belgrade was not only important for the Bosnian Serb political elite under the leadership of the SDS during the war in BiH but also important for ending the war itself. Croatia held similar (irredentist) ambitions, but never really became involved in the Bosnian war in such a systematic way as Serbia did, mainly because of its own war. Although both countries recognised the independence of BiH, they continued to be important in a symbolic, spiritual and material sense for the Bosnian Croats and Bosnian Serbs (Biermann, 2014, 496). Third, no leading political party of the three ethnic groups supported the DPA from the start (Basta, 2016). The Bosniak SDA thus sought a strong central government from the outset, but had to recognise two autonomous political entities, including a state without an army, police or direct funding. For example, Basta (2016, 950–952) shows SDA opposed the system of power sharing within the extremely complex Federation of Bosniaks and Bosnian Croats (the FBiH) from the beginning, which was transferred to the state level. On the other hand, the Bosnian Croat political elite led by HDZ BiH was dissatisfied with not having its own (third) autonomous political entity. Unlike them, the Bosnian Serb political elite could be more satisfied in the SDS framework since they had their own political entity under the name Republika Srpska but could renounce their "own independence" (Zdeb, 2017).

Gromes (2008, 8) starts the discussion in a very interesting way by pointing out that after the DPA was signed, all three ethno-political elites tried to achieve 'victory' such that in the period of peace they would gain back what they had lost in BiH during the war. In this sense, the social environment in RS did not change excessively because in September 1996 SDS again achieved victory at the elections. In this way, practically, the entire political elite in place during the Bosnian war remained in their positions. President of SDS Biljana Plavšić, better known for her interwar statements, indicated right after the war had ended that she "wants the unification of all Serbs into one country, which will be called Serbia" (Gromes, 2008). However, given this was unfeasible at the time, the Bosnian Serb political elite had to settle for its own political entity, which it began to "imagine as a *de facto* state" (Björkdahl, 2018). This is also why the first operative goal was to maintain the weak state power, which they were dissatisfied with, especially in SDA. HDZ BiH was thinking similarly to SDS—albeit with a slightly different institutional starting point—and, in the year following the war, had to start dealing with the fact that the Bosnian Croat population had begun to reject an independent BiH (in 1995, BiH was supported by 65% of Bosnian Croats, while in 1996 only 31%). Biermann (2014, 496), for example, shows that in 1996 when the Croatian Republic of Herceg-Bosna was merging with the FBiH, HDZ BiH held parallel talks with Croatia on the potential annexation of their cantons.

Such a (secessionist) agenda was ever more in breach of the DPA, which envisaged the sharing of power according to the ethnic principle. For instance, Daalder (2000, 156) shows that the DPA, which otherwise tried to strengthen legitimacy and inclusivity through the provision of "security and protection" with this distribution of power, was mainly based on ethnic quotas, 'entity voting' and an ethnic veto in the event a "vital national interest" of one of the ethnic groups was threatened. Still, the DPA was never created to ensure the functionality of the state in the absence of accepting a compromise. Bieber (2006) thus shows how the DPA became hostage to itself at a time when there was an "institutional power struggle" between the ethno-political elites. This also explains why the material and social environment in BiH practically did not change until 1998. Biermann (2014, 496) notes that by 1998 joint institutions were either not established or 'mere facades', mobility between residents in different political entities was minimal due to the IEBL, and war criminals had commenced to re-establish local networks. Already during the negotiations to sign the DPA, it had become clear that the EU would take on a central role in the Agreement's civilian implementation. Daadler (2000, 157) thus emphasises that the EU demanded from the very beginning that the VP, who was to have the "last word" in BiH, come from the EU (Council of the EU 1995). They succeeded in this largely due to the relative passivity of the USA, which not only allegedly showed no interest in civilian implementation during the negotiations, but even refused to grant any powers to the VP (Bildt, 1998, 130–132; Holbrooke, 1998, 276). At that time, the EU nominated Carl Bildt as the first VP, providing as much as 53% of his budget and a considerable part of his staff (Juncos, 2013). During this period, the EC also established a Delegation in Sarajevo, upgraded the Monitoring Mission in BiH and expanded the mission to Mostar (Juncos, 2013, 99–102). Juncos (2013, 97) shows that in the period 1996–1997 the EU spent EUR 803.3 million on BiH.

Nevertheless, the influence of the EU in the initial post-conflict years in BiH was relative. Another problem was that the Office of the High Representative (OHR), which was originally understood more as a *sui generis* institution that reported not only to the Council of the EU, but to the UN Security Council and the Peace Implementation Council (PIC) as well, started work only 1 year after its establishment. For example, Holbrooke (1998, 324) emphasised that "while the military dimension was extremely tactful and present in the early years, the civilian part (EU) was practically non-existent". At that time, the governments of the EU member states soon realised that the rapid withdrawal of NATO forces above all depended on the degree of successful reconstruction and democratisation since the refugees would only return to their homes on the condition that their homes had been rebuilt, and employment opportunities created (Szewczyk, 2010). Uncertainty was also present at that time in the American administration under the leadership of Clinton, which tried to bridge the dysfunctional OHR by strengthening and expanding the role of its own mission in NATO and the Organisation for Security and Cooperation in Europe (OSCE). He achieved this by sending Richard Holbrooke to BiH quite regularly, and at the same time he built an American embassy in BiH, which was similar to the OHR in personnel profile (Flügger, 2002; Holbrooke, 1998, 315–369). The most active EU member state at that time was Germany, which started implementing projects relatively early on in those post-war environments where it was (militarily) present (Biermann, 2014; Flügger, 2002).

However, dissatisfaction arose not only in the local population but also in the international community. Biermann (2014, 499) points out that awareness that BiH's political elite had started to inhibit the process of civilian implementation of the DPA prompted the EU to begin emphasising the word "conditionality" (Council of the EU, 1995). Conditioning in BiH thus commenced when linking funds for reconstruction with readiness for the repatriation of refugees (Biermann, 2014, 496). Otherwise, it is difficult to talk about the effects of conditioning because in this period, the PIC, which gave the political direction of international policy, along with the USA, which relied on quick and strong interventions, were important international actors. It is nonetheless worth stressing that it was the EU that was primarily in charge of economic recovery and controlled the OHR. In this context, the EU sought to influence the material and social environment of BiH in at least two ways. First, as early as 1996, the EU emphasised that the continued relationship between the EU and BiH would depend on commitment to implementing the DPA, which envisages "BiH as an independent, democratic and multi-ethnic state with secure borders" (European Council, 1995). By so doing, the EC explicitly warned the Bosnian-Croatian political elite in particular that the EU "rejects any attempts to revive the governmental structures of the Croatian Republic of Herceg-Bosnia" (ibid.). Second, the EU did not expect this level of obstruction of DPA implementation from the three core ethnopolitical parties (Biermann, 2014, 497). The Council of the EU (1997), for example, changed the positive conditionality in 1996 to a negative one the following year, causing the OHR to freeze all aid to Mostar, isolate SDS in Pale, take over and close certain radio stations of the Bosnian Serbs, and warn the official Zagreb and Belgrade to not interfere in the internal affairs of Bosnia and Herzegovina. In this atmosphere, the EU decided it would not provide any post-conflict aid to RS if Karadžić were de facto in power and even postponed the third donor conference (Flügger, 2002).

Yet, the EU's influence was minimal in RS, as Szewczyk (2010) and Biermann (2014) describe. Szewczyk (2010), for example, notes that in the absence of functional state institutions, the ethno-political elite in SDS practically created "their own state". The social environment of BiH was mainly denoted by the inability to adopt macroeconomic reforms that would provide people with employment opportunities. The absence of prospects had an irreversible effect by way of radicalising local ethno-political parties (Biermann, 2014). This is also why, via the EU, Germany took the initiative to strengthen the powers and funding of the OHR. In December 1997, the OHR thus received the 'Bon powers' that allowed it to pass laws, change the constitution, appoint judges, freeze bank accounts, overrule/change court decisions and even remove popular representatives. This changed already in 1998 when Milorad Dodik, otherwise the president of SNSD, was elected prime minister of RS by the Parliamentary Assembly of RS. He continued the political fight against Karadžić's SDS by immediately moving from Pale to Banjaluka, freezing funds of the RS leadership in Pale and giving a clear signal to the international community that he would respect the provisions of the DPA (Biermann, 2014).

The very election of Dodik as prime minister in 1998 was strongly affected by the impression of international actors since the RS faced a high unemployment rate (70%) and the absence of foreign direct investment and aid for reconstruction, which was then mostly intended for the FBiH (Holbrooke, 1998). It should also be mentioned that during this period the OHR threatened to transfer the authority for Brčko District to the Bosniaks, which would literally cut off the western and eastern parts of RS (material environment) (ibid.). The newly appointed VP Carlos Westendorp therefore had no problem using the bond powers. Moreover, Holbrooke (1998, 353) showed that Westendorp gave a clear signal to RS that he would be starting a policy of imposing unilateral reforms without cooperation. Negative conditioning therefore paid off, as the EU helped Dodik in the parliamentary elections by promising to release "short-term aid to RS" (Council of the EU, 1998). The European Council announced that the EU would increase its funding for the reconstruction of RS if there were visible progress in the level of democratisation and respect for human rights in RS. In this period, the Cooperation Agreement between

BiH and the EU was also signed (Biermann, 2014, 498). Holbrooke (1998, 356) stated that the first months of 1998 "showed more progress than had been made in the previous two years combined".

Still, Dodik's SNSD failed in September 1998 since SDS again won the elections and appointed the president of RS, creating the continuity of the social environment of RS. Gromes (2008, 14) shows that the political landscape in RS between 1998 and 2000 nevertheless began to experience changes as two blocs were established, one that continued to reject BiH and the other understanding the DPA as "common destiny". It should be emphasised that the general rejection of BiH as a country by the ethno-political SDS grew weaker and weaker. While, for example, in 2000, 32–41% of Bosnian Serbs continued to defend the independence of RS, only 27–29% would unite with Serbia (Gromes, 2008). During this period, SDS also began to speak ever louder about its commitment to a functional BiH. Something similar happened on the side of the Bosnian Croats when in 2000 there were only 2% who advocated unification with Croatia (Gromes, 2008). It should also be stressed that both ethno-political parties—SDA and HDZ BiH—were pushed into the opposition in the FBiH (Gromes, 2008, 17).

This period was particularly important for the social environment of RS, as the first indictments for war crimes in BiH were brought before the ICTY. Duško Tadić and Goran Borovnica were among the first defendants for crimes committed in Prijedor. A year later, in 2001, even Biljana Plavšić took responsibility, having voluntarily surrendered and being charged in June 2003 with planning, encouraging, ordering, aiding and abetting the persecution of the non-Bosnian Serb population in 37 municipalities. However, for the social environment of RS and understanding its role in the creation of the metanarrative then (successfully) promoted by SDS, what happened after the end of Plavšić's sentence in Sweden is important. She said in an interview that "she expected heroes from these men (especially Karadžić and Mladić), that they would tell her that we should all go there, stand before the Hague Tribunal and say that only we are guilty and no one else, least of all the Serbian nation" (Dnevnik, 2011). Plavšić, who during the trial could not rely on (Bosnian) Serb witnesses because of Karadžić, was even attacked by Dobrica Ćosić, one of the central Great Serbian ideologues during the breakup of socialist Yugoslavia (Chronology of the Event, n.d.). He told her, for example, that she "was an American individual and a traitor to the Serbian nation", and she replied that "Ćosić was at the top of the communist regime when 30,000 Serbs were killed in

1944 and that he was a regular visitor to Goli otok, so he should not worry about the nation's identity, as it was destroyed in his time" (Dnevnik, 2011).

The view of what was occurring in Bosnia and Herzegovina during that period was encouraging. Thus, for instance, there was a defence reform, which became synonymous with the progress of post-conflict BiH (Aybet & Bieber, 2011). This merged the three different armies into one on the national level, eliminating all parallel military formations and establishing a national Ministry of Defence while reducing the size of the military on the level of the two political entities by 40% (ibid.). Greenwood and Hartog (2005, 81) even talk about a "seismic shift" in RS. The conditioning and credibility of the EU continued to grow during this time, following programmes like Community Assistance for Reconstruction, Development and Stabilisation (CARDS), the establishment of the Stability Pact and foundations of European security and defence policy (Juncos, 2013). In the coming years, the EU even assumed responsibility for most aspects of the DPA, including the appointing of the VPs who wore 'two caps' with the OHR (2002–2011), taking over the UN police mission in 2003 and the NATO mission in 2004 (Juncos, 2013, 125–162).

Certainly the most important, however, was the expansion perspective based on positive conditioning from the very beginning. But this soon changed since the EC perceived increasingly strong obstruction from RS and the increasing influence of Serbia and Croatia. Therefore, when it comes to BiH's prospects for expansion, the year 2000 was again marked by negative conditioning, including identification of the culprit for the slow reforms. For example, the EC (2002) publicly blamed the "highly decentralised structure of BiH, which prevents and blocks effective governance", and began to underline that "RS must build on the DPA and understand that a strong state is compatible with a strong entity" (EC, 2002, 17). A core reason for these signals from the EU was the preparation of a report on BiH's readiness to start negotiations to sign the SAA. BiH needed almost 2 years to complete all reforms in the 18 priority areas, and it should be noted that meeting the criteria was in most cases done under severe "pressure" (EC, 2003, 28). Later, the Directorate for European Integration of Bosnia and Herzegovina completed a questionnaire that in 2003 formed part of the BiH Feasibility Study. The EC (2005) concluded 2 years later through an ex-post evaluation that the study was an extremely important "factor for the acceleration of reforms".

BiH officially started negotiations for the signing of the SAA in November 2005, which in this doctoral dissertation is signed out as the first critical juncture.

Biermann (2014, 499–500) attributes such successes of the EU between 1998 and 2005 to four structural factors. First, 9 years after the adoption of the DPA, it had become increasingly clear to all three ethnopolitical parties in BiH that the international community had no intention of withdrawing from BiH. Even the EC (2002, 28) stressed this, for example, when saying that "the EU will not withdraw and leave the door open for renewed nationalist and separatist tendencies". Second, in 1999 and 2000, Franjo Tuđman and Slobodan Milošević lost power, respectively, ending 'hopes' that Croatia and Serbia would continue to (financially) support secessionism given that the new political elite was more focused on the process of expansion. Third, the war in Kosovo had shown that NATO member states were ready to impose sanctions and even intervene militarily if needed. Finally, the EU's conditionality was aligned with NATO's conditionality. This, in turn, led to the defence reform, which was also a precondition for BiH's membership in the Partnership for Peace.

The time after 2004, when BiH started negotiations to sign the SAA, is understood as a period of decline (Majstorović & Vučkovac, 2016). Biermann (2014) and Majstorović and Vučkovac (2016) show this was mainly due to a misunderstanding of the context and the EU's poor management of the situation on the ground in BiH. Namely, the EU started by applying strong pressure for the official revision and reforms of the DPA, as also clearly expressed in its Report on the progress of BiH (EC, 2005). In it, the EU noted that the DPA is "too complex and fiscally unsustainable" (EC, 2005, 5; 9–10). Such a discursive turn was extremely risky since any emphasis on a more functional BiH meant the transfer of authority from the entity level to the state level. Noutcheva (2012, 164), for example, showed that this emphasis began to create the feeling among the Bosnian Serb political elite that the Bosniaks would gain more authority and power at the expense of RS. Muehlmann (2008, 13) also stressed this when showing that the push for constitutional reforms had irreversibly opened 'Pandora's box' of the system of dividing powers according to the ethnic key and power between the three ethnic groups. The International Commission on the Balkans (ICB) was one of the first to be aware of this risk and warned the EU that "building the state of Bosnia and Herzegovina cannot be based on the fact that the ultimate goal is centralization", while it mainly criticised "the understanding of federalization as a problem that needs to be solved, instead of as a solution that enables the coexistence of three ethnic groups". The ICB was correct because the failed constitutional reform package, rejected in the BiH Parliament in April 2006, had reinvigorated nationalist rhetoric in the political arena of Bosnia and Herzegovina (Zdeb, 2017).

One problem was the police reform, where the public debates on it coincided with the negotiations to sign the SAA between 2005 and 2007. Biermann (2014, 501) states that this turning point saw BiH return to the path of secessionist friction among the three ethno-political parties. The police reform, which thus sought to recreate a modern and unified police unit to operate on both sides of the IEBL, was an initiative of the EU and the OHR (Juncos, 2011, 379). Yet, for it to succeed, the EU demanded a constitutional amendment with two-thirds support in the Parliament of RS. Even Ashdown's politics did not help them. The EU played the joker card that was understood through the lens of 'bringing SDS to its knees'. Interestingly, Ashdown's policy even saw some reservations from the EU as it began to be increasingly associated with the start of negotiations to sign the SAA (Muehlmann, 2008, 17). Juncos (2011, 381) notes that Ashdown overestimated the EU's strength and credibility of the EU that is claimed to arise from an enlargement perspective. The social environment of RS, which continued to be largely shaped by SDS, resisted and successfully suppressed this initiative. Muehlmann (2008, 20) described how this heralded the final breakdown of "EU conditioning" because "neither the Bonn powers nor the EU carrot could implement top-down reforms that did not have the backing and support of the citizens of BiH". It should be emphasised here that the resistance organised by SDS did not have a secessionist slogan but was principally based on the idea of maintaining the status of RS as prescribed by the DPA. Yet this does not mean that nationalism had not already appeared by the October elections of 2006. Moreover, during the campaign, which was distinctly negative, only 2 parties of the 36 were based on a civic (pluralist) logic (Zdeb 2017, 375). It is notable that the traditional ethnopolitical parties (SDS, HDZ BiH, SDA) tried to tone their rhetoric down during the campaign but were replaced by alternative parties that had adopted their earlier (more radical) positions (SBiH, HDZ 1990, SNSD) (Banović & Gavrić. 2010; Popov-Momčinović, 2012). Rašidagić (2006) and Borić (2010) thus show that the failure of the constitutional reforms in BiH was a key feature of the social environment of BiH (and RS), namely, the radicalisation of relations between Sarajevo and Banjaluka due to Silajdžić's victory, the

split within HDZ and the formation of HDZ in 1990, and Dodik's secessionist rhetoric. Dodik at least 19 times later, namely between 2009 and
2013, 'threatened' to hold a referendum on the secession of RS.

The 2006 elections hence led to new ethno-political elites coming to
power in BiH, with Haris Silajdžić and Milorad Dodik standing out.
Whereas Silajdžić, who received over 60% of all votes and thus became a
Bosniak member of the BiH Presidency, advocated the dissolution of RS
during the campaign, on the other hand, Dodik emphasised the possibility
of a referendum on the independence of RS. He reinforced this, for
instance, when stating that "it is quite natural that we, Serbs, understand
Serbia as our homeland" (Biermann, 2014, 501). During this period, the
social environment of RS was also marked by the ICTY's judgments, the
beginning of the first trials of war criminals before the Court of Bosnia and
Herzegovina, the increasingly present discourse on the 'Bosnian Serb
genocide in Srebrenica' by the Bosniak political elite, the debate on
Montenegrin independence, the question of the status of Kosovo, and the
abolition of the official coat of arms and flag of RS. In this atmosphere,
BiH received a signal that it would be signing the SAA. One of the more
important reactions in the context of the ever greater pressures on the
social environment of RS was changes to the material environment with
the aim of relativising the Other. The central goal was thus to consolidate
the ethnopolitical metanarrative of RS with the aim of trying to build an
(imagined) homogenous Bosnian Serb identity. Hence, for example, the
political elite in RS, which had actually officially apologised for the genocide in Srebrenica in 2004, started to erect numerous monuments around
RS commemorating the fallen soldiers of the ARS during the "civil war"
or the war of "defence of the fatherland". This was a key step in relativising the nature of the war (aggression or civil war) with the intention of
presenting all three sides as being equally complicit (and consequently
guilty) in the Bosnian war. It was particularly desirable—beyond Banjaluka
and Pale—to build monuments where the worst crimes against the non-
(Bosnian) Serb population took place. Accordingly, Prijedor (Omarska),
Bijeljina, Srebrenica (Skelani and Ćosići), Višegrad and Doboj were given
new monuments, assuming the destruction/erasure of the Bosniak Other.

Public opinion polls also detected a similar turn in the social environ-
ment of RS. As soon as Kosovo had declared its independence, 43% of
Bosnian Serbs understood this as a precedent for RS, with which 35% of
Bosniaks and Bosnian Croats agreed (Gallup Balkan Monitor, 2009, 6).
Džihić and Wieser (2008) showed that during the independence of

Kosovo, a letter had been sent to the central authorities of BiH asking them not to recognise Kosovo, and the EU flag had also been burned on the streets of Banjaluka. In this time, another turning point came relative to the social and material environment of BiH (and RS), namely the Prud and Butmir processes, which began in December 2008 and lasted until early 2010 as a response to the failed April constitutional reforms of 2006. The commencement of the Prud process was marked by the appeal made by Sulejman Tihić (SDA) to Dragan Čović (HDZ BiH) and Milorad Dodik (SNSD), which led the three largest ethno-national parties to try to give a signal to the BiH public that they were able to negotiate and seek compromises in the implementation of the necessary reforms. The international community, especially the EU, greeted this rare and unusual situation with firm approval (Morrison, 2009, 17). The negotiations ended quickly, namely on 21 February 2009 when Milorad Dodik issued an ultimatum to Tihić and Čović that the ethnic vote must be preserved, including the status of RS (Halimović & Jelin–Dizdar, 2009). Tihić attempted to continue the talks, which happened at the end of March 2009 when the three leaders again sat down at the table and talked about constitutional changes. It should be noted here that these three actors held only 19 of the 42 seats in the BiH Parliament, with which they tried to prove their 'value' to their own nation that by 2006 was already slowly abandoning them for new (ethnopolitical) parties (Zdeb, 2017, 375). When it became clear that the Prud processes would fail, the international community led by the EU decided to continue the process. This was mainly due to VP Valentin Inzko who invited to the table all three representatives who had negotiated in the Prud processes, and simultaneously decided to invite the representative of the USA and Swedish Foreign Minister Carl Bildt to participate, with the latter being the EU representative at the time due to Sweden holding the presidency of the EU Council (Zdeb, 2017, 376). The idea of the OHR and the EU during this process, which we call the Butmir process, was hence to continue with the necessary constitutional reforms (Bassuener & Weber, 2012, 4).

Between 20 and 21 October 2009, when the second and third meetings of the representatives were held, it became clear that only the Bosniak SDA would accept the proposals. Valery Perry (2015, 8) showed that this initiative attracted strong media coverage, which in a way even created pressure on the representatives of the three ethno-political parties. Parish (2010) and Bieber (2010) point out that the outcome of the Butmir process was not difficult to predict as it took place less than 1 year before the general elections in BiH, amid a growing political crisis in Mostar, and Dodik's policy of constant confrontation with the OHR, with which he tried to strengthen his position within RS. Both processes were unsuccessful largely because of the final goals they envisioned since they would have interfered too strongly with the social environment of BiH (and RS). The two failed processes called for a more "aggressive" EU policy on BiH (McMahon & Western, 2009, 9). The German Foreign Ministry thus began to emphasise that "BiH has only one European future, not several" (Reuters, 2010). Catherine Ashton, then EU VP for Foreign Affairs and Security Policy, warned RS that "it can have as many referendums as it wants, but at the end of the day it's just one country that needs to unite" (Radio Free Europe, 2010). The EU began to condition BiH with the already signed SAA such that it would not become valid until the DPA had been revised according to the judgment of the European Court of Human Rights from 2009 (European Commission, 2013). However, the escalation and the very presence of the EU was declining in this period, including the OHR's use of the Bonn powers (Juncos, 2013, 135).

The EU's efforts were either accompanied by considerable resistance from the local population or overruled by the Constitutional Court of BiH, or it was impossible to reach consensus among the EU member states (ICG, 2011, 7). The decline of the EU's presence could also be sensed on the ground as, for example, the EU Force (EUFOR) numbered 7000 members in 2004, but just 2000 in 2010. Something similar happened with the EU Police Mission in BiH (EUPM), which was closed in 2012. During this period, there was much talk about closing the OHR, although this had been postponed every year since 2006. This period was marked by substantial pessimism among the citizens of Bosnia and Herzegovina, as reflected in a Gallup Balkan Monitor public opinion poll (2009). Thus, for example, less than half the Bosniaks believed the EU was striving for BiH membership, while only 34% of Bosnian Serbs understood EU membership as something "positive" (ibid.). Biermann (2014, 502) hence shows that the central reason for such opinions in RS was Milorad Dodik, who was constantly introducing messages into the social environment of RS suggesting that "Banjaluka will not allow the transfer of powers to Sarajevo" and that "negotiations for EU membership will only continue when it is compatible with our own goals". For example, one of Biermann's interviewees (2014, 503) stressed that Milorad Dodik had become a symbol of "defending the DPA", who made it clear to the Bosnian Serbs that "RS has better preconditions than the FBiH due to its own centralization" and that "separation from Bosnia and Herzegovina is actually a real possibility".

By this time, the ICTY's work was already in full swing, including hearing the first cases of war criminals before the Court of Bosnia and Herzegovina where many of the defendants were (Bosnian) Serbs. For example, out of 161 names that the ICTY considered, there were 94 (Bosnian) Serbs, 29 (Bosnian) Croats, 9 Albanians and 9 Bosniaks, along with 2 Macedonians and Montenegrins each. All of this allowed Milorad Dodik to start talking about the ICTY as an "anti-Serbian court", and in particular, he managed to introduce a narrative into the social environment of RS that the Court of BiH, which had started hearing war crimes cases from 2005 onwards, was an anti-Serbian institution (Kivimäki et al., 2012, 32). An important role in this was played by the Centre for the Investigation of War Crimes of RS, which publicly emphasised that as many as 70% of the defendants were Bosnian Serbs, 16.5% Bosniaks and 12.5% Bosnian Croats (Sadović, 2011). Clearly, one important accelerator of the consolidation of this narrative was the adopted Declaration on Srebrenica of the EP from 2009, in which it was underlined that it was a genocide against Bosniaks. This was also noted by one of the interviewees, who is part of the ruling Bosnian Serb political elite. She said that "the EU has never been able to recognize genocides against Serbs, such as the genocide in Drakulići during the Second World War, but now it expects us to recognize the genocide in Srebrenica". Milorad Dodik made a similar point when telling *Večernje* Novosti that "we cannot and will never accept this event as genocide" (Arslanagić, 2010).

From 2010 onwards, when Milorad Dodik won a second term at the general elections, and until mid-2011, when the government was formed on the BiH level, the social environment of RS was exposed to at least four central ideas: (i) a referendum on whether the inhabitants of RS were in favour of the laws adopted by the OHR, (ii) a referendum on NATO membership, (iii) a referendum on whether the RS inhabitants accept the decisions of the Constitutional Court of BiH and (iv) a referendum on the status of RS (Toal, 2013, 196). When the Parliamentary Assembly of RS adopted the referendum law in April 2011 and published it in its Official Gazette, the two prime ministers, namely Catherine Ashton and Miroslav Lajčák, reacted by immediately meeting with Dodik in Banjaluka, where they agreed that the EU-led talks on structural reforms of BiH's judicial institutions had brought them closer to EU standards, which convinced Dodik not to actually hold the referendum (Toal, 2013, 196). To properly understand the metanarrative the Bosnian Serb political elite is trying to recreate, the year that followed was especially important, that is, during the 20th anniversary of RS organised by Milorad Dodik on 9 January 2012. At the celebration, also attended by Dragan Čović (HDZ BiH) and Boris Tadić (President of Serbia), Dodik mythologised this "historical moment" by emphasising that it was "the year 1992 as the year 1942" and that RS is based on the "anti-fascist" spirit of the Serbian nation, which—more than any other in Europe—paid a high price for the fight against Nazism and fascism" (RTRS, 2012). During his speech, Milorad Dodik also focused on the 'Srebrenisation of BiH'.

A more serious reaction to RS Day followed only 1 year later on 17 January 2013 when Bosniak member of the BiH presidency Bakir Izetbegović asked the Constitutional Court of BiH to assess the constitutionality of the Act on Holidays using the argument that "the Day of RS, which is celebrated on 9th January, symbolises only one of the three constitutive nations in BiH, which clearly distinguishes, excludes, limits and favours only one ethnic group" (Obradović & Čilić, 2020). On 23 October 2013, the Venice Commission also confirmed this, characterising the Day of RS as discriminatory and inconsistent with the universal values of dialogue, tolerance and mutual understanding (ibid.). At the same time, the Commission emphasised that the Day of the RS "is based on historical events that are important only for one nation in the RS, namely the (Bosnian) Serbs" (ibid.). The EU began to strengthen its presence again in 2014 when protests were staged in Zenica, later spreading to Sarajevo, Bihać and Tuzla (Puljek-Shank & Fritsch, 2018). The protests, described as "the most violent since the end of the war in BiH", were among the first acts of civil society resistance against the central government of the (F) BiH due to the poor economic and social situation in the country, which did not have a clear party sign. The EU's reaction was not as aggressive as the OHR's, which responded relatively quickly and stated through Inzko that EUFOR forces were ready to intervene if the situation were to escalate and largely focused on the development of relevant economic programmes. In November 2014, a British-German initiative on the Stability and Growth Pact (SGP) thus introduced a new logic of conditioning in BiH (Majstorović et al., 2015). Majstorović and Vučkovac (2016, 164–167) show that the SGP has become a new way of stressing the need for structural reforms in BiH that will allow it to remain on the 'European path' and also meet the Copenhagen economic criteria.

Still, the period that followed was not marked by the (quite) necessary economic and other reforms as the Constitutional Court of BiH ruled on 26 November 2015 that celebration of the Day of the RS on 9 January was unconstitutional. The Court of BiH emphasised that "it in no way prevents the right of RS to celebrate it, but that it cannot be 9 January, as this date is not acceptable for all residents of RS, or rather, not all residents of the RS experience it as such" (Obradović & Čilić, 2020). From here on, it was not long until the third critical juncture, namely the referendum on the Day of RS, because the Constitutional Court of BiH also ordered that the Parliamentary Assembly of RS change the Act on Holidays within 6 months. This did not happen as the political elite of RS, led by Dodik's SNSD, unanimously decided 3 days after the decision that "the RS will continue celebrating the Day of RS on January 9, which is in accordance with the Act on Holidays, does not contain any element of discrimination or threaten the national and religious identity and equality of the three constituent nations" (ibid.).

At the same time, in a press release, they added that "the law on public holidays in RS follows universal values and European standards". It is important that the leaders of both the coalition and opposition parties sign this statement. All parties in the Parliamentary Assembly of RS also unanimously decided on 15 July 2016 that a referendum on the Day of RS would be held. On the same day, Bosniak representatives in the structures of RS called on the OHR to react and protect the DPA. This—through the PIC—officially happened on 30 August when it "called on the Government of RS not to organise a referendum", and a few days later, the Constitutional Court of BiH officially announced that the objection of the Parliamentary Assembly of the RS had not been accepted and that the RS referendum on this issue was unconstitutional (Radio Free Europe, 2016). This did not bother the political elite in the RS led by Dodik given that 1 week before the referendum on RS Day he had met with Vladimir Putin and Aleksandar Vučić, where he not only sent signals of independence to the social environment of RS (by conducting its own foreign policy), but also continued with the referendum agenda, which had lasted since 2008, with which it de facto does not recognise the central government of BiH. "Performing Statehood", as Björkdahl (2018, 37–39) lucidly argues, saw its epilogue on 25 September 2016 when 55.7% of all eligible voters voted 99.81% in favour of making 9 January the day of RS (RTV BN, 2016). Finally, it should be mentioned that the EU's reaction to the referendum initiative of RS remained on the level of declaratory statements, as it merely warned the political leadership of RS that "such a referendum would seriously challenge the cohesion, territorial integrity and sovereignty of BiH" and that it "undermines all the efforts made in the direction of improving the socio-economic situation in BiH and the European integration of BiH" (Džihić & Wieser, 2008; Rettman, 2016).

3.5   HISTORY IN THE SERVICE OF RECREATING ETHNIC EXCLUSIVISM—AN ATTEMPT TO (RE)CREATE BOSNIAN SERB ETHNIC IDENTITY AND/OR THE ONTOLOGICAL SECURITY OF REPUBLIKA SRPSKA?

The history of the social and material environment of BiH is one of mutual coexistence and also an opportunity for selective remembering and the (re)creation of (at least three) metanarratives by the political elite of the three ethnic groups. While at some stage before the First World War, the material and social environment of today's BiH was based on a relatively high level of tolerance, this changed radically and irreversibly, especially during the Second World War when mass conversions, expulsions and ethnic cleansing led to the rise of the destructive logic of ethnic exclusivism. The identities of (Bosnian) Serbs, (Bosnian) Croats and Bosniaks (also South Slavic Muslims/Bosnian Herzegovinian Muslims/Muslims/Muslims), which were 'imagined' mostly on a religious-cultural basis, therefore only began to gain ground in the period after the First World War.

The most important moment—beyond the initial 'innocent' myths about Rastko and the Vidovdan myth—for understanding (Bosnian) Serb political thinking was certainly the period following the First World War when the myth about 'Serbs as saviours' and the 'creators of Yugoslavia' began to be created, which paved the way for Yugoslav integrism, which was supposed to (finally) resolve the Serbian question. Namely, Yugoslav integrism, even at the expense of Garašanin's Načertanije, became ever more synonymous with the Greater Serbian hegemony, which relatively quickly, even before the Second World War, found its (Croatian) opposite in the Ustasha movement. But violence begets violence, which is why the Ustasha movement developed its own enemy, the Chetniks. From this point on, it became clear that the Second World War, which strong featured BiH, would be used to solve the 'Serbian problem', the 'Croatian problem' and the 'Bosniak/BiH Muslim problem'. The ethnic cleansing, expulsions and violent (religious) conversions that took place in the area, which Velikonja (1998, 342) calls a place of "maximum diversity in a minimal space", overshadowed the national liberation struggle of the partisans under the leadership of Josip Broz Tito. With this victory, which practically suppressed the suffering of the population during the Second World War by recreating the myth of "brotherhood and unity", at the same time opened a window of opportunity to strengthen the counter-narratives that were mainly instrumentalised in the last war. Serbian political thought which, even during the Second World War, was looking for a basis to justify the "Serbian national awakening" under the new socialist rule through the myth of Kosovo and peasant uprisings, soon began to frame the victory of the Partisans as a 'Serbian victory' and the path to 'Serbian unity'. Probably the most lucid example of the logic of stealth by the ethnonational political elite—especially in the last war in BiH and after the war—is the selective remembrance of Draža Mihailović as being anti-fascist.

The era of socialist Yugoslavia, marked by the cult of Josip Broz Tito and the mythology of the national liberation struggle, played a big role in the construction of ethnic identities in BiH. This was because the development of Yugoslav political thought led to the preservation and development of exclusivist identities, primarily through religious institutions, which otherwise were legally 'cut off' from the Yugoslav public space. This was most visible after the death of Josip Broz Tito, which opened Pandora's box of the uneven development of the Yugoslav republics, a major economic crisis, and the sporadic relativisation of the Yugoslav regime in the absence of a strong leader. Thus, for example, the Bosnian Croats and Muslims (Bosniaks) started the process of 'de-romanticising' the common life during socialist Yugoslavia with the apparition of the Virgin Mary in Medjugorje and the trial of Izetbegović because of the Islamic Declaration. Yet all of this was, when seen through an ethnopolitical lens—except for the assassination in Marseille—quite benign compared to the SANU memorandum that openly started a policy of exclusion, accusation and consolidation of the narrative of 'victim' and the fragmentation of the Serbian nation. The memorandum was later institutionalised in the official national(ist) policy of Slobodan Milošević, which had a permanent impact on the political landscape in BiH. Having initially functioned in Bosnian Serb circles as a reference point for framing Muslims as an internal Other (the Muslim threat), this soon also became important for framing another internal Other: the Bosnian Croats. The antipode to the national(ist) politician Milošević, who was portrayed by Franjo

Tuđman and who started the process of imagining the Croatian identity, only further dismantled the concept of coexistence in BiH, which was becoming more and more ethnicised.

Ethnically motivated incidents in the 1990s and the creation by the new ethno-political elite in BiH of a narrative about a 45-year period of relative peace in the common Yugoslav space being an 'illusion' led to a new dark period in the country's history. This period, when it comes to the attempt to build a Bosnian Serb ethnic identity by the ethno-political elite of the Bosnian Serbs, began with the creation of a divide between 'real' and 'false' (Bosnian) Serbs. Another important moment for the further consolidation of ethno-political exclusivism was the convincing victory of three ethno-political parties at the first multi-party elections with which, on one hand, BiH's political arena started to become a place of banal nationalism (asphalt roads, ownership, flat tyres, etc.), and on the other hand, it became a space of completely concrete policies of ethnic engineering via 'regionalisation' of the Bosnian Serb space. The delegitimisation and relativisation of BiH's spirit of coexistence, which then drove the process of imagining the ethnopolitical imaginary of SDS, brought a reaction from the Bosnian Croat and Bosniak ethnopolitical elite. With the adoption of the Memorandum on the Sovereignty of BiH, they paved the way for establishing RS, which, through the process of uniting municipalities with a majority Bosnian Serb population, made it clear that the goal was to remain in socialist Yugoslavia, which at the time was facing a growing crisis. The failed Carrington-Cutileiro plan led to BiH's independence referendum, which led to a bloody 3-year war that displaced nearly 2.2 million people and killed around 100,000.

The Bosnian War, marked by the policy of ethnic engineering, ethnic cleansing and the genocide in Srebrenica, was significantly shaped by the Second World War in social and material terms. Imagining and finding parallels between fascist movements, such as the Ustashe, Chetniks and Handžar division, held such ideological potential that the incitement and incitement by the ethno-political elites went practically without any serious opposition. The war in question was largely important because of the (violent) change in the material environment which, along with the logic of destroying cultural/religious and other objects, forced displacement, and changed the names of cities and streets, aimed to destroy all evidence of the existence of the Other. In this way, the ethnopolitical elite strove to strengthen the ontological security of their own (proto)political entity and, consequently, the population in this social and material environment. The end of the Bosnian war, which was extremely complex and far from unambiguous in terms of pacts and cooperation, was chiefly ensured by the international community, which in a few months achieved the cessation of hostilities before the DPA was signed and thus outlined the post-war arrangement of Bosnia and Herzegovina. BiH, which became a decentralised consociational federation and relatively weak relative to the two autonomous subnational political entities (RS and FBiH), soon became 'hostage' to its own constitution. The post-war material and social environment of the RS, which in an ideological sense was largely built on resistance to socialist Yugoslavia or its policy of not confronting the difficult legacy of the Second World War, became a space for imagining statehood on the part of the Bosnian Serb ethno-political elite. In many ways, this is based on Serbian political thinking, yet in the early years, it started with a policy of invasive intervention in the material environment with the aim of creating a metanarrative about the past war as a civil war, or a war 'in defence of the fatherland'. In this context, the presence of the EU, which can roughly be divided into three periods, was made difficult. Namely, the EU worked primarily to change the constitution, centralise and strengthen the central government of BiH, with a view to reducing friction among the three ethnic groups. While it was able to do this up until around 2006, the period thereafter, due to the emergence of new and much less predictable ethno-political parties, practically returned the social environment of BiH to the pre-war period. The RS' policy of resistance to the OHR, the 'Srebrenisation of BiH', the manipulation of historical facts and events during the war, the construction of new monuments that exclusively commemorate the previous war, and the increasingly open 'hostility' between the official Banjaluka and Sarajevo had an irreversible impact on the process of 'implementing the statehood of RS'. The latter only strengthened after 2010—among others in the period after the failed Prud and Butmir processes—when Milorad Dodik convincingly won the general election, and merely deepened the metanarrative promoted by SDS in RS from 1996 onwards.

Thus, the commemoration of the genocide against (Bosnian) Serbs during the Second World War was mainly joined by the creation of counter-narratives concerning the last Bosnian war when central BiH institutions—especially the judiciary—became 'anti-Serbian'. In this way, Milorad Dodik achieved the next step in strengthening the ontological security of RS which therefore—by (re)creating a metanarrative about the social and material environment of the RS—began to significantly build on a clear difference between Serbia and an independent political imaginary, namely with the referendum agendas. Finally, the agenda in question, which was essentially aimed at building an (imagined) special Bosnian Serb ethnic identity, reached its epilogue in 2016 when RS held a referendum on celebrating 9 January as the Day of RS. In so doing, a new element of the social environment of RS was introduced into the modern metanarrative, which the ethno-political elite in RS successfully built and promoted by way of securitisation of the internal other (BiH institutions 'led by the FBiH elite'). This served as resistance against any changes that the international community and especially the EU were striving for. The concept of 'European (non)standard' became extremely important, for instance, during the unconstitutionality of the Act on Holidays of RS, the Police Mission, and the proposed amendments to the DPA. This also explains why in the following chapter there is a need to analyse the attitude of the Bosnian Serbs—who at the last elections voted for the ethnopolitical imaginary created by SNSD and SDS—towards the EU, their perception of the EU, and the EU's role in the post-war governance of BiH (Table 3.1).

Table 3.1 "Roadmap" of the social and material environment and the elements of imagining the (Bosnian) Serb ethnic identity from the sixth century until today

	Sixth century until 1945	1945–1990	1990–1995	From 1995 onwards
Social environment	1180–1204—The reign of Ban Kulin	1945–1980—Mythology of national liberation struggle	1990—SDA, SDS and HDZ BiH victory on first multiparty elections	1995—DPA and the creation of RS
	1219—The cult of Rastko/Sava and autocephality of SOC	1945–1980—The cult of Josip Broz Tito	1990 onwards—Attempt to erase common history, relativisation of neighbourliness	From 1995 onwards—Ethnic veto
	1326—Kotromanić dynasty	1966–1971—Croatian spring		From 1995 onwards—Construction of more than 2000 objects, which consolidate (Bosnian) Serb identity (churches, monuments of Mihalović and Princip)
	1353—Stefan Tvrtko I.	1970—Islamic declaration		
	1389—Vidovdan myth	1974—New (Yugoslav) constitution		
	1593—"Saint Sava rebellion"/SOC losing all of the privileges	1980—The death of Josip Broz Tito	1991—Idea of establishing three TV channels	1996—Another win of SDS, SDA and HDZ BiH
	1829—Edirne Peace Agreement	1986—SANU memorandum	1991—Declaration on the BiH's independence	From 1996 onwards—OHR and EU conditionality
	1829—Garašanin and Načertanije	1986—The rise of Milošević	1991—Karadjordjevo Agreement	From 1996 onwards—Political blockades and radicalization of the political parties
	1852–1862—Rebellion of non-Muslim peasantry	1987—Corruption scandal in Agrokomerc	1992—Referendum	
	1878—Annexation of BiH	From 1987 onwards—Relativisation of the Yugoslav regime and 'brotherhood and unity'	1992–95—Bosnian War	1998—Start of trials in front of the ICTY
	1896—The movement of Serbian intellectuals	1988—Anti-bureaucratic revolution	1995—Genocide in Srebrenica	From 2006 onwards—"Srebrenization of BiH"
	1908—The end of the 'dreams of the Greater Serbia'	1989—Establishment of HDZ	1995—First ICTY indictments	
	1914—Young Bosnia, Princip and 'Serbia as a Balkan Piedmont'	1990—Establishment of SDA, SDS and HDZ BiH	1995—Bosnian Serbs as 'winners'	
	From 1914 onwards—'Serbs as saviours'	1990—Life in SFRY as an 'illusion'		
	1929—Yugoslav integrism	1990—Supporters of SFRY becoming 'Islamised Serbs'		
	1933—Ante Pavelić and Ustashe	1990—Ethnically motivated incidents		
	1941—NDH and crimes against (Bosnian) Serbs			
	1912–1945—Josip Broz Tito and the Partisans			
	1945—The unity of Serbs as 'false unity'; the goal is federalization			

(continued)

Table 3.1 (continued)

	Sixth century until 1945	*1945–1990*	*1990–1995*	*From 1995 onwards*
Material environment	Start of the sixteenth century—Ottoman Empire and 'Islamisation' 1557—Mehmed Paša Sokolović and the restoration of the patriarchate of Peć 1844—Načrtanje and the idea of homogenization of Serbian space 1912–1913—Serbian occupation of Kosovo 1942–1945—Jasenovac and Drakulići	1945 onwards—Construction of 'Yugoslav' monuments 1948—Factories, urbanisation, and industrialisation as a space for inter-ethnic collaboration	From 1990 onwards—Local self-governance premised on 'ethnic key' From 1991 onwards—Renaming streets, cities and schools From 1991 onwards—Ethnic homogenization	From 2006 onwards—Construction of monuments that commemorate the Bosnian War From 2006 onwards—Non-restoration of demolished buildings that symbolise the presence of the Other /
(Bosnian) Serb ethnic identity	Ninth century—Christianisation 1054—the great schism 1180–1204—Bogomilstvo (godliness) 1189—Ban Kulin's letter 'in Bosnian language' 1430—Heresy and new wave of re-Catholisation 1850—Conservative Bosnian elite against the reforms Nineteenth century—Millet system Nineteenth century—The process of equating the Orthodox faith with Serbia 1882—Benjamin Kallay and Bosnian identity 1929 onwards—'Muslims as Asians and parasites'	1945 onwards—Secularisation 1945 onwards—Integral/organic model of Yugoslavia 1974—Muslims as a nation; the narrative on the 'fragmentation of the Serbian nation' 1984—"Muslims as ethnic Serbs and Croats"	1991— Underrepresentation of Bosnian Serbs and the question of the Cyrillic in BiH 1991—Muslims as a threat, Izetbegović as a "Serbophobe" 1992—"Interreligious war is imminent"	

References

Aleksov, B. (2014). Forgotten Yugoslavism and anti-clericalism of young Bosnians. *Prilozi, 43*, 79–87.

Anđelić, N. (2003). *Bosnia-Herzegovina: The end of a legacy.* Frank Cass Publishers.

Andrić, I. (1980). *Most na Drini.* Mladinska knjiga.

Anzulović, B. (1999). *Heavenly Serbia: From myth to genocide.* New York University Press.

Arslanagić, S. (2010, December 3). Dodik Again Denies Srebrenica Genocide. *Balkan Insight.* Available at https://balkaninsight.com/2010/12/03/dodik-slams-international-community-for-referring-to-srebrenica-massacre-as-genocide/

ATV. (2020, February 2). *Ustaški zločin u Drakuliću se pamti: Srbe ubijali bez ijednog ispaljenog metka.* Available at https://www.atvbl.com/vijesti/drustvo/ustaski-zlocin-u-drakulicu-se-pamti-srbe-ubijali-bez-ijednog-ispaljenog-metka-2-2

Aybet, G., & Bibeber, F. (2011). From Dayton to Brussels: The Impact of EU and NATO Conditionality on State Building in Bosnia & Herzegovina. *Europe-Asia Studies, 63*(10), 1911–1937.

Banac, I. (1988). *The National Question in Yugoslavia: Origins, History, Politics.* Ithaca: Cornell University Press.

Banac, I. (1996). Bosnian Muslims: From religious community to socialist nationhood and postcommunist statehood, 1918–1992. In M. Pinson (Ed.), *The Muslim of Bosnia-Herzegovina: The historic development from the middle ages to the dissolution of Yugoslavia* (pp. 129–153). Harvard University Press.

Banović, D., & Gavrić, S. (2010). Ustavna reforma u Bosni i Hercegovini. *Politička misao: časopis za politologiju, 47*(2), 159–180.

Bassuener, K., & Weber, B. (2012). *Croatian and Serbian policy in Bosnia-Herzegovina: Help of Hindrance* (DPC policy study). Democratization Policy Council. Available at http://www.democratizationpolicy.org/pdf/dpc_neighbors_study_final.pdf

Basta, K. (2016). Imagined institutions: The symbolic power of formal rules in Bosnia and Herzegovina. *Slavic Review, 75*(4), 944–969.

Bataković, D. (1996). *Prelude to Sarajevo: The Serbian Question in Bosnia and Herzegovina 1878–1914.* Institute for Balkan Studies. Available at https://www.balcanica.rs/balcanica/uploaded/balcanica/balcanica27/06%20D%20Batakov ic.pdf

Bataković, D. (n.d.). *The Balkan Piedmont – Serbia and the Yugoslav question.* Available at https://www.academia.edu/2537078/The_Balkan_Piedmont_Serbia_and_Yugoslav_Question

Becherelli, A. (2015). Remembering Gavrilo princip. In A. Biagini & G. Motta (Eds.), *The First World War: Analysis and interpretation* (pp. 17–33). Cambridge Scholars Publishing.

Bečirević, E. (2006). *Bosnia's "Accidental" Genocide*. Global Voices Balkans. Available at https://iwpr.net/global-voices/bosnias-accidental-genocide

Begenišić, L. (2019, 9 September), Prisvajaju povelju Kulina Bana: Dragulj srpske pismenosti proglašavanju za temelj Bosne, Novosti. Available at https://www.novosti.rs/vesti/naslovna/drustvo/aktuelno.290.html:817134-PRISVAJAJU-POVELjU-KULINA-BANA-Dragulj-srpske-pismenosti-proglasavaju-za-temelj-Bosne

Bergholz, M. (2013). Sudden nationhood: The microdynamics of intercommunal relations in Bosnia-Herzegovina after World War II. *The American Historical Review, 118*(3), 679–707.

Bethlehem, D., & Weller, M., Eds. (1997). *The Yugoslav Crisis in International Law*. Cambridge: Cambridge University Press.

Bieber, F. (2006). *Post-War Bosnia: Ethnicity, inequality and public sector governance*. Palgrave Macmillan.

Bieber, F. (2010). *Constitutional reform in Bosnia and Herzegovina: Preparing for EU accession* (Policy Brief, 1). European Policy Centre. Available at https://www.files.ethz.ch/isn/115432/PB_04_10_Bosnia.pdf

Biermann, R. (2014). Coercive Europeanization: The EU's struggle to contain secessionism in the Balkans. *European Security, 23*(4), 484–508.

Bildt, C. (1998). *Peace journey: The struggle for peace in Bosnia*. Weidenfeld and Nicolson.

Biserko, S. (Ed.). (2006). *Bosna i Hercegovina – Jezgro velikosrpskog projekta*. Helsinški odbor za človekove pravice. Available at https://yuhistorija.com/serbian/doc/Bosna%20i%20Hercegovina%20-%20Jezgro%20velikosrpskog%20projekta.pdf

Björkdahl, A. (2018). Republika Srpska: Imaginary, performance and spatialization. *Political Geography, 66*(1), 34–43.

Björkdahl, A., & Kappler, S. (2017). *Peacebuilding and spatial transformation: Peace, space and place*. Routledge.

Borić, F. (2010). Bošnjaci u Saboru: Odiseja 2010. *STATUS: Magazin za političku kulturu i društvena pitanja, 14*, 56–62.

Bougarel, X. (1996). Bosnia and Herzegovina – State and communitarianism. In D. A. Dyker & I. Vejvoda (Eds.), *Yugoslavia and after – A study in fragmentation, despair and rebirth* (pp. 87–115). Longman Publishing.

Bringa, T. R. (1995). *Being Muslim the Bosnian way: Identity and Community in a Central Bosnian Village*. Princeton University Press.

Burg, S. L., & Shoup, P. S. (1999). *The War in Bosnia-Herzegovina: Ethnic conflict and international intervention*. Armonk.

Carmichael, C. (2015). *A concise history of Bosnia*. Cambridge University Press.

Cigar, N. (2000). *Uloga srpskih orijentalista u opravdanju genocida nad muslimanima Balkana.* Institute for researching crimes against humanity. Available at http://www.institut-genocid.unsa.ba/userfiles/file/Cigar%20Dio%20 1(1).pdf

Clark, J. N. (2012). Fieldwork and its ethical challenges: Reflections from research in Bosnia. *Human Rights Quarterly, 34*(3), 823–839.

Ćorović, V. (2001). *Istorija srpskog naroda.* Ganus. Available at http://www.rastko.rs/rastko-bl/istorija/corovic/istorija/index.html

Council of the EU. (1995). *Conclusions of the Council on Former Yugoslavia.* Available at https://www.cvce.eu/content/publication/1997/10/13/ 98e4b1f7-d93a-4a23-9dd2-2b2ec702e687/publishable_en.pdf

Council of the EU. (1998). Joint action of 2 February 1998 (98/117/CFSP).

European Council. (1998). Compliance with the conditions in the council conclusions of 29 April 1997. Operational Conclusions. Brussels, COM (98) 237.

Daadler, I. H. (2000). *Getting to Dayton: The making of America's Bosnia policy.* Brookings Institution Press.

Dizdarević, R. (1999). *Od smrti Tita do smrti Jugoslavije: svjedočenja.* OKO.

Dnevnik. (2011, October 23). Biljana Plavšić: Od heroja Ratka Mladića pričakujem, da prevzame krivdo nase. *Dnevnik.* Available at https://www.dnevnik. si/1042455811

Donia, R., & Fine, J. (1994). *Bosnia and Herzegovina: A tradition betrayed.* Columbia University Press.

Đukić, S. (2001). Lovljenje vetra. *Časopis za suvremenu povijest, 38*(3), 1150–1152.

Džihić, V., & Wieser, A. (2008). The crisis of expectations – Europeanisation as "acquis démocratique" and its limits. The case of Bosnia–Herzegovina and Serbia. *L'Europe en Formation, 349–350*(3/4), 81–98.

Ekmečić, M. (1982). *Ustanak u Hercegovini i istorijske pouke.* Available at http:// iis.unsa.ba/wp-content/uploads/2019/09/19-Prilozi-Članak-Milorad-Ekmečić.pdf

Europa Publications. (2003). *The Europa world year book 2003.* Taylor and Francis.

European Commission. (2002). *Bosnia and Herzegovina. Stabilisation and association report, SEC 202/340.* Available at https://www.europarl.europa.eu/ sides/getDoc.do?pubRef=-//EP//TEXT+REPORT+A5-2002-0338+0+DO C+XML+V0//EN&language=EN

European Commission. (2003). *Stabilization and association report* (Second yearly report). Available at https://eur-lex.europa.eu/LexUriServ/LexUriServ.do?u ri=COM%3A2003%3A0139%3AFIN%3AE N%3APDF

European Commission. (2005). *Report on yearly progress of BiH, 561.* Available at https://op.europa.eu/en/publication-detail/-/publication/07107c89-75ad-4a96-91f3-4b9a5d36a165/language-en

European Commission. (2013). Report on Bosnia and Herzegovina, 415, 16 October. Available at https://ec.europa.eu/neighbourhoodenlargement/ sites/near/files/pdf/key_documents/2013/package/ba_rapport_2013.pdf

European Council. (1995). *Guidelines for former Yugoslavia*. Dostopno prek. https://www.cvce.eu/content/publication/1997/10/13/98e4b1f7-d93a-4a23-9dd2-2b2ec702e687/publishable_en.pdf

Feldman, D. (2005). Renaming cities in Bosnia and Herzegovina. *International Journal of Constitutional Law*, *3*(4), 649–662.

Feldman, A. (2017). Kállay's dilemma: On the challenge of creating a manageable identity in Bosnia and Herzegovina (1992–1903). *Review of Croatian History*, *13*(1), 103–117.

Filipović, M. (1997). *Bosna i Hercegovina – najvažnije geografske, demografske, historijske, kulturne i političke činjenice*. Publishing House Sarajevo.

Flügger, M. (2002). Civil implementation of a peace agreement: Inside the office of the high representative in Sarajevo. In R. Biermann (Ed.), *German conflict resolution in the Balkans* (pp. 195–212). Nomos.

Friedman, F. (1996). *Francine Friedman, The Bosnian Muslims: Denial of a Nation*. Boulder: Westview Press.

Gagnon, V. P. (2006). *The myth of ethnic War: Serbia and Croatia in the 1990s*. Cornell University Press.

Gallup Balkan Monitor. (2009). *Perception of the EU in the Western Balkans*. Available at http://wbc-inco.net/object/document/7242/attach/Gallup_Balkan_Monitor-Focus_On_EU_Perceptions.pdf

Gašić, R. (2015). Struggling with Yugoslavism in the first Yugoslavia: The Belgrade elite and the public debate. *East Central Europe*, *42*(1), 29–47.

Gow, J. (1997). *Triumph of the lack of will: International diplomacy and the Yugoslav War*. Hurst and Co.

Greenwood, D., & Hartog, M. (2005). Bosnia and Herzegovina. In D. Greenwod (ur.), *The Western Balkan candidates for NATO membership and partnership* (pp. 77–84). Groningen: Centre for European Security Studies. Available at https://ciaotest.cc.columbia.edu/wps/cess/0018167/f_0018167_15581.pdf

Gromes, T. (2008). *Common democracy, divided society: The impossibility to implement a peace strategy for Bosnia and Herzegovina* (HSFK, 9). Hessische Stiftung Friedens.

Hajdarpašić, E. (2010). But my memory betrays me: National master narratives and the ambiguities of history in Bosnia and Herzegovina. In W. Petrisch & V. Džihić (Eds.), *Conflict and memory: Bridging past and future in (South East) Europe* (pp. 201–215). Nomos.

Halimović, D., & Jelin–Dizdar, T. (2009, March 31). *Mostarski sastanak, prudski sporazum i Dodik*. Radio Free Europe. Available at https://www.slobodnaevropa.org/a/dodik/1565408.html

Hoare, M. A. (2013). *The Bosnian Muslims in the Second World War: A history*. Hurst & Co.

Holbrooke, R. (1998). *To end a war*. Random House.

Human Rights Watch. (2000). *Unfinished business: The return of refugees and displaced persons to Bijeljina*. Available at https://www.hrw.org/reports/2000/bosnia/BOSN005.pdf
ICTY. (2001, February 26). *Prosecutor v. Dario Kordic and Mario Cerkez (Trial judgement)*. IT-95-14/2-T.
ICTY. (2006, September 27). *Prosecutor v. Momčilo Krajišnik (Trial judgement)*. IT-00-39-T. ICTY.
Imamović, M. (1997). *Bosnia and Herzegovina: Evolution of its political and legal institutions*. Sarajevo: Magistrat.
Imamović, M. (2006). *Bosnia and Herzegovina: Evolution of its political and legal institutions*. Magistrat.
International Crisis Group (ICG). (2011). *Bosnia: Europe's time to act* Briefing, 59). The International Crisis Group. Available at https://www.crisisgroup.org/europe-central-asia/balkans/bosnia-and-herzegovina/bosnia-europe-s-time-act
Irwin, R. (2011, 17 June). Court Told of Serb Crisis Staff Role. Global Voices. Available at https://iwpr.net/globalvoices/court-told-serb-crisis-staff-role
Jerotijević, D., Bogavac, Ž., & Stamatović, L. (2020). Customs war of the Kingdom of Serbia and the Habzburg Monarchy at the beginning of the 20th century. *Ekonomika, 66*(4), 95–103.
Juncos, A. (2011). Europeanization by decree? The case of police reform in Bosnia. *Journal of Common Market Studies, 49*(2), 367–389.
Juncos, A. (2013). *EU foreign and security policy in Bosnia: The politics of coherence and effectiveness*. Manchester University Press.
Kalik, M. (2018). *Revolucionarne ideje i duh Mlade Bosne (Veliki rat 1914–1918)*. Faculty for media and culture. Available at https://www.researchgate.net/publication/329649128_Mario_Kalik_-_Revolucionarne_ideje_i_duh_Mlade_Bosne_Veliki_rat_1914-1918_2016
Kamberović, H. (2011). *Hod po trnju: Iz bosanskohercegovačke historije 20. stoljeća*. Institute for history. Available at https://www.researchgate.net/publication/280039656_Hod_po_trnju_Iz_bosanskohercego   vacke_historije_20_stoljeca
Karabegović, D. (2012, 4 April). Sjećanje na zločine u Bijeljini. Radio Svobodna Evropa. Available at https://www.slobodnaevropa.org/a/sjecanje_na_zlocine_u_bijeljini/24537462.html
Kivimäki, T., Kramer, M., & Pasch, P. (2012). *Dinamika konflikta u multietničkoj državi Bosni i Hercegovini*. Friedrich Ebert Stiftung.
Lampe, J. R. (1996). *Yugoslavia as History*. Cambridge University Press.
LeBor, A. (2006). *Complicity with Evil: The United Nations in the Age of Modern Genocide*. Yale: Yale University Press.
Lorenčič, A. (2010). Gospodarske razmere v Jugoslaviji v obdobju 1968–1988: na poti v razpad. In V. Z. Čepič (ur.), *Slovenija – Jugoslavija, krize in reforme*

1968/1988 (str. 261–279). Institute for Contemporary History. Available at https://www.sistory.si/publikacije/prenos/?urn=SISTORY:ID:15562

Lovrenović, I. (2015). *Kulturni identitet(i) Bosne i Hercegovine.* Available at http://ivanlovrenovic.com/public/clanci/bosna-argentina/kulturni-identiteti-bosne-i-hercegovine

Maček, I. (2009). *Sarajevo under siege: Anthropology in wartime.* University of Pennsylvania Press.

Macqueen, A., & Mitchell, P. (1995). The death of Yugoslavia. *BBC.* Available at https://www.youtube.com/watch?v=DdS9M7oSVOg

Madžar, B. (1982). Pokret Srba Bosne i Hercegovine za vjersko-prosvjetnu autonomiju. Sarajevo: Veslein Masleša.

Majstorović, D., & Vučkovac, Z. (2016). Rethinking Bosnia and Herzegovina's post-coloniality challenges of Europeanization discourse. *Journal of Language and Politics, 15*(2), 147–172.

Majstorović, D., Vučkovac, Z., & Pepić, Z. (2015). From Dayton to Brussels via Tuzla: Post-2014 economic restructuring as europeanization discourse/practice in Bosnia and Herzegovina. *Southeast European and Black Sea Studies, 15*(4), 661–682.

Maksić, A. (2017). *Ethnic mobilization, violence, and the politics of affect: The Serb democratic party and the Bosnian war.* Palgrave Macmillan.

Malcolm, N. (1996). *Bosnia: A short history.* Papermac.

Malešević, S. (2017). The mirage of Balkan Piedmont: State formation and Serbian nationalisms in the nineteenth and early twentieth centuries. *Nations and Nationalism, 23*(1), 129–150.

Mannergren Selimović, J. (2013). Making peace, making memory: Peacebuilding and politics of remembrance at memorials of mass atrocities. *Peacebuilding, 3*(1), 334–348.

McMahon, P. C., & Western, J. (2009). The death of Dayton: How to stop Bosnia from falling apart. *Foreign Affairs, 88*(5), 69–83.

Miljanović, M. (1991, 5 January). Ko i kako zastupa Srbe. *Javnost.*

Morrison, K. (2009). *Dayton, divisions and constitutional revisions: Bosnia & Herzegovina at the crossroads.* Defence Academy of the United Kingdom. Available at https://www.files.ethz.ch/isn/105340/2009_08_Dayton.pdf

Muehlmann, T. (2008). Police Restructuring in Bosnia-Herzegovina: Problems of internationally-led sector reform. *Journal of Intervention and Statebuilding, 2*(1), 1–22.

Noutcheva, G. (2012). *European foreign policy and the challenges of Balkan accession.* Routledge.

Obradović, A., & Čilić, U. (2020, January 9). *Dan RS: 28 godina neustavnog praznika.* Radio Svobodna Evropa. Available at https://www.slobodnaevropa.org/a/30366683.html

Okey, R. (2009). *The Habsburg 'civilizing Mission' in Bosnia, 1878–1914.* Oxford University Press.

Parish, M. (2010). Paradigms of state-building: Comparing Bosnia and Kosovo. *Journal of Eurasian Law, 3*(3), 1–33.

Pellet, A. (1992). *The opinions of the Badinter arbitration committee: A second breath for the self-determination of peoples.* Available at https://web.archive. org/web/20110529223410/, https://207.57.19.226/journal/Vol3/No1/art12-13.pdf

Perry, V. (2015). Constitutional Reform in Bosnia and Herzegovina: Does the Road to Confederation go through the EU? *International Peacekeeping, 22*(5), 490–510.

Pirjevec, J. (1995). *Nastanek, razvoj ter razpad Karadjodjevićeve in Titove Jugoslavije.* Lipa.

Popov-Momčinović, Z. (2012). Parlamentarne političke stranke u BiH. In S. Gavrić & D. Banović (Eds.), *Parlamentarizam u Bosni i Hercegovini* (pp. 251–293). Friedrich Ebert Stiftung.

Prometheus. (2013). *Pojedinačan popis broja ratnih žrtava u svim općinama BiH.* Available at http://www.prometej.ba/clanak/drustvo-i-znanost/pojedinacan-popis-broja-ratnih-zrtava-u-svim-opcinama-bih-997

Puljek-Shank, R., & Fritsch, F. (2018). Activism in Bosnia-Herzegovina: Struggles against dual hegemony and the emergence of "Local First". *East European Politics and Societies: and Cultures, 33*(1), 135–156.

Radio Free Europe. (2010). *Strani mudžahedini i Armija Bosne i Hercegovine.* Available at https://docs.rferl.org/sh-SH/specials/al_kaida/05_strani_mudzahedini_i_armija_bosne_i_hercegovine.htm

Radio Free Europe. (2016). *Ustavni sud BiH: Odbijena apelacija Narodne skupštine RS, 9. januar neustavan.* Available at https://www.slobodnaevropa.org/a/27997304.html

Radušić, E. (n.d.). Pitanje ustanka 1875 – 1878. u bosanskohercegovačkoj historiografiji: između historijske istine i multiperspektivnosti. *ANUBiH, 47*(1), 99–130.

Ramet, S. P. (2005). *Thinking about Yugoslavia: Scholarly debates about the Yugoslav breakup and the Wars in Bosnia and Kosovo.* Cambridge University Press.

Rašidagić, E. K. (2006). *Politics in Bosnia and Herzegovina.* Available at https://d1wqtxts1xzle7.cloudfront.net/30468900/Politics_in_Bosnia_and_Herzegovina.pdf?1358867912=&response-content-disposition=inline

Redžić, E. (2005). *Bosnia and Herzegovina in the Second World War.* Routledge.

Rettman, A. (2016, September 21). *Bosnia referendum makes mockery of EU step.* EUObserver. Available at https://euobserver.com/foreign/135176

Reuters. (2010, April 21). *Envoy slams Bosnia Serbs for questioning Srebrenica.* Available at https://www.reuters.com/article/idUSLDE63K0E2

Richter. (2008). Ende einer Odyssee in Bosnien-Herzegowina. SWP-Aktuell no. 41. Berlin: Stiftung Wissenschaft und pokitik.

RTRS. (2012, May 9). *Antifašističke vrijednosti utkane u Srpsku*. RTRS. Available at https://lat.rtrs.tv/vijesti/vijest.php?id=61194

RTV BN. (2016, September 26). *Na referendumu glasalo 55,7% gradana*. RTV BN. Available at https://www.rtvbn.com/3834595/na-referendumu-glasalo-557-gradjana

Sadović, M. (2011, April 1). *The trials of Bosnia's war crimes court*. Global Voices Balkans. Available at https://iwpr.net/global-voices/trials-bosnias-war-crimes-court

Samarčić, R. (1971). *Mehmed Sokolović*. Srpska književna zadruga.

Stjepanović, N. (2015, December 24). *(Nad)realna slika ratne Banjaluke*. Peščanik. Available at https://pescanik.net/nadrealna-slika-ratne-banja-luke/

Szewczyk, B. M. J. (2010). *The EU in Bosnia and Herzegovina: Powers, decisions and legitimacy* (Occasional Paper, 83). EU Institute for Security Studies. Available at https://www.iss.europa.eu/sites/default/files/EUISSFiles/Occ83.pdf

Toal, G. (2013). "Republika Srpska will have a referendum": The rhetorical politics of Milorad Dodik. *Nationalities Papers, 41*(1), 166–204.

Troch, P. (2010). Yugoslavism between the world wars: Indecisive nation building. *Nationalities Papers, 38*(2), 227–244.

United States Holocaust Memorial Museum. (2020). *Jasenovac*. Available at https://encyclopedia.ushmm.org/content/en/article/jasenovac

Vauhnik, V. (1972). *Nevidna fronta*. ČGP Delo.

Velikonja, M. (1998). *Bosanski religijski mozaiki*. Sophia.

Velikonja, M. (2003). *Religious separation and political intolerance in Bosnia-Herzegovina*. Texas A&M University Press.

Velikonja, M. (1997). *Bosanski religijski mozaiki*. Ljubljana: Sophia.

Žanić, I. (2007). *Flag on the mountain: A political anthropology of war in Croatia and Bosnia*. Saqi Books.

Zdeb, A. (2017). Prud and Butmir processes in Bosnia and Herzegovina: Intra-ethnic competition from the perspective of game theory. *Ethnopolitics, 16*(4), 369–387.

CHAPTER 4

Discourse Analysis of Securitisation Acts of the Political Elite in Republika Srpska

The following chapter consists of three parts that refer to the identified critical junctures. They are analysed through qualitative and quantitative discourse and content analysis ($N = 4133$). In the first section, I offer qualitative and quantitative analysis of the discourse during the period of negotiations on signing the Stabilisation and Association Agreement (2005–2007). The second section focuses on analysis of the Prud and Butmir processes (2009–2010), while the third section presents discourse and content analysis for the period between 2015 and 2016 when the political elite in RS announced and held an (unconstitutional) referendum on the Day of RS. In this way, the chapter intends to understand how the Europeanisation process was unfolding at the critical junctures and whether the domestic political elite framed it as a source of ontological insecurity.

© The Author(s), under exclusive license to Springer Nature
Switzerland AG 2023
F. Kočan, *Identity, Ontological Security and Europeanisation
in Republika Srpska*, Central and Eastern European Perspectives
on International Relations,
https://doi.org/10.1007/978-3-031-46169-9_4

4.1   Discourse Analysis of Media Reports in the Negotiating Period for Signing the Stabilisation and Association Agreement (2005–2007)

In the first part, I analyse the discourse during the negotiations to sign the Stabilisation and Association Agreement (SAA) of BiH between 2005 and 2007. The SAA constitutes the EU's most important framework for realising the potential of EU membership and may thus be roughly seen as generally reflecting the 'general progress' made by a candidate country on its way to EU membership.

Quantitative analysis of discourse with respect to a sample of 1769 media contributions from Radio Television of Republika Srpska (RTRS), Radio Television of Bijeljina (RTV BN), Glas Srpske and Nezavisne novine between 2005 and 2007 showed that in 68% of cases negative language (polarised speech) was not detected. In 11.5% of the contributions, moderate speech based on facts was used, whereas in 364 contributions (20.5%) partly polarising (16.2%) or strongly polarising (4.3%) language was identified when the political elite in RS was speaking about the SAA. A relatively similar trend appeared while analysing emotionality as a factor, with 71.2% of cases showing no negative language, 22.6% being marked as moderately emotional and 6.2% extremely emotional. It should be stressed that polarisation (and the associated emotional marking of discursive actions) in the mentioned 20.5% of cases took place on three levels: (i) within RS and primarily by SNSD against SDS, (ii) outside RS and mainly against the 'Bosniak' political elites on both the level of the FBiH and BiH (internal Others) and (iii) outside RS and mostly against international actors (the EU and other external actors) (Table 4.1).

Table 4.1   Results concerning polarity

	Frequency (N)	Relative frequency (%)
No polarising language	1201	67.89
Moderate speech	204	11.53
Partly polarising language	288	16.28
Strongly polarising language	76	4.3

Analysis of polarisation within RS, which during this period was chiefly carried out by SNSD and its president Milorad Dodik, established that it was not directly related to the negotiating process for signing the SAA. It was used as a context to projecting the image of SDS as a "treasonous" party the international community supports in its reform efforts (Nezavisne novine, 2007a, 2; Glas Srpske, 2007a; RTV BN, 2007a). For example, Dodik began to emphasise that "he has information that SDS is talking to the international community about joining the coalition", with which "the party wants to bring the pot to external influences in order to break the unity of the SNSD leadership" (Nezavisne novine, 2007a, 2). In this regard, Dodik—in view of the internal political polarisation—was also helped by the fact that even when Dragan Čavić (SDS) was in power, "the party council did not agree with his proposal to support the three principles of the EU" (Glas Srpske, 2005a, 5). It should also be noted that during the rule of SDS (until 2006) polarisation could also be found within the coalition. The leader of the Socialist Party of RS (SPRS) Petar Đokić highlighted in 2005 that "the politics of SDS lost, as the leadership said for years and years that it would not allow any changes and that it would protect RS at any cost from external efforts aimed at reforming the Dayton Peace Agreement (DPA)" (RTV BN, 2005a).

Unlike the polarisation within RS conducted with the aim of maintaining internal political legitimacy and/or the ruling position, the polarisation occurring outside RS and the securitisation of the internal Other (primarily the Bosniak political elite) was more intense. This started relatively early, namely in May 2005 when Petar Kunić, a professor of administrative law, stressed in an interview for Glas Srpske (2005b) that the reform efforts to sign the SAA are "reform soup of Sarajevo's political kitchen", whereby the "solutions are not acceptable to all three constituent nations". A similar position was held by Nikola Špirić (opposition SNSD) who described Adnan Terzić as "replaceable" and someone who "does not have the support of the international community for reforms, but for humiliating others who should participate in reforms" (Nezavisne novine, 2005a, 6). This was further instrumentalised by Petar Kunić about 9 months later in a second interview for Glas Srpske (2006a, 52) during which he stated that "the centralisation of Bosnia and Herzegovina, right after the 'breaking up' of the former Yugoslavia, is an idea of the Bosniaks who through their lobbyists have been using European integration to centralise the state since the war". Even though Petar Kunić's status as a university professor means he did not possess the leverage to take extraordinary measures, he nevertheless successfully paved the way for the political elite to start emphasising such ideas. Thus, Dragan Čavić, president of SDS, just before handing power over to SNSD, stressed that "any deviation from the DPA would be a return to the previous state and the return of the status of RS as a country, which would not make anyone happy, especially not the Bosniaks, who are completely identified at the state level" (Glas Srpske, 2006b, 5) (Table 4.2).

Polarisation, mainly caused by Dodik's statements, therefore became more intense after the change in power. Already in August 2006, he centred his rhetoric around the irreconcilable differences between RS and (F) BiH while saying during a conversation about joint solutions to the challenges in BiH that "BiH's political parties can find a solution to every issue in BiH", but not "with incompetent jugglers and brokers like Adnan Terzić" (Nezavisne novine, 2006a; RTRS, 2006a). He reiterated promoting this attitude towards the internal Other later in 2007 when stating that "no one is so crazy that he knows that the reform proposal is coordinated with Sulejman Tihić and that the situation from 20 years ago is occurring, when the majority nation did not want to listen to others" (RTV BN, 2007b; Nezavisne novine, 2007b). During this period, it is also worth mentioning the political messages emanating from outside of the ruling coalition, that is, from the Democratic Party of Srpska. The party's president Predrag Kovačević emphasised that "BiH could enter the EU much faster than in the way being promoted by the politicians from Sarajevo" (Glas Srpske, 2007b). He also stressed that "like it or not, Republika Srpska is a country" (ibid.).

When it became clear that the failure of BiH's reform efforts meant the EU would not (yet) sign the SAA (2007), the securitisation of the internal Other by the political elite in RS grew even more intense. Milorad Dodik announced in a press release that "the decision of the EU not to initial the SAA is a consequence of Sarajevo's scheming and charlatan policy of the

Table 4.2 Results concerning emotionality	Frequency (N)	Relative frequency (%)
No emotionality	1260	71.23%
Moderate emotionality	400	22.61%
Extreme emotionality	109	6.16%

unconstitutional centralisation of BiH" (Glas Srpske, 2007c). He rein-forced such rhetoric at a press conference when he declared that "if some-one wants to abolish RS, we will have a response to that", and that "we should not be placed in a situation where we have to put this question on the agenda in RS" (RTRS, 2007). Relatively soon after these statements, a column written by Petar Kunić followed in Glas Srpske (2007). Kunić highlighted that "Sarajevo's unrealistic and unfounded ambitions had led to the disintegration of the political fabric in BiH, which maintained the capacity to deal with the European integration process and the develop-ment of democratic relations in BiH".

The third level of polarisation, which emerged relative to the external Other (the international community), is observable both indirectly (as the context for securitisation of the internal Other) and directly (the external Other as an object of securitisation). In this respect, the polarisation vis-à-vis the international community arose relatively quickly within the studied framework, that is, in April 2005 when the President of SPRS Petar Đokić stated in an interview for RTRS (2005a) that "there is neither progress nor development in BiH [...] which caused the European Parliament to react and as part of which we got a resolution that seeks changes to the DPA". About 1 month later, the EU also contacted the ruling SDS for the first time, where it was stressed that "nothing special happened in the negotiations for the EU and that the negotiations would not have started even if RS had accepted a compromise and started with the police reform" (Nezavisne novine, 2005b). Glas Srpske (2005c) also reported on this statement to the public and, on top of what has already been written, noted that "RS is ready to compromise, but the EU must show a greater level of understanding of the interests of the Serbian nation in BiH". One of the last securitisation acts of SDS during its rule in the analysed period was describing the then high representative of the OHR, Paddy Ashdown, as someone who "supports failed politicians in power like Adnan Terzic", for which we should start "talking on redefining the function of the high representative and reducing his powers" (RTV BN, 2006a).

Securitisation practices in RS became more visible following changes in this political entity's political leadership. For example, Dodik declared in October 2006 that "the SAA is not respected because the decisions on reforms are made by foreigners" and that "they are not sheep who will be led by certain international officials who—for the sake of their own careers—tell them what is good and what is not" (Nezavisne novine, 2006b, 4). Dodik thereby stressed that "if the international community continues with threats, they will not regret the fact that the EU had refused to sign the SAA" (ibid.). More serious polarisation and instrumentalisation continued in 2007, where it is worth highlighting the columnist Slavko Mitrović who discussed the 'three principles' of the EU (police reform) and claimed that they were not "European, but Ashdown's" (Nezavisne novine, 2007d, 8). In this way, he framed VP Ashdown as "a cynic who failed with the police reform and—in accordance with the request of the Bosniak political elite—invented principles" (ibid.). Similar rhetoric was adopted by other members of the political elite in RS when Milan Jelić (President of RS) announced that the Constitution of Bosnia and Herzegovina does not stipulate that "High Representative Ashdown would invent reforms in Sarajevo and then present them to the EU as a precondition for signing the SAA" (Glas Srpske, 2007d, 5). Also of note is the statement by Igor Radojčić (SNSD), the president of the National Assembly of RS, who stated that "the High Representative has turned a new chapter in his activities, but the Bosniak side, by rejecting this, has shown that it is not up to the police reforms, nor to the SAA or the EU, but only to a radical institutional change in BiH" (Nezavisne novine, 2007e, 9).

If the securitisation practice of the political elite in RS in the period under study suggested that in the context of the negotiations and signing of the SAA the OHR (and not the EU) was being securitised, this was finally clarified just prior to the signing. For example, the Bosnian Serb member of the BiH Presidency, Nebojša Radmanović, declared that BiH will soon sign the SAA and, thus, "it would be logical to get rid of the OHR and the high representative after that" (Glas Srpske, 2007e, 6). In his statement, Radmanović also emphasised that "if this does not happen, the thesis that there is a certain number of people in Europe and the world who do not want BiH in the EU will be confirmed" (ibid.). Finally, unlike Radmanović, who was working on the BiH level, Dodik took a different tactic just before signing the SAA. Namely, he started promoting the narrative that "he had succeeded in consolidating the status of RS as a permanent category and an equal partner of the international community", while "media houses in another political entity offer false information and lies about Milorad Dodik" (Glas Srpske, 2007f, 4).

An important element of the discourse analysis was the possibility of a solution, which defines a strategy for dealing with the challenge, which is framed as a security problem. In the context of negotiating to sign the SAA, three strategies dominated: (i) an institutional solution (48.1%), (ii) no possibility of a solution (35.1%) and (iii) compromise/negotiations/ cooperation with the other side (10.9%). Here, it should be stressed that the institutional solution was then understood in both a positive and a negative sense with respect to the reform efforts of the international community. For example, analysis of media content in the period between 2005 and 2006 showed the political elite in RS was emphasising that they were cooperating with the ICTY, which was understood as one of the conditions for signing the SAA. For example, Dragan Čavić (SDS), then president of RS, described how "the Peace Implementation Council welcomed the progress of RS in cooperation with the Hague Tribunal" and that "good cooperation with the ICTY is a prerequisite for success with BiH's European integration" (Glas Srpske, 2005e, 2; 2005d, 4). It should additionally be noted that the narrative about the "good cooperation of RS with the ICTY" during this period was consolidated by both summarising the discursive actions of the political elite of RS and reporting on the meetings between the political elites of the Republic of Serbia and RS, where one could observe the narrative of handing over war criminals to the ICTY (Nezavisne novine, 2005c, 2; RTRS, 2005b) (Table 4.3).

After 2006, when a change occurred in the political leadership of RS, I observe the discursive actions of the political elite that offered an institutional solution during the SAA negotiation process in a more negative light. The reform efforts of the international community and the political elite in BiH were hence presented by the ruling SNSD in RS as a matter that threatens the interests of RS by calling for an amendment to both the Constitution of BiH and the DPA. For example, Dodik began to

Table 4.3 Results concerning treatment option

	Frequency (N)	Relative frequency (%)
No possibility of solution/without compromise or negotiations	622	35.16
Evolution/gradual change	17	0.96
Revolution/radical and fast change	5	0.28
Compromise/dialogue with the other side	193	10.91
Without compromise/dialogue	1	0.06
Peaceful	46	2.6
Violent	8	0.45
Institutional solution	851	48.11
Solution based on culture and/or identity	26	1.47

emphasise that such reform efforts would "destroy the internal structure of the entity" (RTRS, 2006b), and if the reforms were to go in the direction of establishing state institutions and transferring political power from the level of political entities to the state level, "RS would seek its own solutions with which it would at least maintain its current autonomy" (Glas Srpske, 2006d; RTV BN, 2006b). Still, most media contributions that envisaged an institutional solution were reform initiatives with the aim of signing the SAA and including BiH and framed the process of European integration as positive and desirable (RTRS, 2005c; Glas Srpske, 2006c, d; Nezavisne novine, 2006c, d).

A similar logic (positive/negative) as for an institutional solution as a strategy for the challenges during the period of signing the SAA emerged in the analysis of contributions in which those responsible for discursive actions did not offer a solution to the identified challenges. The analysis shows that the period between 2005 and 2006 may be characterised by more positive discursive actions since the strategy of not offering any solution envisaged investing efforts in reforms with the goal of signing the SAA (Nezavisne novine, 2005h, 3; RTRS, 2005e). For example, in 2006, Dodik told RTV BN (2006b) that RS "wants to be part of European integration and that this is their voluntary and long-defined decision". In this period, President of the National Assembly of RS Igor Radojičić (SNSD) held a similar attitude when stressing that "everyone in BiH wants European integration and regional cooperation" (Glas Srpske, 2006d, 52). In the period following April 2006, however, analysis of media contributions in relation to the studied factor (no possibility of a solution) showed the opposite trend, namely in a more negative direction. For instance, Dodik began to 'warn' that "RS would not accept the abolition of the police and the Ministry of Internal Affairs of RS, even if that means the end of negotiations to sign the SAA" (Glas Srpske, 2006e, 3). Around this time, Prime Minister of RS Dragan Čavić (SDS) made a similar point while saying that "every historical category and every administrative category is the result of certain historical circumstances", which will not lead to the abolition of the police structures in the RS (Glas Srpske, 2006f, 46–47). Finally, the analysis detects compromise/negotiation/collaboration with the opposite party as the third-most exposed solution option. The analysis revealed that this was visible in most cases in 2005 and in the first months of 2006 when RS was highlighting the importance of both cooperating with the ICTY and solving this issue with the goal of BiH's

Table 4.4 Results concerning references to the past

	Frequency (N)	Relative frequency (%)
No references to the past	1511	85.42
Second World War	7	0.4
Communism in Yugoslavia	5	0.27
Bosnian War	164	9.27
The Kosovo question	81	4.58
Other historical events	1	0.06

integration into Europe (Nezavisne novine, 2005c, 4; RTRS, 2005e; RTV BN, 2005b) (Table 4.4).

Analysis of media content in terms of references of the past showed that 85.5% of cases did not centre around such references. The majority of media articles that referred to the past made reference to the Bosnian War (9.3%). In relation to the analysed period, there was primarily a discourse on cooperation with the ICTY and the issue of handing war criminals over. More interesting than the reference to the Bosnian War is the mention of the Kosovo question (4.6%) evident in two periods: (i) during the time of the legal proceedings brought by BiH against Serbia and Montenegro for war aggression and genocide and (ii) at the end of 2007 when it had become increasingly clear that Kosovo would be declaring independence. At the time of BiH's legal proceedings against Serbia and Montenegro, the Kosovo issue was principally linked to RS' cooperation with the ICTY in the context of meeting the conditions to sign the SAA. In this regard, the discourse of the political elite in RS was relatively coordinated. For example, Borislav Paravac (SDS) said that "BiH's legal proceedings against Serbia and Montenegro are illegal and illegitimate because they are not supported by RS and the Serbian people in BiH" (Glas Srpske, 2005e, 2), while Igor Radojčić (SNSD) declared that "the legal proceedings against Serbia and Montenegro for war aggression and genocide are very danger-ous and unacceptable for RS" (Nezavisne novine, 2006c, d, 5). The sec-ond period of making references to the Kosovo question shows similar coordination, except that here the political elite in RS connected the Kosovo question with the legitimacy of the OHR in BiH. The most active in this sense was the Bosnian Serb member of the BiH Presidency, Nebojša Radmanović, who stressed that "the international community is black-mailing BiH" and that "BiH will not follow the EU" on the Kosovo question as they understand the Kosovo issue to be an "internal political issue of Serbia" (Nezavisne novine, 2007a, 3).

Analysis of the presence of narratives, symbols and myths mobilised by the political elite in the social and material environments of RS revealed that this was the case in only 19.2% (social environment) and 2.7% of cases, respectively (material environment). Regarding the (re)creation of the metanarrative of the political elite of RS, the discourse analysis showed that this process can be divided into two periods: (i) the period from January to the start of 2006 and (ii) the period from 2006 onwards. The first identified period, marked by the political elite within the SDS party framework, is characterised by an emphasis on the cooperation of RS with the international community (ICTY), which was associated with the process of negotiating to sign the SAA. During this period, the political elite of RS also stressed that the process of European integration was important for the general progress of BiH, and that membership in the EU is a long-defined goal. It is noted that the political elite under the SDS leadership had then already begun to frame two important narratives, which only deepened and consolidated in the second period. While the first narrative touched on the question of the OHR's legitimacy in BiH, the second narrative focused on the question of the police reform, which was then seen as a precondition for signing the SAA (Nezavisne novine, 2005; RTV BN, 2005c). There was also an indirect mention of the material environment, that is, the inter-entity border (IEBL) that the political elite in RS had envisioned as the "territorial integrity of RS" (Nezavisne novine, 2005e, 4). In this time period, therefore, discursive actions that framed the relationship with respect to the external other (primarily the OHR and the ICTY) were mainly in the foreground.

The second identified period, denoted by the political elite within the SNSD framework, may be characterised by the stress on narratives that framed the relationship of RS to the internal and external Other in an antagonistic manner. Accordingly, the issues of "the interests of the Bosnian Serbs, which could not be pursued with the proposed reform agenda of the international community" (Nezavisne novine, 2005i; RTV BN, 2005d) rose to the surface, leading to discursive actions highlighting the "extortion of the international community" to revise the DPA (through the police reform), which in turn was leading to the "disappearance of RS" (Glas Srpske, 2006i, j, k; Nezavisne novine, 2006f; RTRS, 2006c). Such discursive actions of the political elite included antagonism towards the internal Other, as members of the elite began to stress that the reform initiatives were being "coordinated with Sarajevo", that the constitutional changes were "anti-Serbian", that "the FBiH is working against RS", as a result of which "any deviation from the foundations of the DPA and the constitutional position of RS could lead to the self-determination of RS through a referendum on independence" (RTV BN, 2006; Nezavisne novine, 2006; Glas Srpske, 2006). It is also interesting to observe that they also introduced a victimisation narrative into the discourse when declaring that "RS is not to blame for the failed reforms" and that "the time has passed when Sarajevo could blame RS for everything" (Nezavisne novine, 2006a, 2). It should also be noted that the political elite of RS started in this period to combine the social environment with the material environment of RS, stressing that "RS is a permanent territorial category" (Glas Srpske, 2006).

This period, which also encompasses the end of the (successful) negotiations to sign the SAA, is therefore characterised by accelerated antagonism of the attitude to the internal and external Other, which at some point were even connected (e.g., the claims that the reforms of the international community were being coordinated with Sarajevo). However, the political elite of RS' attempt to recreate a metanarrative during the negotiations to sign the SAA, which lay in the domain of the EU, is that the EU as an institution was itself not presented in a negative light, but mainly the OHR. This is also demonstrated by the last analysed factor, namely the presence of the EU in the discourse, which was mentioned in a neutral way in 80.4% of cases. In just 3.4% of cases, the EU was mentioned in a negative way, while 12.5% of the analysed contributions mentioned the EU in a positive sense. In 3.9% of cases, it happened that the reform efforts of the international community (the police reform and the 'European principles') were presented in the media in such a way that the EU was not even mentioned (Table 4.5).

Table 4.5 Results concerning the presence of the EU in the discourse

	Frequency (N)	Relative frequency (%)
The EU is not mentioned	68	3.84
The EU is mentioned in a neutral way	1422	80.38
The EU is mentioned in a positive way	220	12.44
The EU is mentioned in a negative way	59	3.34

A more detailed analysis of the discourse of media contributions that frames the EU as positive showed that in some cases the EU was understood as a platform for "finding solutions with the aim of creating an effective police in accordance with EU standards" (Glas Srpske, 2005g, 3) and that "the signing of the SAA is not only in the interest of RS, but also represents a great victory for RS" since membership in the EU represents the "all-round progress of BiH" (RTV BN, 2006c). Among the 3.4% of contributions that portrayed the EU negatively, one may observe discursive actions that frame the EU's reform efforts as "primarily coordinated with the political leadership in Sarajevo" with the goal of "centralising BiH" or "invented principles without any basis in any EU framework" (Glas Srpske, 2005h, 5; 2006j, 2). The other direction of "negative understanding of the EU" went in the direction of "rejection of the SAA", which "would be the biggest blow to Europe" (Nezavisne novine, 2006j, 5). Here, it should be underscored that the biggest share of contributions describing the EU as something negative is perceived after July 2007 when Milorad Dodik (SNSD) began to stress that European standards in the field of police "do not exist" and that RS "is ahead of the false dilemma of signing the SAA for something that does not exist" (Glas Srpske, 2007h, 4; 2007i, 1).

Finally, when it comes to the actors and objects of securitisation, the analysis shows that representatives of SNSD (244) are in the lead, followed by SDS representatives (46). It is noted that the analysis detected the presence of a significant number of representatives (216) of the international community (largely the OHR and the High Representative of the EU) in the discursive acts of the political elite of RS. More detailed analysis of the factors highlighted above (polarisation of speech, reference to the past/revival of the past, mention of the social and material environments of RS) revealed that Milorad Dodik (SNSD), Milan Jelić (SNSD), Igor Radojčić (SNSD) and Dragan Čavić (SDS) were the actors more engaged with the securitisation. For example, the analysis shows that Dodik (SNSD) followed the principle of polarisation with his discursive actions in almost 50% of cases in the analysed period, while in only 11.6% of his speeches he stressed the insurmountable differences between RS and the (F)BiH or the international community. In 37.5% of cases, the analysis identified partly polarising language (moderate criticism). Much more 'concrete' than Dodik was Branko Dokić, then a member of SPRS. While analysing individual securitising actors regarding polarising acts, it is important to point out that it was not only representatives of the political elite of RS who engaged in polarising behaviour since the analysis found that such strategies were used by representatives of both the internal Other(s) (Sulejman Tihić and Adnan Terzić from SDA) and the external Other(s) (notably Paddy Ashdown).

4.2 Discourse Analysis of Media Reports During the Prud and Butmir Processes (2009–2010)

In the second part, I analyse the discourse at the time of the Prud and Butmir processes between 2009 and 2010. The Prud and Butmir processes were the next important attempt to alter the institutional framework of BiH, as prescribed by the DPA. The goal of both processes, in which representatives of the key political parties (SDA, SNSD, HDZ BiH) as well as the EU and the USA were involved, was to reform the DPA with the aim of creating a more functional BiH. Analysis of a sample of 1267 media contributions in RTRS, RTV BN, Nezavisne novine and Glas Srpske between 2009 and 2010 showed that in 60% of cases negative language (polarisation of speech) could not be detected. In 4.9% of the contributions, moderate speech based on facts was used, while in 369 contributions (29.1%) partly polarising or strongly polarising (5.8%) language was detected. A relatively similar trend was seen while analysing emotionality as a factor, where there was no negative language in 58% of cases, moderately emotional texts in 32.5% of them, whereas 9.5% of the contributions were extremely emotional.

In this case too, polarisation (and the associated emotional marking of discursive actions) in the identified 34.9% of cases occurred on three levels: (i) within RS and chiefly by the opposition parties (primarily SDS) against the SNSD coalition, (ii) outside the RS and mainly against the 'Bosniak' political elites on both the level of the FBiH and BiH (internal Other) and (iii) outside RS and mostly against international actors (external Other). In this case, the actors are particularly interesting since securitisation was carried out not 'merely' by the political elite, but also by columnists and even 'non-governmental' organisations where the Republika Srpska Veterans' Association (*Boračka organizacija Republika Srpska*—BORS) stood out (Table 4.6).

Analysis of the polarisation within RS at the time of the Prud and Butmir processes, as mainly engaged in by the opposition SDS and its president Mladen Bosić, showed that SDS' cooperation with Dodik's

Table 4.6   Results concerning polarisation

	Frequency (N)	Relative frequency (%)
No polarising language	761	60.06
Moderate speech	62	4.89
Partly polarising language	369	29.12
Strongly polarising language	74	5.84

SNSD in the Prud process along with Sulejman Tihić (SDA) and Dragan Čović (HDZ BiH) was framed as "a threat to RS" (Nezavisne novine, 2009a, 3). Bosić thus began to emphasise that it was a process targeted at changing the constitutional arrangements of BiH, which the leader of the ruling party in RS cannot decide on its own (RTV BN, 2009a). He continued with such rhetoric in March 2009 when announcing that "SDS will not accept any initiative to reform the BiH Constitution based on the agreement between Dodik, Tihić and Čović", because such an agreement would directly mean "the demolition of the DPA and threaten the political powers and capabilities of RS guaranteed by the Constitution" (Nezavisne novine, 2009b, 2). Bosić also noted that "for the first time in the history of the existence of RS, it had happened that one of the leading politicians, even the Prime Minister of RS, had accepted an invitation to speak about the territorial changes in BiH" (Nezavisne novine, 2009c, 8–9; RTRS, 2009a). This also explains why Bosić stressed that SDS did not view the Prud process as a "legitimate process", as he also clearly demonstrated in October 2009 when again calling on SNSD not to participate in the conversation (RTRS, 2009b). SDS continued its polarisation in 2010 during the general elections when SDS vice-president Vukota Govedarica told the public that "SNSD is the one that is reviving the Prud process", thereby leading a policy of "territorial changes in BiH and directly harming RS" (Nezavisne novine, 2010a, 4–5).

Still, Bosić and his SDS were not the only ones to oppose and publicly 'reckon' with Dodik's SNSD; Milanko Mihajlica, president of the Serbian Radical Party in RS, also did this. He declared the Prud Agreement to be a big mistake because the talks on the division into four regional units were "completely unnecessary", and even called on Milorad Dodik to withdraw from the talks "for the sake of the people of RS, especially those who lost their lives for RS" (Nezavisne novine, 2009d, 14). At this point, it should be noted that the ruling SNSD also led the polarisation in this time period, namely against the opposition Party of Democratic Progress (*Partija demokratskog progresa*—PDP) and Mladen Ivanić, a Bosnian Serb member of the BiH Presidency. Nebojša Radmanović emphasised in the case of PDP that "they will finally get an answer to who is for BiH in the EU", since PDP—unlike SNSD—was against the dismissal or abolition of the High Representative in BiH (Nezavisne novine, 2009f, 5). Rajko Vasić, general secretary of SNSD, argued similarly. He said that "Ivanić is the best interlocutor of the international community in attempts to concentrate political power and authority in Sarajevo" (Nezavisne novine, 2010c, 5; RTRS, 2010a). When talking about polarisation within the SNSD-Ivanić paradigm, it is necessary to stress the securitisation act in May 2010 when Rajko Vasić, in the spirit of the "pre-election clash", connected support for the Butmir process with the genocide in Srebrenica and said that "Ivanić is not behaving responsibly to the RS as it supports the Butmir unitary package and recognises the genocide in Srebrenica" (Nezavisne novine, 2010, 3–4).

Unlike the polarisation within RS, otherwise driven by efforts to preserve the internal political legitimacy of SDS, with the latter already having the next general election in October 2010 in its eyes, the polarisation outside the RS and the securitisation of the internal other (mainly the Bosniak political elite) grew more intense. This started relatively early on, in March 2009, when Dodik started to emphasise that "they cannot talk about demands within the Prud process, but only about principles, with peaceful dissolution being one of those principles" (RTRS, 2009c). He thereby stressed that "official Sarajevo wants constitutional changes with the aim of centralising BiH" (ibid.). This rhetoric continued in October 2009 when Nezavisne novine columnist Dragan Jerinić, professor at the University of Banja Luka Emil Vlajki, and BORS joined the securitisation of the internal Other. They began to stress that "the centralisation of BiH is the desire of the Bosniak side" and that "any compromise is wind in the sails of Sarajevo politics with SDA at the helm" (Nezavisne novine, 2009g, 15; RTRS, 2009e). The political elite within SNSD continued with such rhetoric when member of the BiH presidency Nebojša Radmanović stated that "Sarajevo's political circle wants to rule the whole of BiH, which is shown by everything from the signing of the DPA until today" (Glas Srpske, 2009a, 59–60). In this regard, it is also worth highlighting Nikola Špirić, then president of the BiH Council of Ministers, who had crossed the 'Rubicon' of party polarisation and described how "the key to BiH is the responsibility of the Bosniaks", while "BiH's European path is threatened by religious radicalism, or the attempt to create an Islamic state by the Bosniak political elite" (Glas Srpske, 2010a, 4). In the period after April 2010—in the context of the pre-election campaign—we again observe an increased degree of polarisation and securitisation of the internal Other. For example, Dodik said in April that "there is nothing new in Sarajevo, because it is once again destroying the foundations of the DPA and the rules of two entities and three nations" (Glas Srpske, 2010b, 4), and later made this more concrete when emphasising that Haris Silajdžić (president of SBiH) had "misled both Tadić and Gül" and that he "does not believe in the good intentions of Turkey, which exclusively favours Bosniak (political) interests" (Nezavisne novine, 2010d, e, 3) (Table 4.7).

The third level of polarisation, which took place in relation to the external Other (the international community), was visible both indirectly (as a context for the securitisation of the internal Other) and directly (the external Other as an object of securitisation). Polarisation in relation to the external Other began already relatively early within the studied framework, namely in April 2009 when Dodik stressed that "the Bosniak political elite wants the intervention of the international community", but that the constitutional changes "are not a condition for membership in the EU" (RTRS, 2009e). Yet, the international community soon became the object of securitisation when Milorad Živković, a member of SNSD, declared that "the OHR is responsible for the radicalisation of the situation in BiH" and also singled out the Constitutional Court of BiH, which was being ruled by "foreigners", as a 'culprit' (Glas Srpske, 2009b, 59). This kind of rhetoric continued with Milorad Dodik who during the Butmir and Prud processes even demanded the "abolition of the OHR", saying that it lacked legitimacy in his eyes and "in the eyes of the inhabitants of RS" (RTRS, 2009f). In the period after October 2009, the political elite in RS began to direct attention towards third countries. SDS, for

Table 4.7 Results concerning emotionality	Frequency (N)	Relative frequency (%)
No emotionality	735	58.01
Moderate emotionality	412	32.52
Extreme emotionality	120	9.47

example, noted in a press statement that "they had sent a letter to Vuk Jeremic and Sergej Lavrov", in which they underlined that "the international community is extorting RS" and that it is "dangerous and unacceptable for discussions on the most important issue of the future of RS to be conducted under the auspices of countries that openly advocate the centralisation of BiH" (Glas Srpske, 2009c, 4).

Such logic was developed by Emil Vlajki who stated that "the Americans insist on unrealistic proposals, thereby provoking a sharp reaction and radical moves from RS, which would create the conditions for the destabilisation of BiH or even the renewal of ethnic frictions" (Glas Srpske, 2009d, 6; RTRS, 2009g). In the already tense atmosphere, Milorad Dodik also made his contribution, pointing out the EU as the culprit—in addition to the USA—and that "the ambitions of the USA and the EU do not coincide with the idea of long-term stability in BiH", since "Bosniaks always hide behind the USA and the EU" (RTRS, 2009a). He continued with such rhetoric even when official Moscow was exposed as a kind of "protective force of RS", "which is against interference in the internal affairs of BiH" (RTRS, 2009i). Dodik also said that "there is no love for BiH, only obligations that coincide with the international DPA project" (ibid.). In this respect, the columnist Slavko Mitrović should also be highlighted. In his article "*Tuđe dobre namere*" (Good Intentions of Others), Mitrović wrote that "there may already be scenarios for provocation by the international community, where, for example, NATO would close the borders of BiH, with which it would further criminalise the leadership of RS and weaken its negotiating position" (Nezavisne novine, 2009h, 14).

Securitisation practices in RS became more evident after October 2009, which marks the beginning of the Butmir process. For example, Rajko Kuzmanović (President of RS) started to stress "that he does not understand why Bosniaks do not want to discuss such an important internal matter without the presence of the international community" (RTV BN, 2009b). For instance, Rajko Vasić (Secretary General of SNSD) emphasised that "foreigners are undermining any attempt to agree on constitutional reforms in BiH" (RTRS, 2009i), and Dodik that "progress in BiH is only possible without the OHR" and that "the OHR is inhibiting the Dayton path of BiH" (Nezavisne novine, 2009i, 4–5; 2009k, 2). The polarisation and securitisation of the external Other declined slightly up until the 'election year' when in March 2010 Dodik spoke of BiH as an "unsustainable country" that was "subject to the rule of ambassadors" (*ambassadorocracy*) (Glas Srpske, 2010b, 5). In this regard, it is worth mentioning one of the last actions in the time period under study when the Government of RS led by Milorad Dodik published on its website a list of persons "allegedly responsible for the satanisation of RS" in November 2010–1 month after the elections—that included the American and Swedish ambassadors, Bosse Hedberg and Charles L. English, respectively (RTRS, 2010b). Both responded to these accusations and confirmed that "there is no plan to destroy RS" (ibid.).

An important element of the discourse and content analysis was the possibility of a solution, which defines a strategy for dealing with the challenge framed as a security problem. In the context of the Prud and Butmir processes, three strategies were prominent: (i) no possibility of a solution (54%), (ii) compromise/negotiations/cooperation with the opposite party (15.8%) and (iii) an institutional solution (15.3%). It should be emphasised that all solutions ran in the direction of preserving the "territorial integrity and political capacities of RS". For example, the period January 2009 to October 2009 may be characterised as a period of strengthening the perception of RS as a permanent political category and securitisation of the internal and external Other with a strategy of not offering a solution, while between October 2009 and October 2010 as a period of offering an 'institutional solution', namely, a referendum on the independence of RS or its secession from BiH (Table 4.8).

In the period from January to October 2009, which coincides with the failed Prud process (March 2009) and beginning of the Butmir process (October 2009), the analysis detected primarily discursive actions by the ruling SNSD that systematically emphasised "they have a state

Table 4.8 Results concerning the treatment option

	Frequency (N)	Relative frequency (%)
No possibility of a solution/without compromise or negotiations	681	53.75
Evolution/gradual change	22	1.74
Revolution/radical and rapid changes	4	0.32
Compromise/dialogue with the other side	200	15.79
Without compromise/dialogue	116	9.16
Peaceful	11	0.87
Institutional solution	194	15.31
Solution based on culture and/or identity	39	3.08

institution's stepfather attitude to RS" (Glas Srpske, 2009e, 2–3) and that "the political capacity and territorial integrity of RS are not in question" (Glas Srpske, 2009f, 3; RTV BN, 2009c; Nezavisne novine, 2009l, 2). Milorad Dodik thus noted that "it is absolutely clear to everyone in the world that RS is economically and politically self-sustainable, yet we cannot claim this for BiH", and that BiH is "a sustainable model only because of the international community" (Nezavisne novine, 2009m, 2–3; Glas Srpske, 2009g, 2). We must not overlook the phrases employed by Dodik. One of the most interesting concerned "imagining statehood", with Dodik stating that "RS—within its own territorial and political framework—should function as a federative state, which would enable it to have its own national teams, such as football and basketball, and which could cooperate at international competitions" (Nezavisne novine, 2009n, 4). The period between March 2009 and October 2009, which coincides with both the failed Prud (March 2019) and beginning of the Butmir process (October 2009), can be seen—also in terms of discursive practices—as a period of some kind of (ideological) vacuum. The latter, which in practice means the absence of a clear perspective on the future of constitutional reforms or reform initiatives, was mainly harnessed by the political elite of RS for securitisation on two levels, assuming "a strategy without a solution", namely: (i) mostly against the Bosniak political elite and 'official Sarajevo'; and (ii) primarily against the international community (the OHR), whereby the international community was understood as the context for securitisation of the internal Other. In this period, it was also possible to detect a reference to the search for solutions in the existing constellation of the DPA, especially from July 2009 onwards when Dodik began to emphasise that "referring to the DPA is not an anti-Dayton action" (Glas Srpske, 2009h, 2). Dodik thereby noted that "he has no intention of playing a clown and that, because of Sulejman Tihić's concerns, he will not give away anything that belongs to RS" (ibid.).

It is precisely the reference to the "Dayton settlement of BiH" that coincides with the offering of an "institutional solution"—the use of a referendum to protect the territorial integrity and political capacities of RS. Here, we are discussing another identified time frame, namely between October 2009 and October 2010, which coincides with the start (and end) of the Prud process and the general elections in BiH. An introduction to this was offered by the securitisation act of Milorad Dodik who in November 2009 stressed to RTRS (2009j) that "he will not allow the Serbs in BiH to be in the position of a minority and—in a biological sense—disappear". Just a few days later, he emphasised in a press statement that "RS is prepared for both the possibility of the existence and survival of BiH and the possibility of its end, which is why we should implement a legitimate process, complete with a referendum" (Nezavisne novine, 2009k, 2). During this period, Vladimir Lukić, a former negotiator of the DPA, said that "RS did not get anything more as part of the DPA that it did not already have before; namely, RS already had territory, population and power, which are the elements of statehood" (Glas Srpske, 2009a, 91). Lukić (ibid.) noted that "it would be logical that RS should get its own statehood in the negotiations for the DPA". Such (secessionist) rhetoric even intensified in December 2009 when Dodik declared that "BiH, which was created by the international community, will disintegrate sooner than RS will cease to exist" (Glas Srpske, 2009g, 2). Here, Dodik's connection to the SAA (2005–2007) is even more interesting since he said that "he wants the future political system—through small reforms—to create something impermissible, so the goal of RS is the gradual return of the powers that were given to them yet taken away through legal violence until 2005" (Glas Srpske, 2009j, 5). In this period, the possibility of a referendum was discussed not only by the ruling political elite led by Dodik, but by other actors as well, such as Nezavisne novine's columnist Dragan Jerinić. He emphasised, for example, that "in the current circumstances, it is completely legitimate and justified to talk about the referendum as the last defence mechanism for maintaining equality within BiH" (Nezavisne novine, 2010f, 15). Jelinić underscored that "referendums are a great fear of Sarajevo, but that in the end there will be a referendum, and not just one" (ibid.) (Table 4.9).

Analysis of media content in terms of references to the past showed that 88.8% of cases did not have such focuses. Most media articles that referred

Table 4.9 Results concerning references to the past

	Frequency (N)	Relative frequency (%)
No references to the past	1126	88.87
Second World War	1	0.08
Communism in Yugoslavia	20	1.58
Bosnian War	99	7.81
The Kosovo question	11	0.87
Other historical events	9	0.43

to or revived the past referred to the Bosnian War (7.8%). In the studied framework, there were also nine contributions that referred to other historical events, such as the period of the Ottoman Empire (2), the assassination of the Austrian heir to the throne in 1914 (1), the Kingdom of Yugoslavia (1), the war in Croatia (1), NATO's attack on Serbia (1) and even the Armenian genocide (1), albeit this was a completely negligible trend. The reference to the Bosnian War was therefore much more present where, in terms of securitisation, actors stand out who, in principle, are not connected to the political elite or are not treated as such. Here, we can especially point out Miroslav Filipović, a columnist at Glas Srpska who in his article "Lagumdžija, Serbs and Israel" declared that "in such a social democracy of Lagumdžija it is not difficult to recognise the elements of National Socialism, which in this case deals with the Serbian question" (Glas Srpske, 2009m, n, 4), and Darko Tomić, a reader of Glas Srpske, who underscored in his 'letter' that the "Bosniak political elites want to destroy the Serbs with Islamic radicalism and that RS itself must take responsibility for its own protection on its borders and later deal with the consequences, as was the case many times in the 20th century" (Glas Srpske, 2009k, 58). In this respect, we must not forget the role of nongovernmental organisations, namely BORS and the Association of Non-Governmental Organisations of RS. Both organisations were actively involved in the discussions on the issue of reform changes in BiH, and stressed that "if a change to the Constitution of BiH is necessary, then the right of RS to self-determination is completely legal and legitimate since this is the only possible framework for protecting the inhabitants of RS" (Nezavisne novine, 2009p, 3).

Analysis of the presence of narratives, symbols and myths mobilised by the political elite in the social and material environments of RS revealed that this was the case in up to 31.4% (social environment) and 2.2% (material environment) of cases. This means the political elite employed various symbols, myths and narratives in their discourses that are important for the political identity of RS and the very identity of the Bosnian Serbs. Quantitative analysis of the discourse showed that the process of (re)creating the metanarrative ran in two directions: (i) imagining the social and material environments within BiH and (ii) imagining the social and material environments outside the institutional framework of BiH. The first identified direction, thus denoted by imagining the social and material environments within BiH, is characterised by an emphasis on the narrative of RS as a "permanent (political) category" whose "territory is inviolable"

(Glas Srpske, 2009f, 3; 2009l, 4–5; Nezavisne novine, 2009n, o, 4; RTV BN, 2009c). In this way, the political elite under the leadership of Milorad Dodik above all pointed out the economic, political and social self-sustainability of RS that functions within BiH as a fully autonomous political entity (Nezavisne novine, 2009n, o, 4; Glas Srpske, 2009f, 3). It is also important to stress that the political elite also began to consolidate the narrative of RS as a political entity that—unlike the FBiH—respects the constitutional arrangements of BiH as prescribed by Annex no. 4 of the DPA, and that it was completely legal and legitimate to insist on the "Dayton postulates of BiH" (RTV BN, 2009b). What is particularly interesting here is that Dodik—as regards the external Other in the social and material environments of RS—started to emphasise that "the OHR is to blame for the radicalising of the situation" and that "the OHR is making the Dayton path of BiH impossible". In this regard, Dodik even proposed abolishing the OHR during the Butmir and Prud processes (Nezavisne novine, 2009k, 2). At the same time, in 28 cases (2.2%), the political elite of RS understood or presented the FBiH as some kind of "foreign country" (RTV BN, 2009d; Nezavisne novine, 2010d, e, 5).

The second direction identified, characterised by imagining the social and material environments beyond the institutional framework of BiH, may be denoted by the stress given to narratives that framed the position of RS in an antagonistic way vis-à-vis the internal (mainly Bosniaks) and external other (mainly the OHR and the USA). In relation to this, the question of the ways in which RS should 'defend' its own political capacities in the wider BiH framework was in question, where the issue of the 'entity voting' (Glas Srpske, 2009m, n, 2) rose to the fore. The issue of entity voting also triggered the 'eternal question' of three political entities (Glas Srpske, 2010c, 2–3), paving the way for imagining statehood and independence beyond the institutional framework of BiH. This happened mainly in the period after October 2009, which heralds the commencement of the Butmir processes. The latter is important because, although it emerged from the Prud process, it had the support and active engagement of the international community under the leadership of the EU, OHR and the USA. Accordingly, in this period the political elite of RS tried to (re) create a narrative about BiH as an "(unsustainable) international project" which, assuming the absence of the international community, "requires the search for alternatives for the future institutional arrangement of BiH" (Nezavisne novine, 2009h, 14; RTRS, 2009k). In this setting, the political elite led by Milorad Dodik began to emphasise that "the efforts of the EU and the USA do not aim at the long-term stability of BiH" and that "the legitimacy of the referendum is all the greater if the international community does not support its own international project (the DPA)" (RTRS, 2009g; Glas Srpske, 2010b, 5). This narrative was not simply recreated by the political elite led by Dodik, but by other actors of securitisation as well, such as Petar Kunić, the mentioned columnist for Nezavisne novine (2010g, 14) who, while defending the argument that "BiH is an international protectorate", stressed that "the people of RS strongly identify with their republic", where he not only framed RS as an autonomous political entity, but also as an independent state. In this way, the actors of securitisation—similar to the period when the SAA was about to be signed—re-used the victimisation narrative in the discourse itself by emphasising that they were the only ones who wanted BiH to remain on the 'Dayton path, and that the Bosniak political elite wanted the centralisation of BiH, as part of which the Bosnian Serbs would become a 'minority'. And, in all of this, "foreigners are the ones who are destroying any possible dialogue within BiH regarding its future" (RTRS, 2009c, d).

The second identified direction, which coincides with the period of the "eventual collapse of the Prud and Butmir processes" (RTRS, 2010d) and the general elections in BiH (October 2010), may therefore be characterised by accelerated antagonism, notably regarding the attitude to the internal and external Other(s), that "threatened the existence of the RS political entity". Interestingly, once again the attempt to recreate the metanarrative used by the political elite of RS during the Prud and Butmir processes, which were not exclusively in the domain of the EU (the Prud process was a national project (HDZ BiH, SNSD, SDA), while the Butmir process was later coordinated by the EU, OHR and the USA), shows that the EU itself as an institution was not subjected to securitisation practices and hence presented in a negative light, but mainly the OHR was. Moreover, although the Butmir process (October 2009) was under the direct 'patronage' of the EU, it was in fact not mentioned often in the securitisation practices of the political elite of RS. For example, the analysis shows the EU was not mentioned at all in 528 contributions (41.7%) touching on the Prud and Butmir processes, while in 650 contributions (51.3%), it was mentioned, albeit in a neutral way. In 55 contributions, it was referred to in a positive way (4.3%), and in just 34 contributions, it was viewed as negative (2.7%) (Table 4.10).

Analysis of media coverage framing the EU either positively or negatively revealed the political elite understood the EU as an institution that

Table 4.10   Results concerning the presence of the EU in the discourse

	Frequency (N)	Relative frequency (%)
The EU is not mentioned	528	41.67
The EU is mentioned in a neutral way	650	51.3
The EU is mentioned in a positive way	55	4.34
The EU is mentioned in a negative way	34	2.68

"does not require constitutional reforms for eventual EU membership" (RTRS, 2009d) and as an institution that "is harming the long-term stability of BiH with its efforts" (RTRS, 2009d). Somewhere on the continuum between a more positive and a more negative evaluation, the analysis additionally offers an insight into the fact that the EU as an institution (or membership in it) was also used for the purposes of polarisation within RS. Hence, for example, the ruling SNSD started to emphasise that "everyone who agrees with the preservation of the OHR in BiH is both against the European integration of BiH and the RS" (Glas Srpske, 2009b, 59). Further, in October 2009, the political analyst Obrad Kesić engaged in a securitisation act when telling Glas Srpske (2009m, n, 2) that the Butmir process "was conceived by the Bosniak political elite, which directs its demands against RS through the EU". The EU was thereby being 'used' as a context for the securitisation of the internal Other. It should be reiterated here that the EU as such was hardly present in the discursive behaviour of securitising actors in RS.

Finally, in the case of securitisation actors the analysis showed that SNSD representatives led the way (362), followed by SDS (25). It is noted that the analysis detected the presence of a non-negligible number of representatives (103) of the external Other (mostly the OHR, the High Representative of the EU and the American ambassador) in the discursive actions of the political elite of RS. More detailed analysis of the highlighted factors (polarisation of speech, reference to the past/revival of the past, mention of the social and material environments of RS) revealed Milorad Dodik (SNSD), Nebojša Radmanović (SNSD), Nikola Špirić (SNSD), Igor Radojičić (SNSD), Nikola Špirić (SNSD), Mladen Ivanić (PDP) and Mladen Bosić (SDS) to be the primary securitising actors. The analysis shows, for example, that Milorad Dodik (SNSD) followed the principle of polarisation with his discursive actions in almost 50% of cases during the analysed period, and it is worth noting that a mere 6.7% of his speeches emphasised the insurmountable differences between RS and the (F)BiH or the international community. When analysing individual securitising actors as concerns polarising acts, it is important to state that it was not only representatives of the political elite of RS who engaged in polarisation' since the analysis demonstrated that this strategy was also used by representatives of the internal Other (Sulejman Tihić from SDA, Dragan Čović from HDZ BiH).

4.3 DISCOURSE ANALYSIS OF MEDIA REPORTS DURING THE ANNOUNCEMENT AND IMPLEMENTATION OF THE REFERENDUM ON THE DAY OF REPUBLIKA SRPSKA (2015–2016)

In this final section, I analyse the discourse at the time of the announcement and implementation of the referendum on the Day of RS. This critical juncture is important because it is the first such manifestation of an 'extraordinary measure' taken by the political elite in RS to (re)strengthen the social and material environments of RS. The holding of the unconstitutional referendum is also the first (and to date the only) step of the political elite of RS to imagine it as an independent political entity with its own political capabilities and thereby strengthen the ontological security of this subnational entity. Quantitative analysis of the discourse on a sample of 1077 media contributions between 2015 and 2016 showed that in 36.9% of cases—when the political elite in RS was speaking about the referendum—it was not possible to detect negative language (polarised speech). Moderate factual speech was found in 9.1% of the posts, whereas partly polarising (40%) or highly polarising (14%) language was detected in 582 posts. A relatively similar trend was seen when analysing emotionality as a factor, where there was no negative language in 53.6% of cases, 31.6% of moderately emotional texts and 14.9% of extremely emotional contributions. In this case, polarisation (and the associated emotional marking of discursive actions) in the mentioned almost 54% of cases occurred on two levels: (i) outside RS and primarily against the 'Bosniak' political elite, on both the levels of the FBiH and BiH (internal Other), and (ii) outside RS and chiefly against international actors (external Other). It is particularly interesting here that the political elite of RS did not at this time implement polarisation within RS, but—in a relatively coordinated manner—performed securitisation acts against the 'Bosniak' political elite and the international community. The greatest activity is recorded by the SNSD political elite under the leadership of Milorad Dodik (Table 4.11).

Analysis of the polarisation occurring outside RS and chiefly against the Bosniak political elite (the internal Other), which in this period was mainly conducted by SNSD and the President of RS Milorad Dodik, showed that it started already in April 2015. Milorad Dodik first publicly attacked Bakir Izetbegović and declared that "the constitutional review of the Act on Holidays in RS is a direct attack on RS" (Glas Srpske, 2015a, 4). Dodik framed the holidays as a "symbol of the freedom of the Serbs in this area", since "the freedom of the Serbs in BiH depends on the freedom of RS itself" (Glas Srpske, 2015b, 2–3; RTRS, 2015a). When on 27 November 2015 the Constitutional Court of BiH declared the referendum on the Day of RS unconstitutional, polarisation only grew. Hence, Dodik's initial reaction to the Constitutional Court's decision was the accusation that "the Constitutional Court of BiH is a Muslim court against Serbs and nothing else" (Nezavisne novine, 2015a, 5; Glas Srpske, 2015c, 3). The description of the Constitutional Court of BiH as being "Bosniak" also continued in December when the Government of RS began to introduce messages into the public sphere about the need to reform the Constitutional Court of BiH (Nezavisne novine, 2015b, 4). Regarding this, the Government of RS stated in a press release that "this time, too, two Bosniak judges overruled two Serbian and two Croatian judges, which is merely a continuation of the long-standing practice of using the Constitutional Court of BiH as a political instrument of the Bosniak parties" (Glas Srpske, 2015e, 2; RTV BN, 2015a; RTRS, 2015b).

However, the polarisation in this time period was not simply carried out by the political elite led by Milorad Dodik, but also by regular columnists of the biggest media houses in RS. This included Slavko Mitrović who in his contribution *"Kuhanje Srpske"* (Cooking of Srpska) brought into the

Table 4.11 Results concerning polarisation

	Frequency (N)	Relative frequency (%)
No polarising language	397	36.86
Moderate speech	98	9.10
Partly polarising language	431	40.02
Strongly polarising language	151	14.02

public sphere a discussion about the fact that "Izetbegović's demands have their basis in the Islamic declaration of his father, namely in that part of the declaration in which Alija Izetbegović talks about the fact that Muslims must hide until they become the majority in power, and only then start achieving their goals" (Glas Srpske, 2015d, 4). A relatively similar stance with a clear religious connotation was also taken by a columnist at Nezavisne novine, Anđelko Kozomara, who in his text justified the legitimacy of the referendum on the Day of RS by stating that "the second political entity (FBiH) is overpopulated with Salafists, Shiites and other Arabs who, through capital, control a large part of the FBiH", as a result of which "Croats and Serbs do not feel at all comfortable" (Nezavisne novine, 2016a, 24). It is also worth mentioning the dean of the Faculty of Political Sciences of the Independent University in Banja Luka, Milovan Milutinović, and the Serbian Archbishop of RS, Krizostom. In August 2016, in a column in Glas Srpske (2016a, 4–5), Milutinović wrote that "Bakir Izetbegović's behaviour is under the strong impression of the unrealised war goals of SDA and his father (Alija Izetbegović)", which he justified by referring to the fact that "Alija Izetbegović rejected the Carrington-Cutileiro plan in 1992, which was the reason for the war" (ibid.). Serbian Archbishop Krizostom went one step further in the securitisation of Bakir Izetbegović by noting that "Bakir Izetbegović would not only question the baptismal glories, but would also question the name and the very existence of RS and the Serbian nation" (Nezavisne novine, 2016d, e, 3).

It is particularly interesting that the political elite in RS did not practise polarisation in relation to the other internal Other: the Bosnian Croats. Moreover, the Bosnian Croats had become a 'tool' in the hands of the Bosnian Serb political elite in their struggles against the Bosniak political elite and the international community. For example, Marko Pavić, head of the Democratic National Alliance, announced in December 2015 that "Croats also support the departure of foreigners from the Constitutional Court of Bosnia and Herzegovina" (Glas Srpske, 2015f, 2–3; RTRS, 2015a). SNSD general secretary Luka Petrović said in July 2016 that "the referendum on the Day of RS does not offend Croats and does not threaten their national interest, so I do not understand why it would offend Bosniaks and threaten their national interests" (Nezavisne novine, 2016a, 4) (Table 4.12).

Table 4.12 Results concerning emotionality

	Frequency (N)	Relative frequency (%)
No emotionality	577	53.57
Moderate emotionality	340	31.57
Extreme emotionality	160	14.86

The second level of polarisation, which took place in relation to the external Other (the international community), was observable both indirectly (as the context for securitisation of the internal Other) and directly (the external Other as an object of securitisation). This started relatively early in the framework under study, namely at the end of November 2015 when the Constitutional Court of BiH declared the referendum on the Day of RS to be unconstitutional. At the time, the President of RS Milorad Dodik stressed that "he will request the representative of RS in joint institutions in BiH to withdraw foreign judges from the Constitutional Court of BiH" (Nezavisne novine, 2015c, 3; RTRS, 2015b). Dodik continued such rhetoric in December 2015 when he highlighted that the "Constitutional Court is a political tool of the OHR" (Glas Srpske, 2015e, 2), and in January 2016 when he started to stress that "he is not interested in the appeals of the embassies in BiH regarding compliance with the judgment of the Constitutional Court of BiH" (Nezavisne novine, 2016b, 2–3). In the period November 2015 to August 2016, therefore, polarisation in relation to the external Other was directly noticeable since the international community was the object of securitisation.

Analysis for this period also detects the 'protective forces of the RS'; namely, the Republic of Serbia and Russia. For example, in December 2015, Dodik met with Aleksandar Vučić regarding the decision of the Constitutional Court of BiH where Vučić said that "he would rather be silent, as he does not want any new disputes" (Glas Srpske, 2015d, e, 5). Yet, the media summarised Dodik's statement more comprehensively after his meeting with Vučić, when he stated that "Alija Izetbegović's dream was Sharia law instead of the Constitution, which is confirmed in practice by his son Bakir Izetbegović" (ibid.). On the other hand, Dodik 'praised' Russia since "it has never made its support conditional on the goals of RS" (Glas Srpske, 2016c, 2–3; Nezavisne novine, 2016d, e, 3). Even here, Dodik used the space for further securitisation of the internal Other, saying that "without this country [Republika Srpska], Serbs cannot live peacefully and freely in BiH because we all know what would happen if they were subjects of Sarajevo" (ibid.). Unlike the more positive attitude to Russia and Serbia, we note the more negative attitude of the political elite of RS towards Turkey. This time, too, Turkey was used more as a context for securitisation of the internal Other, namely the Bosniaks. Thus, for example, in July 2016, Dodik described how "Bosniak patriotism is most visible in the fact that they support Ahmet Davutoglu in his insults of RS, when RS commemorated the Day of RS' Army, and the anniversary of the victims in Donja Gradina" (Glas Srpske, 2016, 6; RTV BN, 2016a).

An important element of the discourse and content analysis was the chance of a solution, thus defining a strategy for dealing with the challenge framed as a security problem. In the context of preparing for and implementing the referendum on the Day of RS, three strategies stood out: (i) no possibility of a solution (64%), (ii) an institutional solution (18.2%) and (iii) a cultural identity solution (8%). It should be emphasised that all solutions went in the direction of "preserving the territorial integrity and political capacities of RS". Hence, for example, the period between January 2015 and November 2015 may be characterised as a time of the "consolidation of RS as a permanent political category" assuming possible coexistence within the DPA framework; while the period between December 2015 and December 2016 as a time of strengthening identity-wise the solutions with the ultimate goal of declaring the independence of RS or its complete secession from BiH (Table 4.13).

Table 4.13 Results concerning the treatment option

	Frequency (N)	Relative frequency (%)
No possibility of a solution/without compromise or negotiations	697	64.72
Evolution/gradual change	4	0.37
Revolution/radical and rapid changes	4	0.37
Compromise/dialogue with the other side	19	1.76
Without compromise/dialogue	52	4.83
Peaceful	16	1.49
Institutional solution	196	18.19
Solution based on culture and/or identity	87	9.08

In the period January 2015 to November 2015, around the time the political elite in RS announced the referendum on the Day of RS, the analysis mostly detected accusations made by the Bosnian Serb political elite that the Bosniak political elite did not want peaceful coexistence. For example, Speaker of the RS Parliament Nedeljko Čubrilović from the Democratic Union noted that "by the Bosniak political elite questioning the legitimacy of the celebration of the Day of RS, it is not building a common future and lasting peace in BiH" (Nezavisne novine, 2015a, 4; RTRS, 2015c). Čubrilović added that "any problematisation of the Day of RS or any potential ban directly denies the existence of RS" (ibid.). Dodik continued with similar rhetoric, saying "that he wanted the Constitutional Court of BiH to make a legal decision, not a political decision" (Glas Srpske, 2015f, 2). Dodik made it clear that "commemorating RS holidays and respecting RS symbols is not a violation of the DPA, which prescribes the institutional order of BiH and the position of RS within BiH" (ibid.).

A relatively peaceful period in which the analysis found no specific securitisation acts by the political elite in RS was followed by the Constitutional Court of BiH ruling that the proposed referendum on the Day of RS was unconstitutional. Between December 2015 and December 2016, identity-related solutions appeared, whose (ultimate) goal—according to the discursive acts—was the declaration of the independence of RS. For example, Dodik linked the Constitutional Court of BiH decision to the "destruction of RS", adding that "half the inhabitants of BiH do not identify with BiH, and it has never occurred to anyone to destroy it" (Glas Srpske, 2015g, 3; RTRS, 2015d). He continued by saying that RS was entering a period of "fighting for everything that RS has been guaranteed by the DPA" (RTRS, 2016a). In mid-December, Dodik began to emphasise in media appearances that "the public is putting pressure on him and the political elite of RS and falsely accusing them of wanting to destroy BiH" (Nezavisne novine, 2015d, 3; RTV BN, 2015a). Such rhetoric was not only used by Dodik, but by the SNSD parliamentary group in the Parliament as well, which declared in a public statement before the New Year holidays that "the decision of the Constitutional Court of BiH was completely political, not legal" (Nezavisne novine, 2015e, f, 3). The group also noted that "the aim of the decision of the Constitutional Court of BiH is to deny the legitimacy and legality of RS and the institutional arrangement of BiH prescribed by the DPA" (ibid.).

The rhetoric employed by the political elite led by SNSD only intensified after January 2016. On the first day of the Serbian New Year (January

14), Dodik described in an interview for Nezavisne novine (2016f, 3) how "RS and the Republic of Serbia are his country, whereas BiH is only a place in which he must operate". He even went further: "BiH has been a strategic mistake since 1995" (ibid.). He continued engaging in such discursive acts in March 2016, arguing "that the sincere desire of the Serbs in BiH is to live freely, but freedom without a state does not exist, and the Serbs in BiH have their own state, namely RS" (Nezavisne novine, 2016g, 3). Sredoje Nović and Dušanka Majkić, members of SNSD, took a step farther in terms of integrating elements of cultural identity as a form of solving the (security) challenge when stating that "preventing the celebration of the Day of RS means a direct attack on the identity of the Serbian nation and RS" (Nezavisne novine, 2016h, 2–3; 2016i, 5; RTRS, 2016b). A similar viewpoint (identity-wise) was held by a member of the Socialist Party, Slobodan Protić, who told the Parliament of RS that "any attempt to prevent a referendum in RS must be understood as a judgment on the Serbian nation" (Nezavisne novine, 2016j, 2; RTV BN, 2016b) (Table 4.14).

Analysis of media content in terms of references to the past or revival of the past established that 81.4% of cases did not have such focuses. Among media contributions that referred to the past, the majority referred to the Bosnian War, with the political elite in the SNSD framework standing out in terms of securitisation. Alongside the mentioned discursive actions engaged in by Dodik, like describing BiH as a strategic mistake since 1995 (Nezavisne novine, 2016f, 3), and Čubrilović who declared that the "the Bosniak political elite does not follow the principle of peaceful coexistence and permanent peace after the Bosnian War" (Nezavisne novine, 2015a, 4), it is worth highlighting another two discursive acts that invoked references to the past. Dodik said in January 2016 that "if RS did not exist, the

Table 4.14 Results concerning references to the past

	Frequency (N)	Relative frequency (%)
No references to the past	877	81.43
Second World War	15	1.39
Communism in Yugoslavia	5	0.46
Bosnian War	120	11.14
The Kosovo question	3	0.28
Other historical events	52	5.13

Serbs in BiH would suffer in the same way as they did in the past war" (Glas Srpske, 2016e, 4–5), and in September 2016 argued that "there are clearly war plans from 1995 based on the assumption that RS would not last more than 10–15 days" (Nezavisne novine, 2016g, 4).

Much more interesting is the analysis of the presence of narratives, symbols and myths mobilised by members of the political elite in RS in 'their' social and material environments. This presence was found in 49% (social environment) and 3.2% (material environment) of cases. Regarding the (re)creation of a metanarrative by the political elite in RS, the discourse analysis established that the mentioned process went in two directions: (i) imagining the social and material environments within BiH and (ii) imagining the social and material environments outside the institutional framework of BiH. The first direction is marked by a stress on the narrative of RS as a "permanent (political) category" whose "symbols and territory are inviolable". Here, it is especially important to highlight symbols that are typically understood as elements of an internationally recognised country. Thus, for example, immediately after the Constitutional Court of BiH decision, Dodik started talking about the fact that "following the abolition of the coat of arms, anthem and Day of RS, a systematic campaign is being waged to destroy everything that RS has been provided with under the DPA". The 'campaign' to preserve the social and material environments of RS was continuing at the end of December 2015 when the legal-legislative service of the Parliament of RS expressed in a press release "doubts in the authenticity of the decision of the Constitutional Court of BiH because it did not write its decision down in the Serbian language" (Nezavisne novine, 2015g, 5). Continuity of the narrative about the Constitutional Court of BiH being 'anti-Serbian' is accordingly visible. In January 2016, this was even further instrumentalised in the internal environment of RS when Dane Malešević, the Minister of Culture in RS, announced in a press statement that his department would be "rewarding students for achievements that foster a sense of loyalty to RS, as the latter depends on the willingness of its inhabitants to protect and nurture it at all times" (Nezavisne novine, 2016h, 6). It is significant here that Dodik declared in his discursive acts that "RS is a state, Serbs [are] a free nation, and SNSD [is] the only party that guarantees Serbs their freedom within RS" (Glas Srpske, 2016h, 5; RTRS, 2016c).

The second direction that was identified, denoted by imagining the social and material environments beyond BiH, is characterised by the stress on narratives that frame the position of RS vis-à-vis the internal

Other (mainly Bosniaks) in an antagonistic way. In this sense, the (unconstitutional) referendum was a means of imagining such an environment. Also here, the central securitising actor was Milorad Dodik, who described the referendum as a "fundamental democratic principle of every society" (Nezavisne novine, 2016j, 3) and the Constitutional Court of BiH decision as "a prelude to the end of democracy and the beginning of the rule of the judiciary" (Nezavisne novine, 2016k, 2). Here, it is more important to imagine the social and material environments beyond BiH, which juxtaposes the position of RS against the Bosniak political elite in an antagonistic manner.

In August 2016, the political elite of RS began to highlight the importance of the "(in)stability of BiH" that was the fault of not only Izetbegović's SDA, but also radical Islamic groups. For example, Dodik said, "Izetbegović imagines that he is the state and that with such signals he is only strengthening the position of radical Islamic groups" (Glas Srpske, 2016i, 2; Nezavisne novine, 2016l, 5). Dodik added that "he will not go to Sarajevo and that Izetbegović, with his statements that [Dodik] could end up like Gaddafi, is merely instrumentalising Bosniak and Islamic extremists in order to get at him [Dodik]" (Glas Srpske, 2016j, 2–3). In these circumstances, Dodik also recreated the material environment of RS when speaking of the fact that "49% of BiH territory belongs to RS" and that "the Bosniak political elite in Sarajevo is bothered that this belongs to RS under the DPA" (Glas Srpske, 2016k, 4; RTRS, 2016d). This period also contains one of the rare securitisation acts by Mladen Ivanić, a Bosnian Serb member of the BiH Presidency, and Petar Đokić, the president of the Socialist Party, who, in the increasingly strained relations between the official Banjaluka and Sarajevo, emphasised that "everyone must go to the referendum, because in such a way they are defending what their fighters and civilians were fighting for at the cost of their own lives". Further, they stressed that "the Izetbegović family is abusing its own position within the common institutions to settle accounts with the Serbian nation" (Nezavisne novine, 2016m, 2; 2016n, 3).

It is particularly interesting that beyond the mentioned cases of polarisation vis-à-vis the external Other (primarily the OHR), the latter was not actually subjected to acts of securitisation. This is most apparent with the EU, which was rarely included among the securitisation acts of the political elite of RS. One reason, of course, is that apart from emphasising the need to respect the decision of the Constitutional Court of BiH, the EU was not directly involved in the resolution of the referendum on the Day of RS. This is also shown by the analysis since the EU was not mentioned in 83.4% of cases. Among a total of 1077 analysed media articles, the EU was mentioned in just 179 articles where it was mentioned in a neutral way in 13% of cases, in a positive way in 1.9% and in a negative way in 1.7% (Table 4.15).

Qualitative and quantitative analysis of the discourse thus detected mentions of the EU in the studied period mainly between June and September 2016, when the media summarised the statements of Lars Gunnar Wigemark, then head of the EU Delegation in BiH. He stated "that the referendum is unnecessary and that the EU is ready to help with finding solutions to the issue of holidays in BiH" (RTRS, 2016d; RTV BN, 2016c). The EU delegation in BiH also began to stress that "the referendum does not have an appropriate legal basis for its implementation, which is why RS should stop the continuation of the referendum" (Glas Srpske, 2016j, 2–3). Here, two examples of a more negative portrayal of the EU by the political elite in RS should be presented. Thus, in August 2016, after the referendum on Britain's exit from the EU (Brexit) had taken place, Dodik said that "Great Britain can hold such a referendum, but RS cannot even hold a referendum on the Day of RS" (Nezavisne novine, 2016p, 3). Another example of such a discursive act came in September 2016 when Dodik told RTRS (2016d) that he "has information that Bakir Izetbegović spoke with three ambassadors from the EU about how many weapons the FBiH possesses, and that RS is easy prey". Still, it should be emphasised that these are isolated cases. The analysis showed that even when the political elite of RS engaged in securitisation acts against foreigners with respect to the Constitutional Court of BiH and the OHR, the EU was not mentioned—not even when the EU Delegation in BiH stressed that RS must respect the ruling of the Constitutional Court of BiH.

Table 4.15 Results concerning the presence of the EU in the discourse

	Frequency (N)	Relative frequency (%)
The EU is not mentioned	898	83.38
The EU is mentioned in a neutral way	140	13
The EU is mentioned in a positive way	21	1.95
The EU is mentioned in a negative way	18	1.67

Regarding the actors of securitisation, the analysis showed that SNSD representatives led the way (322), followed by DEMOS representatives (45), PDP (27) and SDS (19). It is necessary to note here that the analysis revealed the negligible presence of actors beyond RS. More detailed analysis of the highlighted factors (polarisation of speech, references to the past/revival of the past, mention of the social and material environments of the RS) established that Milorad Dodik (SNSD), Nedeljko Čubrilović (DEMOS), Mladen Ivanić (PDP), Staša Košarac (SNSD), Željka Cvijanović (SNSD), Nenad Stevadić (SDS) and Siniša Karan (Secretary General of the Government of RS) were the most visible securitising actors. For example, the analysis shows that Milorad Dodik (SNSD) followed the principle of polarisation with his discursive actions in almost 50% of cases (48.3%) during the analysed period, where it is noted that in 26.6% of cases his speeches spotlighted the insurmountable differences between RS and the (F)BiH, or the international community. When analysing individual securitising actors with regard to polarising acts, it is important to point out that the media in RS mainly gave space with respect to media contributions on the topic of the referendum to the political elite of RS, leading to the negligible presence of representatives of the internal and external Other(s). Namely, the external Other—as the first voice—appeared in the analysis only 35 times.

4.4   Conclusion

Based on qualitative and quantitative analysis of the discourse of 4113 media contributions at 3 identified critical junctures, I draw the following conclusions that provide a framework for determining whether Europeanisation was framed as a source of ontological threat to Republika Srpska.

First, with regard to polarisation and the associated emotionality, at all critical junctures the analysis established that it occurred outside the political framework of RS and primarily against the Bosniak political elite (the internal Other) and only secondarily against the international community (the EU as the external Other). By far the most polarising and emotional impact—regardless of whether it was a direct or indirect EU engagement—was found to be framing of the Bosniak political elite as a (security) threat. The analysis showed that securitising acts were chiefly engaged in by the political elite led by Dodik's SNSD, and at a certain point they were helped by both opposition parties and various non-governmental organisations and other individuals (columnists, researchers, analysts, professors). The securitising actors, in a discursive framework that allowed for polarisation, thereby framed the Bosniak political elite as 'enemies of RS', as 'actors trying to delegitimise RS' and to 'centralise BiH to the detriment of the Bosnian Serbs'. To a greater extent, the external Other (mostly the OHR) was primarily used as a context for substantiating such arguments (the OHR and the international community as a political tool in the hands of the Bosniaks to achieve certain goals).

Second, regarding the options for solutions to exit from the 'crisis', the strategy of "no possibility of a solution" prevailed, followed by either an institutional solution or cooperation with the opposite side. In all three cases—regardless of whether the political elite in RS offered a solution in their securitisation acts or not—the dominant solution was thus to maintain the *status quo*. In this way, the political elite in RS sought to preserve the 'territorial integrity and political capacities of RS', using as a starting point the strengthening of the perception of RS as a permanent political category institutionally regulated by the DPA. In fact, it was this initial starting point that forced the political elite in RS while considering any reform to introduce a 'victimisation discourse' into the public sphere, framing RS as a 'victim and hostage of the Bosniak political agenda' and hence trying to preserve the existing social and material environments of RS. When the political elite of RS saw that in some cases (like during the Prud and Butmir processes) BiH had institutional support from the international community for the adoption of certain reforms, it began to publicly promote the referendum strategy as an extraordinary measure, which not only created the feeling of extortion on the part of domestic and international actors, but largely insinuated the possibility of the independence and statehood of RS. In this way, it also strengthened the social and material environments and—at least on the discursive level—managed the anxieties arising from the potential changes. Here, the underlying idea was that by assuring the greater functionality of BiH the latter would become centralised at the expense of the loss of certain political capacities of RS. It should be recalled here that securitisation as such is a technique of governance used by the political elite of RS which, assuming preservation of the institutional *status quo*, simultaneously preserves social antagonisms and thereby legitimises the importance of the existence of RS. At this point, it is worth mentioning the comparative results of the quantitative analysis for all three turning points, indicating that the 'no solution' strategy, including the 'identity-based strategy', became more apparent over time.

In the first period under study, only 35% of contributions did not offer a solution, and just 1.5% were solutions of an 'identity nature'. In the second studied period, the 'no solution' strategy was already present in 53.7% of contributions, with 3% of the solutions being of an 'identity nature'. In the final studied period, the 'no solution' strategy was already present in 64.7% of contributions, and the 'identity' one in 8%. This finding indicates that between 2005 and 2016 the feeling of a 'hopeless' situation grew among the political elite, which in turn was replaced by identity solutions or ones based on (banal) ethnonationalism.

Third, qualitative and quantitative discourse analysis with respect to all three studied critical junctures revealed that the securitisation actors did not refer excessively to the past. By far the most represented reference to the past was concerned with the events in Yugoslavia (before the last war) and the Bosnian War, albeit it was only rarely that the revival of history became an inherent part of a securitisation act. At the same time, this is an extremely telling finding since the starting point of the sociological approach to securitisation is precisely the stress on the psychological-cultural dispositif of the audience. Indeed, this has a great impact on the success of securitisation because the audience is 'confused' with regard to a certain history and memory such as, for example, both common life in the SFRY and the memory of the Bosnian War. This context makes it necessary to look at the findings more broadly, namely by framing the Bosniak political elite and Bosniaks as such as an 'Islamic threat', and the mere equating of the process of the EU's reform initiatives in BiH as attempts to centralise BiH as a form of fear of (bare) survival of RS and its population. The latter was clearly evident in analysis of the third turning point when the political elite of RS emphasised the 'discomfort of Bosnian Serbs and Bosnian Croats' in BiH since the FBiH is controlled by Muslims (especially non-Bosnian–Herzegovinian Muslims) in a political sense. The existence of RS (and its social and material environments) was accordingly understood not simply as a form of security for its own inhabitants, but also as the sole framework possible for the 'freedom' of the Bosnian Serbs.

Fourth, analysis of the presence of narratives, symbols and myths mobilised by the political elite in the social and material environments of RS for the purpose of (re)creating a metanarrative revealed clear continuity at all three critical junctures. Part of the answer lies in the fact that SNSD held power in RS in all three periods, and another part in the fact that the political elite in RS led by Dodik succeeded in consolidating two central frameworks for the mobilisation of narratives, symbols and myths. The first framework envisioned the social and material environments of RS within BiH, while the second imagined the social and material environments of RS beyond the institutional framework of BiH. Both frameworks and the logic of their use in securitisation practices were relatively apparent; when members of the political elite in RS believed they could manage the anxieties associated with changes to the existing institutional framework of BiH (political predictability), they generally talked in public about the fact that 'RS is a permanent political category', that 'RS is a legitimate part of BiH' and that 'it has every right to its own autonomous political activity'. The goal of this (re)creation of a metanarrative was thus to maintain the *status quo* and associated benefits, which are principally enjoyed by the political elite and secondly by the population of RS in relation to the (F)BiH. At times when it had become increasingly clear that the need for reforms was not only strongly present within BiH, but even encouraged by the international community, the political elite of RS started to (re)create a metanarrative about the social and material environments of the RS outside the institutional framework of BiH. In these cases, "RS was presented as a sustainable political project" able to "survive outside the institutional framework of BiH", and additionally framed by the political elite in RS in various narratives such as the one about the 'anti-Serb Constitutional Court of BiH', about 'Bosnia and Herzegovina as an unsustainable international project', about 'the international community and the OHR as a political instrument of the Bosniak political elite', about 'the Bosniaks and the international community as actors who are trying to delegitimise and destroy RS', where the only strategy to have appeared was to implement different referendums, including on independence. In the intervening period, the political elite of RS also—with the aim of strengthening the social and material environments—tended to highlight the issue of Serbian victims in the recent Bosnian War, the attempts to 'Srebrenise Bosnia and Herzegovina' and the unjust understanding of the '(Bosnian) Serbs in general as the culprits on duty for everything bad, what is happening in BiH, both on the part of the Bosniaks and the international community'. With this strategy, which presupposed the antagonism of the internal and the external Other on the premise of strengthening RS' own (political) subjectivity and the ethnic identity of the Bosnian Serbs, the political elite in RS actually gave the impression that any reform (may) irrevocably mean(s) the 'end of RS'. Here, it is worth noting that in the last period under study they already started to underscore that "they have already taken away their anthem, coat of arms and flag", arguing that they "practically took all the symbols of RS, and now they want to take away their holidays as well".

Fifth, the discourse analysis, which determined the degree to which the EU was present in the discourse, showed that the EU—with both its direct (SAA and the Prud and Butmir processes) and indirect (referendum on the Day of RS) roles—was relatively unproblematic. Accordingly, the EU was frequently not mentioned at all in the analysed media articles and, even when it was, it was mostly viewed in a neutral way. A possible reason for this is that the role of the 'problematised' external Other has always been played by the OHR. While the first period considered may be mainly characterised as emphasising the benefits of European integration and membership in the EU, this understanding by the political elite in RS was more the exception than the rule by the second turning point. This weakening understanding was even more evident at the third critical juncture where the EU otherwise had a more indirect role in implementation of the unconstitutional referendum on the Day of RS. As soon as the Constitutional Court of BiH decision on unconstitutionality was reached, the EU, via the EU Delegation in BiH, began to make this clear to the socio-political environment of BiH, although the issue was either ignored or not addressed. It is also difficult to say that the OHR itself is not an actor of Europeanisation given that not only is it mostly financed by the EU, but it is also largely coordinated with the EU's goals in BiH; i.e., the stabilisation of BiH and the transfer of the EU's economic, political, social and cultural framework to the social and material environment of BiH. Here, it is also worth noting the finding of the quantitative analysis that the EU became a less and less relevant actor throughout the three periods. While in the first period the EU was not mentioned in only 3.8% of cases and was presented in a neutral way in 80% of them, this had already changed by the second period. At that time, the EU was not mentioned in 41.7% of the contributions and mentioned in a neutral way in only 51%. By the third critical juncture, however, the EU was not mentioned in 83% of the contributions, yet defined as neutral in just 13%.

All of this suggests that Europeanisation should not be understood as a source of ontological insecurity of RS, but instead as a context (the Prud and Butmir processes as the best example) that political elites employ to antagonise and securitise the internal Other (mainly Bosniak political elites). In fact, it is precisely the presence of the (F)BiH and the Bosniak political elite in the discourse used by the political elite in RS in all periods of the analysis which indicates that the internal Other was understood as a source of ontological insecurity of RS. The political elite in the RS thus framed it as a security problem and thereby tried to strengthen their own metanarrative of the ethnic identity of the Bosnian Serbs, the political identity of RS as such and its social and material environments. In this way, the Europeanisation process—which must be understood more broadly, and no longer simply as an attempt to transform ethnic identities—became a lever for strengthening the ontological security of RS.

References

9. januar proglašen neustavnim, RS ne odustaje od praznika. (2015a, 27 November). *Nezavisne novine*, p. 5.

Amerikanci žele da izazovu sukobe u BiH. (2009d, 15 October). *Glas Srpske*, p. 6.

Bajden pokreće ustavne promjene. (2009c, 17 May). *Nezavisne novine*, spp. 8–9.

BiH jedino može da opstane na dejtonskoj osnovi. (2009h, 20–22 November). *Glas Srpske*, p. 91.

BiH kao savez država. (2009m, 15 February). *Nezavisne novine*, pp. 2–3.

BiH se dobro pripremila za pregovore s EU. (2006e, 8 February). *Nezavisne novine*, p. 5.

BiH u tri izborne jedinice. (2010c, 22 October). *Glas Srpske*, pp. 2–3.

Bosić: RS je u opasnosti. (2009a, 2 February). *Nezavisne novine*, p. 3.

Brexit potresao svijet, RS nema te ambicije. (2016p, 12 September). *Nezavisne novine*, p. 5.

Butmirski paket osmislili lobisti (2009m, 22 October). *Glas Srpske*, p. 2.

Butmirski put. (2009g, 7 October). *Nezavisne novine*, p. 15.

Čerupanje RS. (2016h, 26 August). *Glas Srpske*, p. 4.

Čorba iz sarajevske kuhinje. (2005b, 25 May). *Glas Srpske*, p. 5.

Da, biće još referenduma. (2010f, 5 January). *Nezavisne novine*, p. 15.

Dan Republike niko ne može ukinuti. (2015g, 28–29 November). *Glas Srpske*, p. 3.

Dejton ostaje, Srpska ostaje. (2005d, 5–6 February). *Glas Srpske*, p. 5.

Dejtonski referendum. (2016j, 15 September). *Glas Srpske*, p. 4.

Delegati SDS-a s istoka RS protiv Čavićevog prijedloga. (2005a, 24 August). *Glas Srpske*, p. 2.

Dodik nudi izlaz iz krize. (2007a, 21 November). *Nezavisne novine*, p. 2.

Dodik: OHR smeta dejtonskom putu BiH. (2009k, 20 November). *Nezavisne novine*, p. 2.

Dodik: RS država, Srbi slobodarski narod, a SNSD stranka pobjednik. (2016i, 29 August). *Glas Srpske*, p. 5.

Dosta je pritisaka. (2006i, 1 February). *Glas Srpske*, p. 5.

Ešdaun se požalio na nerazumijevanje reforme. (2005e, 9 March). *Nezavisne novine*, p. 4.

Evropa Čeka reforme. (2007f, 8 October). *Glas Srpske*, p. 32.
Evropa ili Evropa. (2007d, 27 June). *Nezavisne novine*, p. 11.
Fasciniranost državom. (2010g, 20 October). *Nezavisne novine*, p. 14.
Formiranje vlasti, pa promjena Ustava. (2006b, 23 October). *Nezavisne novine*, p. 3.
Glas Srpske (2006d). U BiH se ostvaruje napredak u programu reform:.
Izbacite strance iz Ustavnog suda BiH. (2015c, 28–29 November). *Nezavisne novine*, p. 3.
Još jedna godina izazova. (2006e, 8 March). *Glas Srpske*, p. 52.
Kao garanti uključite se u odbranu Dejtona. (2009c, 9 October). *Glas Srpske*, p. 4.
Ključ za BiH odgovornost Bošnjaka. (2010a, 21 January). *Glas Srpske*, p. 4.
Ko ovdje nije normalan? (2006a, 8–9 July). *Glas Srpske*, p. 52.
Ko ruši Republiku Srpsku, ruši i Bosnu i Hercegovinu. (2006f, 3–4 Ĵune). *Glas Srpske*, pp. 46–47.
Kompromis je jedini put. (2005c, 21 August). *Glas Srpske*, p. 4.
Konfederalno uređenje budućnost BiH. (2007b, 22 February). *Glas Srpske*, p. 2.
Koraci ohrabrenja. (2005e, 8 March). *Glas Srpske*, p. 2.
Korumpiranje razuma. (2006j, 5 December). *Glas Srpske*, p. 2.
Krah lažnih reformista. (2005b, 21 May). *Nezavisne novine*, p. 4.
Kuvanje Srpske. (2015d, 21 December). *Glas Srpske*, p. 4.
Lagumdžija, Srbi i Izrael. (2009n, 20 January). *Nezavisne novine*, p. 4.
Na sceni plan rušenja institucija RS. (2015e, 14 December). *Nezavisne novine*, p. 3.
Napredak moguć samo bez OHR-a. (2009i, 18 November). *Nezavisne novine*, pp. 4–5.
Nasljedniku kraća "krila"? (2005g, 19 May). *Glas Srpske*, p. 3.
Nečemo fotelje, nego – promjene. (2006k, 11–12 March). *Glas Srpske*, p. 52.
Nelegalni napadi na Srpsku. (2009k, 28 February). *Glas Srpske*, p. 58.
Nema političkog ambijenta za privlačenje investitora. (2009j, 18 December). *Glas Srpske*, p. 5.
Nepotrebno dizanje tenzije o Danu RS. (2016i, 21 July). *Nezavisne novine*, p. 5.
Neupitna pozicija Republike Srpske. (2009f, 28 January). *Glas Srpske*, p. 3.
Neupitna RS uslov nastavka razgovora. (2009o, 20 February). *Nezavisne novine*, p. 4.
Neutemeljeno u ustavu. (2006b, 18 August). *Glas Srpske*, p. 5.
Nije povrijeđen vitalni interes Bošnjaka. (2016n, 23 December). *Nezavisne novine*, p. 2.
Niko se sa RS ne može igrati. (2015a, 22 April). *Glas Srpske*, p. 4.
O granicama regije nije bilo ni riječi. (2009l, 28 February). Glas Srpske, pp. 4–5.
O policiji i trećem entitetu. (2007i, 3 September). *Glas Srpske*, p. 1.
Odluka o Danu RS stigla u skupštinu. (2015f, 26–27 December). *Nezavisne novine*, p. 3.

190   F. KOČAN

Odluka o referendumu ujedinila partije u RS. (2016m, 3–4 December). *Nezavisne novine*, p. 2.

OHR i Ustavni sud BiH odgovorni za radikalizaciju situacije. (2009b, 6–7 June). *Glas Srpske*, p. 59.

One koji kleČe ne vole ni oni pred kojima kleČe. (2007c, 12 December). *Glas Srpske*, p. 11.

Opozicija: SNSD oživljava prudski sporazum. (2010a, 20 May). *Nezavisne novine*, pp. 4–5.

Osporavanjem Dana RS ne gradi se pomirenje. (2015d, 18-19 April). *Nezavisne novine*, p. 4.

Paljenje hrama unijelo nemir i strah među Srbe. (2016d, 22 August). *Nezavisne novine*, p. 3.

Pobjeda demokratije Čvrst dokaz snage Srpske. (2016c, 16 May). *Glas Srpske*, p. 5.

PoČela realizacija prudskog sporazuma. (2009l, 23 January). *Nezavisne novine*, p. 2.

PoČeli pregovori BiH i EU. (2006c, 26 January). *Nezavisne novine*, p. 3.

PoČeli pregovori sa EU. (2005h, 26 November). *Nezavisne novine*, p. 3.

Policija na Čekanju. (2005i, 17 September). *Nezavisne novine*, p. 7.

PolitiČki udar na Dan RS. (2015f, 24 November). *Glas Srpske*, p. 2.

PolitiČki udar Ustavnog suda BiH na Dan Republike. (2015c, 27 November). *Glas Srpske*, p. 3.

Predsjednik RS: BiH nije ljubav već moranje. (2016f, 14 January). *Nezavisne novine*, p. 3.

Prekinuta vladavina ambasadorokratije. (2010b, 23 March). *Glas Srpske*, p. 5.

Prudski sporazum krupan promašaj. (2009d, 15 April). *Nezavisne novine*, p. 14.

Puna ovlašČenja još godinu dana. (2007e, 28 February). *Glas Srpske*, pp. 1–2.

Razbijen plan za izazivanje haosa. (2016k, 20 September). *Glas Srpske*, p. 2.

Razvoj ekonomije zavisi od politićke stabilnosti. (2006a, 15 September). *Nezavisne novine*, p. 11.

Referendum o Danu RS Hrvate ne vrijeđa. (2016a, 22 July). *Nezavisne novine*, p. 4.

Referendum o Danu RS na Ustavnom sudu. (2016k, 28 July). *Nezavisne novine*, p. 3.

Referendum o Danu RS prvi u nizu. (2016j, 25 July). *Nezavisne novine*, p. 3.

Referendum treba da otkloni bol i nepravdu. (2016e, 7 September). *Nezavisne novine*, p. 3.

Reforma policije mora biti plod dogovora. (2006f, 19 July). *Nezavisne novine*, p. 6.

Republika Srpska postala lider u BiH. (2009e, 8-9 January). *Glas Srpske*, pp. 2–3.

Republika Srpska traži poštovanje i uvažavanje. (2016b, 11 January). *Nezavisne novine*, pp. 2–3.

Revizija Dejtona poraz politike SDS. (2007a, 18 April). *Glas Srpske*, p. 6.

RS neće odstupiti od svojih stavova. (2006j, 23 October). *Nezavisne novine*, p. 5.

RS neće odustati od svog statusa. (2016g, 1 March). *Nezavisne novine*, p. 3.

RS nije bljesak vremena, ona je izraz naše slobode. (2015b, 6-9 January). *Glas Srpske*, pp. 2–3.

RS samoodrživa, BiH nije. (2009g, 19 February). *Glas Srpske*, pp. 2.

RS treba više jedinstva da spriječi njenu demontažu. (2016a, 1 August). *Glas Srpske*, pp. 4–5.

RTRS. (2005a, 4 February). Čavić–Matijašević: Napredak u odnosima sa Briselom, saradnje RS s Hagom.

RTRS. (2005b). Ministarstvo odbrane–EUFOR: Pitanje ratnih zločina prioritet!

RTRS. (2005c). Ivanić: Nova faza razvoja BiH.

RTRS. (2005e). Ivanić: Početak pregovora sa EU – nagrada za BiH.

RTRS. (2006a, 18 May). Terzić: Onaj ko nudi tehnički mandat savjeta ministara, protiv je države.

RTRS. (2006b). Kandidati SNSD-a usmjeriće BiH ka EU.

RTRS. (2006c). Schwarz-Schilling: Više neće biti nametenih rješenja. Savjet ministara treba da preraste u vladu BiH. (2006d, 18 August), *Nezavisne novine*, p. 8.

RTRS. (2007, 13 April). OHR protiv novih pregovora.

RTRS. (2009a). Kuzmanović započeo konsultacije uoči sastanka na Butmiru.

RTRS. (2009b). Beograd: Lideri stranaka iz RS sa Tadićem.

RTRS. (2009c). Dodik: Sarajevo traži ustavne promjene radi centralizacije BiH.

RTRS. (2009d). BORS: Srpska ne smije biti oštećena.

RTRS. (2009e). Dodik: Ustavne promjene nisu uslov za ulazak u EU.

RTRS. (2009f). Dodik: "Prudska trojka" traći ukidanje OHR-a?

RTRS. (2009g). Vlajki: Butmirski proces nameće unitarnu BiH.

RTRS. (2009i). Vasić: Stranci miniraju svaki pokušaj dogovora.

RTRS. (2009j). Dodik: Srbi neće biti manjina.

RTRS. (2009k). Dodik: Nema ustupaka na štetu Srpske, Moskva protiv nametanja u BiH.

RTRS. (2010a). Vasić optužuje Ivanića za odbranu "butmirskog paketa".

RTRS. (2010b). Ingliš-Hedberg: Ne postoje planovi o uništenju RS.

RTRS. (2010d). Vasić optužuje Ivanića za odbranu "butmirskog paketa".

RTRS. (2015a). Dodik: Referendum o pravosuđu biće održan u martu ili aprilu.

RTRS. (2015b). Kecmanović: Srpskoj prijeti i promjena imena.

RTRS. (2015c). Na idućoj sjednici NSRS o odluci o referendumu.

RTRS. (2015d). Ivancov: Inicijativa o referendumu o Srpskoj – demokratski način reagovanja.

RTRS. (2016a). Anđekovović: Ustavni sud nova udarna brigada protiv Srpske.

RTRS. (2016b). Ćeranić: Ustavni sud ne može više donositi neustavne odlike.

RTRS. (2016c). Dodik: Volja naroda se ne može suzbiti pravnim nasiljem.

RTRS. (2016d). Dodik: Narod će biti pitan o ulasku u NATO.

RTV BN. (2005a, 11 April). RS ne može prebaciti obaveze prema Haškom tribunalu na institucije BiH.

RTV BN. (2005b). RS ne može prebaciti obaveze prema Haškom tribunalu na institucije BiH.

RTV BN. (2005c). Čović sumnja u dobar ishod procesa.

RTV BN. (2005d). Dukić: Zločini nad Srbima smišljeni državni projekat.

RTV BN. (2006a). Do jeseni punom parom.

RTV BN. (2006b). EU apelovala na nastavak reformi u BiH.

RTV BN. (2006c). U BiH se ostvaruje napredak u programu reformi.

RTV BN. (2007a, 19 October). Političari umjesto integracije izabrali izolaciju.

RTV BN. (2007b, 13 October). Nedostatak dialoga usporava put ka EU.

RTV BN. (2009a). Novi sastanak trojke na Čekanju.

RTV BN. (2009b). RS je dokazala da je samoodrživa.

RTV BN. (2009c). Zvaničnici Srpske spremni na povlačenje.

RTV BN. (2009d). Dodik: Nema ustupaka na štetu Srpske, Moskva protiv nametanja u BiH.

RTV BN. (2015a). Dodikov strašni sud.

RTV BN. (2016a, 26 September). Na referendumu glasalo 55,7% građana.

RTV BN. (2016b). Građani masovno da izađu na referendum o Danu Republike.

RTV BN. (2016c). Zavetnici: Poziv građanima da izađu na referendum.

Sarajevski politički krug hoće da vlada cijelom zemljom. (2009a, 5-6 December). *Glas Srpske*, pp. 59–60.

Savjet ministara treba da preraste u vladu BiH. (2006g, 18 August). *Nezavisne novine*, p. 8.

SDS protiv preuređenja BiH. (2009b, 27 March). *Nezavisne novine*, p. 2.

Silajdžić doveo u zabludu Tadića i Gula. (2010d, 28 April). *Nezavisne novine*, p. 3.

Slijede hapšenja haških bjegunaca. (2005c, 4 November). *Nezavisne novine*, p. 2.

Složni u odbrani Dana RS. (2015h, 30 November). *Glas Srpske*, pp. 2–3.

SNDS ne prihvata uslove PDP-a. (2009f, 26 January). Nezavisne novine, pp. 2–3.

SPONA: Još jedan napad na RS. (2009p, 21 February). *Nezavisne novine*, p. 3.

Srpska na evropskom kursu. (2007h, 1 February). *Glas Srpske*, p. 4.

Srpska slavi slobodu. (2016e, 11 January). *Glas Srpske*, pp. 4–5.

Sude srpskom sudu. (2016l, 3–4 December). *Nezavisne novine*, p. 2.

Svoju sudbinu moramo uzeti u svoje ruke. (2007d, 6–9 January). *Glas Srpske*, pp. 54–55.

Terzić je Ešdaunova mjenica bez pokrića. (2005a, 26 May). *Nezavisne novine*, p. 6.

Teško do dogovora o reformi policije. (2007e, 5 September). *Nezavisne novine*, p. 9.

Tihić i Silajdžić bojkotovali, Lagumdžija napustio sastanak. (2007b, 23 February). *Nezavisne novine*, p. 2.

Traže odluku Ustavnog suda BiH na ćirilici. (2015g, 29 December). *Nezavisne novine*, p. 5.

Tuđe dobre namjere. (2009h, 20 October). *Nezavisne novine*, p. 14.

Tužba BiH protiv SCG neprihvatljiva za RS. (2006d, 7 March). *Nezavisne novine*, p. 8.

U BiH nema dogovora o krupnim pitanjima. (2009n, 14 July). *Glas Srpske*, p. 2.

Unitarizacija BiH bez budućnosti. (2006c, 8–9 April). *Glas Srpske*, pp. 53–54.

Ustavni sud političko oružje Bošnjaka i OHR-a. (2015e, 9 December). *Glas Srpske*, p. 2.

Ustavnom sudu BiH potrebne reforme. (2015b, 9 December). *Nezavisne novine*, p. 4.

Vasić optužuje Ivanića (2010c, 3 February). *Nezavisne novine*, p. 5.

Vasić: Uvredljive poruke. (2010e, 17 May). *Nezavisne novine*, p. 3.

Vodenica sa tri točka. (2005h, 21 November). *Glas Srpske*, p. 5.

Zakon o Ustavnom sudu BiH na Čekanju. (2016h, 24 May). *Nezavisne novine*, pp. 2–3.

Zakon po zakon, Evropa. (2006d, 27 February). *Glas Srpske*, p. 3.

CHAPTER 5

Conclusion

This book has several main goals: (1) to examine how it is possible that Europeanisation can strengthen the sense of ontological insecurity in RS; (2) to make sense of the importance of Europeanisation for the material and social environments, which in turn reinforces the sense of ontological insecurity in RS; (3) to determine in what way Europeanisation through the desecuritisation of ethnic identities enables the integration of ethnic and political identities on the micro (Bosnian Serbs in RS), meso (RS in BiH) and macro levels (BiH in the EU). For all three general research goals, particular aims were pursued at the same time, giving further support for the conclusions. In this sense, the conclusion that follows is structured so as to: (1) answer the research questions and synthesise the findings and (2) reflect on the development of the concept of ontological security and its importance for both theory and practice arising from the studied phenomenon. Some findings concerning each of the three research questions have already been presented in each chapter, and thus below they are elaborated on in terms of both the integration of the particular and general objectives and with respect to the findings of the entire analysis (the findings outlined in all of the chapters are complemented and woven together).

© The Author(s), under exclusive license to Springer Nature
Switzerland AG 2023
F. Kočan, *Identity, Ontological Security and Europeanisation
in Republika Srpska*, Central and Eastern European Perspectives
on International Relations,
https://doi.org/10.1007/978-3-031-46169-9_5

The starting point in answering the first research question of '*what context is shaping the Bosnian Serb identity*' is understanding the historical trajectory of imagining the Bosnian Serb identity. In this sense, it is necessary to underscore that one only started talking about the Serbs as a nation in the modern sense of the word in the late nineteenth century. An important emphasis here is that even though it is only possible to talk about some kind of proto forms of identities, one cannot neglect the inherent quest to mould separate historical events, certain social relations, and religious determinants to (re)create 'the sense of a common origin'. The latter, understood from today's point of view, could begin via the process of political self-awareness in medieval Bosnia, itself the outcome of the religious distinction between the Bosnian church and the Eastern and Western forms of Christianity. This is simultaneously the 'first critical juncture' when we talk about the justification of 'objectively different' or even exclusivist national or ethnic categories from today's viewpoint. Namely, some Serbian authors have stressed that the Bosnian Church was Orthodox, some Bosniak authors have associated the Bogomils with Islam and Bosniak identity, and some Croat authors have argued that they were Bohemian Croats who later converted to Islam.

However, this process commenced in the nineteenth century, not in the tenth century, as is often claimed these days (by the political elite). If we were to transport ourselves back to the twelfth or fourteenth century, we would probably characterise both historical events (the escape of Stefan's brother Rastko to the Holy Mountain to the monastery of St. Panteleimon and the Vidovdan myth about Prince Lasar Hrebeljanović), which are today ascribed with great importance, as relatively unimportant. Yet, since the nations strove to create the sense of a common origin while imagining their own collective, one may describe them as the 'myths of all myths', or the myths that have become the go-to sources of 'Serbian ethnic self-awareness'. In so doing, the Serbs crucially—and even more so in the case of BiH—have relied on the religious dimension of (ethnic) identity, as already indicated by the early period of the Ottoman Empire's presence in the territory of today's BiH. This was mainly possible because of the 'Millet system' that (un)consciously distinguished between ethnic/religious groups and also significantly contributed to the rebellions arising in the second half of the nineteenth century. Although these rebellions primarily had an economic basis (non-Muslims began to realise that they were in a disadvantaged position), they (already) had quite a clear political connotation since the rebellions—as historical analysis shows—held a deeper meaning referring to the efforts of 'Serbs' to unite the Ottoman provinces with a majority Serbian population within the common state of Serbia. The first seed of the idea of 'homogenisation of the Serbian space', as taken care of by Ilija Garašanin and his *Načertanije*—these days understood as a foundational text for the idea of Greater Serbia, also considerably coincides with this period. Here, it should not be forgotten that the process of equating the Orthodox faith with Serbia began at the same time, as substantively conceived by authors like Vuk Stefanović Karadžić, Petar Petrović II. Njegoš, Dositej Obradović, Ljubomir Kovačević, Lukijan Mušicki and Jovan Sterija Popović, who have succeeded in elevating the 'epic struggle and sacrifice of Prince Lasar' to the level of collective martyrdom. This point onwards provides the first (identity-wise) reference point for the legitimate search for the right to Serbian national self-determination.

Even though all of these historical events should not be ignored and should be understood as events that over time became myths and have successfully turned into general pillars of today's social (and material) environment in RS, they are understood as an unproblematised aspect in the efforts to create the sense of a common origin. This is especially the case when comparing them with those that mainly started to take place after 1910 with the establishment of Young Bosnia. The latter organisation is important not only in terms of the institutionalisation of 'pro-Yugoslav' or 'pro-Serbian' political thinking, but above all with respect to the actions for which Young Bosnia and its infamous member Gavrilo Princip are responsible. Princip not simply assassinated the Austrian heir to the throne, but his act ensured that the very instrumentalisation and politicisation of his action sought to show that members of Young Bosnia were prepared to do anything (at a certain stage, also at any cost) for the common (Yugoslav) state. The idea of 'Serbs as saviours' or the 'creators of Yugoslavia' came to fruition soon after the First World War when the Kingdom of Serbs, Croats and Slovenians (1918) and later the Kingdom of Yugoslavia (1929) were formed. In this way, the path was paved for 'Yugoslav integrism' with which the Serbian question was meant to be (finally) resolved, but at the same time, the oppression of other nations (mainly Croats) became synonymous with Greater Serbian hegemony.

That is also why the events that marked the beginning of the First World War, and the interwar events, are much more important for understanding today's attempt to (re)create a metanarrative undertaken by the Bosnian Serb political elite and the social and material environments of

RS. Namely, even before the start of the Second World War, the territory of what is today BiH was exposed to (at least) two nationalist movements that remain an important part of the public debate in BiH's society these days (in both a symbolic and completely tangible sense). This refers to the Ustasha and Chetnik movements, which—sooner or later—began working hand in hand with Nazi Germany and fascist Italy after 1941 when the Kingdom of Yugoslavia capitulated and the NDH was established. The Second World War, which was intense in the area of what is today BiH, thus—at least from today's perspective—became the framework for solving the 'Serbian', 'Croatian' and 'Muslim/Bosniak' question(s). The Partisan movement's victory under the leadership of Josip Bros Tito heralded a new era of building ethnic and national identities in the expanded version of the Yugoslav state: the SFRY. Yet, this process had to take place 'unofficially' in that it had to bypass the official state policy. This means the suffering of the population during the Second World War and the political massacres thereafter were suppressed through the process of imagining a collective (Yugoslav) identity, one largely fuelled by the myth of 'brotherhood and unity'. The period of Tito's SFRY is important in a historical sense, principally due to the strengthening of counter-narratives to the official version of collective remembrance, the imagining of exclusivist identities primarily through religious institutions (otherwise legally and formally 'cut off' from the state) and the process of imagining the Yugoslav victory as a 'Serbian' victory engaged in by the Serbian political elites. This was especially observable in the last war in the area of BiH—a good example being the process of framing Draža Mihailović as an anti-fascist.

Another (Yugoslav) turning point important for understanding the historical 'momentum' and offering an appropriate basis for the process of forming the present-day metanarrative of the Bosnian Serb political elite within the social and material environments of RS is the death of Josip Bros Tito (1980). His death caused a political vacuum, which—particularly in the context of the uneven development of the Yugoslav republics, the great economic crisis, and the sporadic relativisation of the Yugoslav regime—the nationalist political forces with Slobodan Milošević at the helm were able to exploit. He harnessed the 'infamous' SANU memorandum (1985–1986) to consolidate the narrative of Serbs as being 'victims' of the Yugoslav political system, which ensured the fragmentation of the Serbian nation. The goal was therefore not only the collectivisation of the nation within Serbia but also the homogenisation of 'suffering' as a characteristic of all Serbs, from Croatia to Kosovo. Yet, this is also a critical juncture—until the collapse of the SFRY—which we must understand as the next important historical event to have shaped the modern metanarrative about the ethnic identity of the Bosnian Serbs, an identity the political elite in RS is trying to (re)create. Not only were there ethnically motivated incidents in the 1990s and the creation of a narrative about the 45-year period of relative peace in the common Yugoslav space being an 'illusion', but also the beginning of the creation of a separate political elite (from Serbia) led by Radovan Karadžić. He used the increasingly burdensome (and fertile for nationalism) Yugoslav context to frame the internal Other (both Muslims/Bosniaks and Bosnian Croats) as a 'threat'. This was no longer understood merely in a legal-political or institutional sense—i.e., the preservation of BiH within the SFRY—but also in a purely physical sense, as further indicated by the logic of creating a clear dividing line between 'real' and 'false' (Bosnian) Serbs. It should also be emphasised that the Bosnian Serb political leadership started to increasingly associate the above-mentioned 'threat' with terror against Serbs during the Second World War, with Jasenovac (from August 1941 to April 1945) and the massacre in the village of Drakulići (7 February 1942).

The period immediately before the Bosnian War (1991–1992), the period during the Bosnian War (1992–1995) and the period following the Bosnian War (after 1995) are extremely significant for understanding the modern metanarrative about the ethnic identity of the Bosnian Serbs and the social and material environments of RS. The first multi-party elections in BiH in 1991 and the victory of three ethnopolitical parties (SDS, SDA and HDS BiH) paved the way for banal nationalism on one hand (for example, which village has paved roads and who owns what real estate) and, on the other, more applied nationalism, which SDS implemented through spatialisation. Hence, for instance, in 1991, SDS began by uniting municipalities in which the majority population was Bosnian Serb and commenced interfering with the social and material environments with tangible acts (erecting and changing monuments, street names and, finally, renaming municipalities, etc.). In this way, not simply the relativisation, but even the delegitimisation of BiH's spirit of coexistence and common life (*komšiluk*) took place.

The decisive moment denoting the start of the actual legal and political institutionalisation of 'independent life' or the independent political identity of RS was the signing of the Memorandum on the Sovereignty of BiH. The latter was signed by the Bosnian Croat and Bosniak political elite as a response to the increasingly violent intervention of the Bosnian Serb political elite in the social and material environments of BiH. The key goal of this union of municipalities by SDS was the preservation of the 'Bosnian Serb environment' in the SFRY. A failed international agreement to reduce the friction between the Bosniak, Bosnian Serb and Bosnian Croat political leaderships led to the Bosnian referendum on independence (held between 29 February 1992 and 1 March 1992), and in turn to a bloody 3-year war (6 April 1992 to 14 December 1995). The latter was denoted by a policy of ethnic engineering (about 2.2 million people were displaced), a huge number of deaths (about 100,000 people) and the first genocide on European soil since the Second World War (Srebrenica— the deaths of 8372 Bosniaks; 11–22 July 1995). The Bosnian War is the most important for the modern metanarrative of the ethnic identity of the Bosnian Serbs and the political identity of RS, which the political elite of RS continues to try to (re)create. At the same time, it is about establishing such a social and material environment of RS in which the destruction of cultural-religious and other objects took place on the assumption of the historical legitimacy of the 'old' material and social environment, changing the names of streets and roads with the aim of destroying all material proof of the existence of the Other. The results of the discourse analysis also reveal that the Bosnian War is the most critical for the creation of the modern material and social environments of RS. Most examples of discursive acts that referred to the past were focused on the Bosnian War.

Even though the Bosnian War ended with the international community's intervention and the attack on Bosnian Serb military targets following the intervention of NATO, the result of the war is still—in a narrow ethnopolitical sense—understood as a 'victory' of the Bosnian Serbs who were given their own (autonomous) subnational political entity in the DPA. The process of imagining its own statehood—despite us continuing to speak about one of the two political entities within the institutional framework of BiH—began relatively early, rendering any EU presence that sought to create the institutional capacities of BiH as a state difficult. The key historical event contributing to the very stagnation of socio-political life in BiH was the victory of Milorad Dodik in 2006, who with his rhetoric, practically returned RS to the pre-war period.

From this point on, we note the consolidation of the policy of resistance to the OHR by RS, the manipulation of historical facts and events during the war, the construction of new monuments (since 1996, over 2500 new monuments have been built in BiH, most of which

commemorate the last war), the increasingly open 'hostility' between official Banjaluka and Sarajevo, and the start of the creation of a narrative
about the 'Srebreninisation of BiH'. This continued even after 2010 when
Dodik's SNSD again convincingly won the elections and carried on (re)
creating a metanarrative about RS being an endangered political entity,
about BiH being an international project, and about the international
community's reform efforts being the beginning of the end of the political
capabilities of RS. It should be stressed that the period after 2010 (the
failed Prud and Butmir processes) is important for the modern metanarrative concerning the ethnic identity of the Bosnian Serbs and the political
identity of RS, which the political elite is trying to (re)create. This is principally because Dodik started to promote the differentiation between the
Republic of Serbia and RS, namely through the reform agendas. The latter
saw its epilogue in 2016 when RS successfully held an unconstitutional
referendum on celebrating 9 January as the Day of RS. In this setting, it
should be underlined that the events immediately before the last Bosnian
War, during the Bosnian War and what happened after the Bosnian War
are the most important for the modern metanarrative being recreated by
the ethnopolitical elite of RS. They were also crucial for the social and
material environments of RS. This was additionally clearly established in
the discourse analysis as most references to the past—where they could be
detected—related to the last Bosnian War. Simultaneously, these findings
shed light on a (second) narrower research goal in an empirical sense, that
is, to determine how the attempt to (re)create a metanarrative functions as
a legitimate framework for the creation of an internal Other (Bosniaks and
Bosnian Croats) and an external Other (the international community).

Stemming from this, the answer to the second research question, i.e.,
'*do the political elites in RS construe EU integration as a threat to the collective identity of Bosnian Serbs and political identity of RS?*', primarily relies
on the analysis of discourse at the three critical junctures. The starting
point is to return to the classical understanding of Europeanisation. This
means that I must start from the understanding of Europeanisation as a
process that makes sense of the level of normative integration of the country in the EU based on a meaningful choice conditioned by identity. The
central reason for this is that the goals of the SAA (2005–2007) and the
Prud and Butmir processes (2009–2010) were subjected to the logic of
adapting the institutional framework of BiH to make it better prepared for
European integration/EU membership. In this sense, the logic of the
transformation of the logic of Self–Other, or an attempt to relativise the

antagonistic relations between ethnic groups in BiH, was in the 'second plan', or understood as a kind of 'by-product' of the reform processes in BiH. Precisely at this point, there was securitisation of the internal and external Other, not necessarily connected to the EU itself. It should be highlighted here that the signing of the SAA, which is typically understood as a clear sign of a country's 'progress' and an opportunity for further 'development' with the goal of full EU membership, was (also) viewed as something negative, as something that 'takes away from the RS' and gives to 'the (F)BiH', as something that weakens the political capabilities of RS, and hence as a thing that must be 'fought against'. The framing of the reform efforts by the international community (and the EU) as potentially fatal for the future of RS was also visible during the Prud and Butmir processes (2009–2010), which were even more vividly understood as a 'Bosniak agenda', that—if successful—would have spelled 'the beginning of the end of RS'. It is also worth mentioning here the results of the quantitative analysis of media contributions since—comparatively speaking, through the studied three critical junctures between 2005 and 2016— the EU became ever less relevant. While the EU was mentioned in 80% of the analysed contributions by the first turning point, it was mentioned in just 20% of them by the third turning point.

To summarise, the reform efforts, or the attempt to direct the reform agenda (adjusting the institutional and legal order to make it better harmonised with the EU framework) with the aim of creating a 'more functional state' (actual attempts at centralisation), are those aspects of Europeanisation that act as a source of securitisation of internal and external Other. At least two issues must be re-iterated; first, the qualitative and quantitative analysis of the discourse revealed that the presence of the external Other was employed as a context for the securitisation of the internal Other (mainly the Bosniak political elite and official Sarajevo, i.e., as a technique of governance). Second, this external Other is not the EU directly so much as the international community as such, and above all the OHR, which actually holds the power to change the social environment of RS and the (F)BiH through the Bonn powers. All in all, the situation overall dictates that Europeanisation—at least in the case of RS and the (F) BiH—is no longer understood only in the sense of adapting the legal, political, administrative and economic framework of the chosen country to the one established by the EU, but more broadly as a process of transferring the liberal world order, to which the EU is also subject. This is therefore the notion of stabilisation as an ideological socialisation, which foresees the transfer of the EU's economic, political, social and cultural framework. In this case, it was mainly the international community—not the EU—that was repeatedly subjected to securitisation acts. This is also crucial for the ontological security theory itself and the distinction between fear (securitisation) and anxiety (ontological security). Indeed, the securitisation acts were directed against the entire international community ('BiH as an international project', 'BiH as an international protectorate', 'the rule of ambassadors in BiH'), suggesting that the 'threat' is not solely targeted at one actor (in our case, the still dominant OHR), but to the international community itself.

The third research question, i.e., '*which are the effects of constructing internal and external Others for integrating RS with the rest of BiH and the EU*', should be understood as calling for a meta synthesis of the whole book. In this respect, I answer the question by focusing on five points. First, by understanding that the classical aspects of Europeanisation are (mis)used as a context in which the securitisation unfolds, this would mean that Europeanisation would achieve (potential) desecuritisation only on the assumption that in its efforts it would not try to radically interfere with the social, political and legal institutional aspects of BiH. Arising from this, the second point is that such Europeanisation does not manifest as something positive in the existing political constellation of RS, or as something that could reduce antagonism between ethnic groups, assuming the strengthening of the political capacities of BiH as a country. Such logic—at least at the first critical juncture, where the EU is directly involved—in the discursive sense leads to a process of political disintegration on the meso (BiH) and macro levels (EU), yet also strengthens political integration on the micro level (RS). Third, strengthening political integration on the micro level (RS) therefore works as a mechanism for managing the anxieties produced by the EU reform agenda. The analysis thus shows that the securitisation acts of the political elite in RS in the Europeanisation context may be understood as an attempt to strengthen the sense of ontological security of the political entity of RS. In this way, I have managed to demonstrate the overlaps of Europeanisation, securitisation and ontological security, which was a narrower research goal from a conceptual point of view.

Fourth, this strengthening of the sense of the ontological security of RS as a political entity does not simply aim to create a new kind of social and material environment for RS, but above all to preserve the existing environment of RS. In this regard, it should be emphasised that while it may be claimed that the first two scrutinised critical junctures (SAA and the Prud and Butmir processes) only aimed to preserve the existing social and material environment of RS, the third critical juncture (the referendum on the Day of RS) may be understood as a direct attempt to reinforce the sense of ontological security. By successfully holding an unconstitutional referendum on the celebration of January 9 as the Day of RS in 2016, RS completed the process of 'performing statehood' in a discursive sense and in terms of building an appropriate social (and material) environment for performing this. In this way, it also succeeded in consolidating the meta-narrative of RS being an independent political entity that can 'survive and exist' independently, outside the framework of BiH. The results thus—at least in terms of the discourse analysis—do not indicate that Europeanisation could act as a strategy for the desecuritisation of antagonisms between ethnic groups and thereby contribute to integration on the meso (BiH) and/or macro level (EU). This is also important because the analysis at no point suggests that the presence of the EU or potential membership in it can be understood, for example, as a central mechanism for strengthening the sense of the ontological security of RS.

At the same time, analysis of the securitising acts of the political elite of RS also does not indicate that Europeanisation as such would be understood as the beginning of the end of RS. However, this was clearly shown—in relation to the discursive acts of the political elite—especially with respect to the OHR or the wider international community. In this respect, it is also worth pointing out that at the second and third critical junctures external actors became ever more important, notably Serbia and Russia, towards which RS maintained a clear—friendly—foreign policy position. RS understood both countries as protective forces vis-à-vis the international community (mainly the OHR and the EU) and the 'Bosniak political elite'. I accordingly also offer an insight into the narrower research goal from a theoretical point of view, namely how the concept of ontological (in)security in the context of European integration and Europeanisation, which is mostly understood as the central transformational potential of the EU in the process of post-conflict reconciliation and peace-building, and the relativisation of (national and ethnic) antagonisms, can be contextualised.

It is also worth highlighting the most important findings regarding the concept of Europeanisation as a context that enables the transformation of ethnic identities and its placement in the intertwining theories of securitisation and ontological security. The substantive contribution in question is—from the aspect of the interweaving of concepts (Europeanisation, ontological security and securitisation)—the preparation of a conceptual model. The latter is employed to empirically test the thesis that Europeanisation, or the efforts of the EU in a post-conflict country, can create (existential) insecurities of collectives, which are then managed by the political elite by relying on securitisation as a governance technique. This model enables the analysis of two outcomes of the use of securitisation as a technique of governance in the context of Europeanisation. First, it permits an understanding of how the political elite instrumentalises Europeanisation with the goal of maintaining the position of power in its political entity. It succeeds here by framing the EU as a source of insecurity for the existence of both ethnic identity and political identity in the political entity in which it governs. Second, the model also provides a proposal for understanding how such a way of governing prevents the otherwise expected social, political, economic and cultural changes of both the ethnic group of the political elite and the wider political entity. I tested the model on the problem of the Bosnian Serb political elite's exploitation of Europeanisation to maintain or even deepen antagonisms between ethnic groups in RS, although it is certainly applicable to other (sub)national post-conflict environments addressed by the EU. With this, the contribution of such interweaving of concepts is not only conceptual, but analytical as well. This is because it carves the operationalisation to scrutinise why the transformational potential of Europeanisation in post-conflict societies does not have the same effect as was shown in the case of the integration of Western European post-conflict countries after the Second World War.

The understanding of Europeanisation as the context that enables the transformation of ethnic identities (from antagonism to agonism) assumed that this is one of the central effects of the EU through stabilisation as an idea of socialisation and integration into the political, economic, cultural and social framework of the EU. The experience of post-war European integration also (and above all) indicates this, or that it is even in some way (due to the logic of integration) imminent. The results at some points (e.g., the discourse analysis) indicate that by attributing to Europeanisation the role of such a transformation with the goal of an agonistic dialogue (or peaceful coexistence) between the three ethnic groups, they also show the seeds of (theoretical) idealism. Indeed, practice has revealed that such an aspect of Europeanisation in its 'ideal form' did not develop in the case of BiH. Stemming from this, it can be understood primarily as a by-product of 'classical' Europeanisation, which strives for a reconfiguration of the institutional, political and administrative order of the chosen country by (re)creating institutions to make it more in line with the EU framework. Therefore, such an aspect of Europeanisation in practice is not traceable. This also explains why potentially desecuritising effects are difficult to notice. However, the book has shown that the interplay of Europeanisation, securitisation and ontological security is possible if the socio-political and security situation in RS and (F)BiH is seen through constructivist glasses. From the perspective of this interplay—i.e., of constructed realities—one of the main results is the argument that the EU does not possess genuine potential for successfully promoting the civic model of identification in BiH, assuming its coexistence with ethnic ones. Any attempt at the EU's more active engagement in terms of reform was framed as a 'Bosniak agenda', as also shown by an observation in the field, that is, that only Bosniaks can identify with the civic identity (Bosnian and Hersegovinian). One of the more important empirical findings is that, in the case of BiH, the approach to the EU or a clearer European perspective does not out-weigh the potential loss that the political elite in RS would 'suffer'. The latter, in the case of RS, means the potential loss of the status of a subna-tional entity with a large degree of autonomy within BiH. These losses are likely not mainly understood in terms of identity but used to justify the rejection of the EU's efforts.

Although perhaps the studied aspect of Europeanisation in the case of BiH did not show the potential it held in the post-Second World War period and regarding the transformation of the relationship between, for example, France and Germany, it is still an extremely useful concept. The first argument in support of it is that Europeanisation as such should not be limited to EU-isation and can only be understood through the prism of adaptation to the particular institutional, political and economic order that rules the EU. Instead, Europeanisation must be understood more broadly, namely, in the context of the process of 'exporting' the liberal Western model (thus also the EU's cultural, political, social and economic framework), which is a characteristic of the entire Euro-Atlantic external environment (in addition to the EU, for example, the OHR). Another realisation of potential interest for both the theory of securitisation and ontological security is that the very process of Europeanisation in a broader sense can—if understood as something negative in a certain society—be understood as either a purely targeted threat or a broader manifestation of anxiety, where the 'enemy' is unknown, but defined instead as 'the international community'. At the same time, this is important because it confirms the sense of the pluralistic framework used in this book as it offers a dialogue in the field of security studies (at least those arising from the constructivist paradigm) to some extent since certain questions move relatively quickly from the field of individual security to a broader societal and even a (sub)national level of (in)security. Here, too, a methodological note is required given that the creation of the perception of (in)security is analysed through the actions of the political elite, which directs the debate and in some ways—quite legitimately—manages all kinds of anxiety felt by the population.

This makes it important that securitisation and ontological security highlight different aspects of understanding the concept of security and simultaneously enable a more complex treatment of the appearance of the 'threat' itself, which is both identity and political. It can also be primarily the latter, whereby the identity issue is merely a 'handy' tool for achieving political goals. It should be explicitly emphasised that such a framework in no way depicts the entire reality, which is why it is reasonable here to also call for further analysis of the interplay between ontological security and securitisation in BiH, and to carry out a similar analysis in the FBiH or even on three levels (RS, FBiH and connection to the whole of BiH). The third realisation is that a subnational entity, such as RS in the case under study, can be the 'carrier of subjectivity' when it comes to ontological security itself. This suggests that in the future, research will also have to turn to those regions or areas and entities that traditionally—due to the element of non-recognition of their independence—are not understood as subjects of international relations. Yet, it should be stressed that RS— unlike, for example, Abkhasia, Transnistria or Somaliland—is organised differently and is not categorised as a de facto *state* in the existing literature. This is because RS is constitutionally conceived in such a way that it possesses a high degree of autonomy within the institutional framework of BiH. Of course, this does not mean that such political entities cannot implement or imagine their own statehood, as the case of RS vividly demonstrates. It must be stated that BiH (and RS) in this case acts as *a sui generis* example for determining the interplay of fear and anxiety, noting that such a conceptual model of the relationship between the concepts of Europeanisation, securitisation and ontological security can also be used to investigate the relationship between Serbia and Kosovo, or to understand the Turkish Republic of Northern Cyprus, both within that political entity and relative to the Republic of Cyprus.

Finally, the conclusion provides space for reflection on the concept of securitisation and ontological security in both theory and practice with a view to a case study, namely of RS. First, BiH as a post-conflict environment is not significantly different from any other post-conflict environment in Europe (e.g., Cyprus) or more broadly (e.g., Sri Lanka or the Republic of South Africa) since it is largely a question of either strengthening or preserving political capabilities or power. Such a description also applies to other countries that have not experienced war in such a devastating way, and the objective dividing line between them is merely the instrumentalisation of what Fukuyama (2018) calls identity politics. These, however, can—assuming the instrumentalisation of past events, irrespective of how relatively non-significant they may be—recreate the feeling of exclusion, deprivation and threat to their 'community'. All of these are elements of which both the theory of securitisation and ontological security anticipate and, accordingly, permit understanding. This also results in one of the key reservations, which should be discussed in a more concrete manner in the future in the discipline of IR (as well as more broadly), since the theory of ontological security in particular enables the 'justification' of the policy of exclusion or takes it as an element grounding the strengthening of the sense of ontological security. It is similar to the theory of securitisation but, on the other side of the coin, by understanding desecuritisation as a process for returning security issues to the field of 'normality', the latter is mainly seen through Western liberal glasses. This means that any deviation from the liberal world order or the search for intermediate alternatives within the framework of the Euro-Atlantic external environment to desecuritise the isolated security issue will never be truly understood as 'real' desecuritisation. Indeed, such an understanding (may) make impossible the scientific interpretation of a 'true' return to the field of 'normality', as prescribed by the global liberal order.

Finally, if I look back at RS (and BiH) vis-à-vis the existing literature, field work and my writing of various contributions on this topic—a process that started even before I commenced writing this book—I can hardly claim that this book reveals information that has not been brought to light by now, or some new fact that enables a rewriting of history in the area of today's BiH or the proposing of completely new policies. Being aware that—especially for the area of the former Yugoslavia—it is typical that some key agreements among the political elites have remained secret or in the spirit of any 'serious' research in the region (in a pub over coffee or so on else), I can talk about the fact that the book sensibly combined the information available in an analytical and synthetic way, and qualitatively and quantitatively checked and deepened it and illuminated it from a new angle (securitisation, ontological security). It is also in this spirit that the conclusions of this book should be read—with a pinch of salt and with awareness and understanding that the book pertains to the field of the social sciences, which have different laws to respect than the natural or technical sciences and where the context is always redefined and inconclusive conclusions are drawn based on the information available at a given time and place.

CHAPTER 6

Appendix

6.1 Qualitative and Quantitative Analysis of the Discourse: Operationalisation

To perform qualitative and quantitative analysis of the discourse, news articles from four media outlets were used: Radio Television RS (RTRS), Radio Television Bijelina (RTV BN), Glas Srpske, and Nezavisne novine, which are among the most widely read media and newspapers in RS (Vukojević, 2015; RTVFBiH, 2018). The discourse analysis included: (i) 1769 units in the period between 2005 and 2007, (ii) 1267 units between 2009 and 2010 and (iii) 1077 units between 2015 and 2016. Only newspaper articles (Nezavisne novine and Glas Srpske) and articles published on web portals (RTRS and RTV BN) were analysed since the archives of television broadcasts were only available from 2015. The unit of analysis was therefore newspaper articles or web articles. In analysing the discourse, the theory of securitisation was applied and operationalised using the seven variables presented below. For the variables, the operationalisation proposed by Ejdus and Božović (2016, pp. 6–12) was followed while adding two additional variables related to: (i) the material and social environments of RS and (ii) framing of the EU. These variables significantly upgrade both the element of making references to or reviving the past and

© The Author(s), under exclusive license to Springer Nature   211
Switzerland AG 2023
F. Kočan, *Identity, Ontological Security and Europeanisation in Republika Srpska*, Central and Eastern European Perspectives on International Relations,
https://doi.org/10.1007/978-3-031-46169-9_6

understanding the external 'Other' (EU), as defined in contextual terms by both the Copenhagen and Paris Schools.

The first variable is **polarisation** because the theory assumes there is a positive correlation between a high degree of polarisation and the intensity and frequency of securitising acts (Ejdus & Božović, 2016; Fermor & Holland, 2019; Kurylo, 2020). This variable was encoded at four levels (Ejdus & Božović, 2016, p. 6):

0—no polarising language;
1—moderate speech (language based on facts);
2—partly polarising language (moderate criticism); and
3—strongly polarising language (demonisation).

The second variable is the **treatment option**, which defines preferences for tackling a challenge that is framed as a security problem (Coskun, 2011; Ejdus & Božović, 2016). Here, the theory assumes that the level of emotionality has a positive effect on the persuasive power of the 'securitising actor' through the media discourse (Ejdus & Božović, 2016, p. 6). This variable was encoded over five levels according to Ejdus and Božović (2016, p. 6), where three codes have two diametrically opposite ends, defined as (a) and (b), hence:

0—without the possibility of a solution;
1—evolution/gradual change;
2—revolution/radical and rapid changes;
3a—compromise/negotiations/cooperation with the other party;
3b—without compromise/negotiations/cooperation with the other party;
4a—peaceful settlement of the dispute;
4b—violent dispute resolution;
5a—institutional solution; and
5b—identity solution.

The third variable is **emotions** to which Van Rythoven (2015), Hagstrom and Hanssen (2015), Ejdus and Božović (2016) and Senn (2017) attribute an important role at both the very beginning of and during the securitisation process. This variable was encoded at three levels (Ejdus & Božović, 2016, p. 6):

0—without emotions;
1—moderately emotional; and
2—extremely emotional.

The fourth variable is **media bias,** used to analyse the extent to which the media has been biased in enabling discursive actions by securitising actors. In securitisation theory, bias is important as it is assumed that a relatively high level of biased media reporting can deepen social polarisation between the two 'camps', i.e., between those supporting the discursive actions of the securitising actor and those who do not (Vultee, 2010, p. 42; Ejdus & Božović, 2016, p. 7). This variable was encoded over four levels (Ejdus & Božović, 2016, p. 7):

0—neutral (does not contain biased messages);
1—balanced (contains biased messages, yet these are balanced on both sides);
2—moderately biased; and
3—biased.

The fifth variable is **references to the past** or its **revival,** as already envisaged by the Copenhagen School and is considerably upgraded by the Paris School via the psychological–cultural disposition. The latter determines the process of securitisation due to its own limitations in history and memory (Balzacq, 2005, p. 172). This variable was encoded through the identified critical junctures concerning the ethnic identity of Bosnian Serbs, namely (Ejdus & Božović, 2016, p. 7):

0—without references to the past/revival of the past;
1—the Second World War;
2—common life in the SFRY;
3—disintegration of the SFRY and the referendum on the independence of BiH;
4—NATO's intervention in BiH;
5—signing of the DPA;
6—the Kosovo question; and
7—other historical events.

As a sixth variable, the **EU's presence is introduced into the discourse** given its importance in terms of the studied potential of Europeanisation on ethnic identities. Special attention was devoted to framing the EU's presence as something either positive or negative. The variable was encoded at four levels:

0—The EU is not mentioned;
1—The EU is mentioned in a neutral way;
2—The EU is mentioned in a positive way; and
3—The EU is mentioned in a negative way.

The final, seventh variable is **direct references to the social and material environments** of RS. This is predicted by the theory of ontological security that points out the importance of the stability of (ethnic) identities. The variable was encoded on four levels:

0—The social and material environments of RS are not mentioned;
1—Only the social environment of RS is mentioned;
2—Only the material environment of RS is mentioned; and
3—The social and material environments of RS are both mentioned.

REFERENCES

Balzacq, T. (2005). The three faces of securitization: Political agency, audience and context. *European Journal of International Relations, 11*(2), 171–201.

Coskun, B. B. (2011). *Analysing desecuritisation: The case of the Israeli-Palestinian peace education and water management*. Cambridge Scholars Publishing.

Ejdus, F., & Božović, M. (2016). Grammar, context and power: Securitization of the 2010 Belgrade pride parade. *Southeast European and Black Sea Studies, 17*(1), 1–17.

Fermor, B., & Holland, J. (2019). Security and polarization in Trump's America: Securitisation and the domestic politics of threatening others. *Global Affairs, 6*(1), 55–70.

Hagström, L., & Hanssen, U. (2015). The North Korean abduction issue: Emotions, securitisation and the reconstruction of Japanese identity from 'aggressor' to 'victim' and from 'pacifist' to 'normal'. *The Pacific Review, 28*(1), 71–93.

Kurylo, B. (2020). The discourse and aesthetics of populism as securitisation style. *International Relations, 0*(0), 1–21.

RTVFBiH. (2018). Gledanost TV stanica u BiH tokom cijelog dana u julu 2018. Available at http://www.rtvfbih.ba/loc/template.wbsp?wbf_id=94

Senn, M. (2017). The art of constructing (in)security: Probing rhetorical strategies of securitisation. *Journal of International Relations and Development, 20*(2), 605–630.

Van Rythoven, E. (2015). Learning to feel, learning to fear? Emotions, imaginaries, and limits in the politics of securitization. *Security Dialogue, 46*(5), 458–475.

Vukojević, B. (2015). Mediji u Republici Srpskoj: publike i sadržaji u kontekstu teorije koristi i zadovoljstva. *Časopis za komunikaciju i medije, 34*(10), 29–52.

Vultee, F. (2010). Securitisation: A new approach to the framing of the "war on terror". *Journalism Practice, 4*(1), 33–47.

Index[1]

---

[1] Note: Page numbers followed by 'n' refer to notes.

© The Author(s), under exclusive license to Springer Nature   217
Switzerland AG 2023
F. Kočan, *Identity, Ontological Security and Europeanisation
in Republika Srpska*, Central and Eastern European Perspectives
on International Relations,
https://doi.org/10.1007/978-3-031-46169-9